TOURISM MARKETING

Service and Quality Management Perspectives

Eric Laws

D1513497

Stanley Thornes (Publishers) Ltd

First published in 1991 by:
Stanley Thornes (Publishers) Ltd
Old Station Drive
Leckhampton
CHELTENHAM GL53 0DN
England

British Library Cataloguing in Publication Data

Laws, Eric
    Tourism marketing: service management perspectives.
    1. Tourism. Management 2. Tourism. Marketing
    I. Title
    910.68

    ISBN 0-7487-0428-0

PO 2491

Typeset by Tech-Set, Gateshead, Tyne and Wear
Printed and bound in Great Britain at The Bath Press, Avon

Contents

PART ONE   SERVICE AND QUALITY MANAGEMENT ANALYSIS

List of Figures

List of Tables

Preface

As the final draft of this book was being completed, the author attended a meeting of the Institute of Travel and Tourism at which Gunter Nischwitz, Director of the German National Tourist Organisation in London, discussed the wide ranging effects on tourism of the political events in Eastern Europe. The following paragraphs are based on his presentation, and provide a concise insight into many of the themes developed in this book. [Gunter Nischwitz was Chairman of ANTOR (The Association of National Tourist Office Representatives in the United Kingdom) in the period 1985–7].

The fundamental basis of tourism is individual freedom to travel; without that there can be no modern tourism industry. The political relations between nations too often act as barriers to travel and set artificial directions to people's perceptions of travel opportunities, but the opening of Eastern Europe as a series of more democratic regimes were established at the end of the 1980s has had an immediate impact on the European travel industry.

Nowhere was this more evident than in Berlin. It was a joyous feeling for an entire generation of German people to walk through the Brandenburg Gate without any significant restrictions; initially a great deal of curiosity was satisfied as people were able to cross the Berlin Wall in both directions with the minimum of restrictions. For 40 years after the Second World War the eastern section had been virtually closed so interest was naturally directed elsewhere; youngsters knew very little of the geography of half of their native country. Suddenly the media began to pay daily attention to political, cultural, economic and personal interest news stories from Eastern Europe, stimulating interest and awareness on several levels, with direct effects on the demand for travel. At the present time, the contrasts between East and West attract a great deal of interest, going to the Eastern sector seems like stepping back to the immediate post war period, and is a poignant experience as city centres are still devastated by bomb damage, and the every day conditions of life are so different.

An immediate result of the more relaxed political climate has been a lot of civic twinning projects, and private visits between the two halves of Germany are also a strong feature of the new situation: this is occurring at all levels of society. Business travel into Eastern Germany has increased very rapidly in response to the many commercial opportunities, and as capital investment needs are recognized. There is already a demand for holiday travel to Western resort areas such as the Canary Islands from East German residents, but this is constrained by the country's currency restrictions and by the more pressing economic needs of its population for household durables and so on, which can now gradually be satisfied.

The interest in these events from other countries has meant a big boost in business for hotels in West Berlin, where the tourism infrastructure is much more developed than in the Eastern sector. West Berlin is an ideal base for day excursions to places of great historical and cultural interest in the GDR, as it provides comfortable accommodation and good international transport links. After the War, many West German towns such as Ratzeburg and Coburg had suddenly lost a large part of their traditional hinterlands under the division, and so had been subsidized by the Federal Republic. Natural regions of great interest to tourists such as the Harz and the Rhon Mountains had effectively been cut in two, but now they are well placed to benefit from the new tourism axis between West and East Germany. In the longer term these changing patterns of travel perceptions and behaviour will stimulate the realignment of transport networks throughout Germany, and the establishment of new international gateways.

What is important about this development in tourism is that individual people are now able to form their own opinions based on direct observation and contact, rather than relying on the views of politicians or journalists. Restrictions on individual liberty intimidate people, and have negative effects on their attitudes, but freedom gives a great boost and travel reinforces the growing confidence that individuals are now gaining.

Eric Laws

Introduction

This book draws together a number of important perspectives on the people, organizations and places which together make up the tourism industry. The unifying theme is rooted in the author's belief that the central issue emerging for tourism managers as the twenty-first century draws closer is a concern with the nature and quality of tourism experiences.

Three groups of people have stakes in the creation and enjoyment of tourism services; this book explores ways in which their differing needs can be understood and satisfied. The first of these groups are those who work in the many and varied businesses which depend on or contribute to the tourism industry. The second group whose interests are considered in this book are the residents in tourism destinations whose everyday lives may be altered by the many consequences of tourism such as changed patterns and opportunities of work, rapid local development or the introduction of new social values. The third group are the tourists, those people for whose benefit and enjoyment investments have been made in aircraft and airports, coaches and parking lots, resorts, hotels and shopping centres, and for whom entrepreneurs have developed excursions, entertainment, activities and inclusive tours. Sometimes, and perhaps to an increasing extent, the interests of these three groups, workers, residents and tourists, are in conflict. But it is often forgotten how recent a phenomenon mass tourism is, and the opportunities to develop an industry which is more sensitive to the issues raised in this book, and more responsive to everyone's needs are demonstrated and discussed.

Tourism, like any other human activity, has both beneficial and adverse consequences. These need to be understood by planners and tourism principals, and are increasingly becoming the concern of tourists themselves. Three major classes of negative effects can be identified; one area of concern is the consequences of mass tourism on local life in the destination areas. Traditional employment sectors come to seem less attractive as tourism develops, and its new style of work distorts the supply of labour while increasing the demand for labour; the result is increasing wages and the inflow of workers. Capital and skilled managers are often imported to provide the standards of service expected by international travellers, while much of the profit which tourism generates flows overseas. Secondly, the structure of societies will change rapidly under the pressure of high spending, free living temporary incomers. Against this, there are opportunities to develop more responsible tourism which recognizes rather than exploits the needs of host communities. The third type of problem is the increase in pollution and congestion which tourism development can cause, and the resultant damage to a region's physical environment or natural wildlife habitats.

Many organizations play a vital role in the delivery of complex tourism services, and their contribution can best be understood from a systems perspective. This approach highlights the appropriateness of the services they provide to tourists, the overall effects on workers and residents, and the interdependent nature of tourism enterprises. The tourism industry is a complex system because the organizations which contribute to it are extremely varied in several important characteristics. Some may be publicly owned while others are private companies. Many operate for a profit while others do not even charge for their services. Some provide the services they create directly to tourists, others act as wholesalers or agents for tourism principals. Some specialist companies are wholly dependent on tourism, others exist primarily to serve other client groups, but also cater to the specialized needs of tourists in the course of their main business activities. The scale of organizations operating in the tourism sector ranges from very small, proprietor-operated seasonal businesses such as guest houses, to international regulatory bodies such as IATA (the International Air Transport Association).

The approaches taken in Part One of this book draw on research and technical literature dealing with tourism, and management theory dealing with the service industries. The theory reviewed in the book provides readers with a multidisciplinary base from which to understand the challenges and issues with which tourism managers have to deal and establishes a framework to evaluate potential solutions. Each chapter is followed by a short list of books which were selected either because the chapter was largely based on them, or because they offer contrasting perspectives on the topics covered in the chapter. Most lecturers will have their own preferred texts which they might wish to recommend to their students; the readings and questions offered here are intended to guide the further thinking of independent readers, suggesting also ways in which the themes of each chapter might be applied in readers' own situations.

Part Two of the book provides readers with a series of case studies drawn largely from managers' own accounts of recent situations. Each case can be understood using the various approaches discussed in this book, and further developed in the specialized literature cited in the text. The cases were selected because they represent a turning point of some kind for each organization, or because they illustrate an innovative and effective approach to particular situations. But in each of the cases, decisions had to be taken by individual managers or teams, based on their own experience and insights, and in the light of the specific and unique circumstances confronting each case at that point in time.

The contribution which the author intends for this book is that the insights it offers will help managers working in the tourism industry, and inspire students on advanced courses who aspire to careers in tourism to continue to improve the quality of tourism services for all with a stake in the success of this growing industry, whether they are staff, residents or tourists. The quality of tourism services seems likely to become a central factor for future managerial decisions; this book offers a way of analysing tourism processes which will enhance readers' understanding of the service aspects of tourism management.

Prospects for the continued growth of tourism are very favourable. Societal influences seem likely to further stimulate demand for recreation and travel, and continuing reductions in the real cost of air travel will bring new destinations within the budget of increasing numbers of tourists. Many governments will probably continue to encourage both domestic and incoming tourism, for its beneficial effects including job creation, economic diversification and foreign exchange earnings.

Against the developmental push of competing destinations, resorts, hotel groups, airlines, attractions, tour operators and retail travel agencies which together expand the demand for tourism, a number of forces restraining tourism growth can be identified. Foremost amongst these are the social and economic factors discussed in the book. As the Preface indicated, tourism also plays a part in promoting understanding and trust among people of different nations, but the industry depends entirely on freedom to travel.

Acknowledgements

This book could not have been written without the support, advice and encouragement of many people. The case studies depend entirely on the detailed knowledge and expertise of the managers who discussed them at length with the author, and the assistance of the following organizations is gratefully acknowledged: Hawaii Visitors Bureau in Honolulu, the Big Island HVB Chapter in Hilo, the Hawaii State Department of Planning and Economic Development, the Parker Ranch, British Airways, Hilton International, Ladbroke Group PLC, the English Tourist Board, the Holiday Inn Lhasa, London Entertains, Premier Travel, and Raitt Orr Associates. The author wishes to thank all managers who shared their experiences, and who found the time to comment on and improve early drafts of the case studies, but accepts any errors as his own responsibility.

Amongst the many other tourism enthusiasts to whom the author expresses his gratitude are two main groups; the first are his students and colleagues, many of whom have contributed to the development of the ideas advanced in this book. The second group includes all the experts who have presented their views for discussion and debate at the meetings and in the publications of the Tourism Society, the Chartered Institute of Marketing Travel Industry Group, the Institute of Travel and Tourism and the Travel and Tourism Research Association.

To all these, and his travelling companion over the years, the author extends his thanks.

Eric Laws
1990

Service and Quality Management Analysis

CHAPTER ONE

The Analysis of Tourism Service Systems

Introduction

Modern tourism has an interesting historical and social origin; the Industrial Revolution changed the patterns of work and leisure which had been established in mediaeval times. Large conurbations developed, breaking the direct link to agricultural work cycles and skills which most people had accepted, and substituting machine paced labour for traditional skills. The economy shifted from subsistence and exchange to cash for wages and purchasing, and with the development of transport and communications systems the natural interest which people had in other places and their need for a break from routine could begin to be satisfied commercially. Later, statutory paid holidays and increasing awareness of distant cultures, climates and countries fuelled the demand for tourism. While it remains a central concern for society and most adults, work has become less dominant as the economy moves towards a post industrial stage of evolution where personal goals of self development become attainable through greater awareness of opportunities, more disposable income, and increased leisure time at most levels in society.

Technical definitions of tourism indicate its scope and importance in modern Western culture, society and economics. Tourism encompasses activities and travel carried out for leisure, and family or business reasons (other than commuting). Leisure travel may satisfy any of three purposes: rest, entertainment or personal development. Riordan (1982, quoting from Karabuga, 1969) has drawn attention to the Russian authorities' views of tourism at that time: 'Tourism includes more or less lengthy journeys with the aim of active rest and better health, tempering the organism, acquiring new knowledge and experience and performing socially useful work.' The seminal definition by Burkhardt and Medlik (1981) provides the framework for the analysis of tourism throughout this book, 'the temporary short term movement of people . . . and their activities during the stay at these destinations'.

Tourism commands increasing attention amongst businesses, government and the public. Tourism activities overlap recreation and leisure, while the enterprises satisfying tourists' demands include specialists in entertainment, sport, catering, transport and accommodation, as well as retailing and tour operations. A large number of organizations provides the wide range of services required to satisfy the many needs of tourists, leading to the following definition: 'Travel and tourism is the vast complex network of business engaged in the lodging, transportation, feeding and entertaining of travellers' (American Express, 1989). The base for the analysis presented in this book is peoples' decisions regarding their investment of time and money in tourism or other purchases.

Models of the tourism industry

Theories and models provide an abstract, simplified way of visualizing the many components of complex situations, and offer a framework for the analysis of their interactions in a functioning system. A feature of research into tourism which also occurs in studies of other sectors is that a variety of models are available to aid in understanding. In part, this is the result of the varying backgrounds in management, economics, anthropology, geography, psychology and so on which researchers have brought to this relatively new area of study. In a more fundamental way, this diversity also reflects the complexity of the tourism phenomenon.

Concepts are the building blocks for models, but although any particular concept presents the analyst with an ordered view of the subject under scrutiny from a particular perspective, it has limitations. Two in particular need to be noted. In the first place a model is a simplification; it generalizes from reality and does not offer a complete consideration of all factors germane to each situation, rather it stresses the common elements which are found in different situations. Secondly any model, theory or concept is based on assumptions. Many of these can be made explicit, or can be teased out of the argument offered, but others are deeply imbedded in the cultural values from which the researcher constructed his (or her) theory. As such, these assumptions are seldom visible, either to researchers or to others who read and attempt to apply their theories because they often share a similar cultural background. Models such as those explored in this book can be used in one of two main ways; either to explain events which have occurred, or to predict what may occur in the future. This match to reality is the test of a traditional model's strength, and as weaknesses or limitations are revealed, the need for a new theory or model is demonstrated, and so scientific theory progresses to deeper levels of understanding and application.

The basic tourism model

The simplest travel package consists of two service elements — return travel and activities at the destination. Therefore, the basic model of tourism has three components, shown in Figure 1.1.

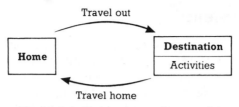

Figure 1.1 The basic tourism model

This model highlights the set of organizations which together create or respond to a demand for tourism experiences from the public. The underlying feature of interest to organizations supplying tourism services is the varied reasons why people might wish to travel. Chapter 2 reviews theories of tourist behaviour and the motivations which lead to their demands for travel; the model above summarizes these as 'activities'. The term 'activity' enables this simple model to represent day visit tourism, but with the addition of accommodation services it can readily analyze the more complex tourism system catering to the needs of those who spend one or more nights away from home.

It is already apparent from the basic tourism model that the tourism sector encompasses a wide range of business activities and tourism opportunities for clients. Many holiday makers purchase travel in the form of packages and the tour operators improve on the basic tourism model by including additional services. Examples of the enhancements to travel packages include transfers at the destination, the services of representatives and through them opportunities for a variety of leisure, cultural, sporting or entertainment activities. These additional service elements are a managerial tool, by which managers can distinguish their organization's style from that of competitors' along dimensions such as completeness of holiday experience and its cost, quality or convenience. More significantly, all these aspects are included in the client's perception of the overall holiday experience. Many other benefits can be incorporated into the various stages of the tour package, including insurance, assistance with airport check-in, home transfers, parking or predeparture accommodation.

Development of the basic model reveals the complexity of the tourism industry and identifies the many components of the tourists' experience. However, the purpose of models is to simplify, and the challenge for analysts is to select the most salient features from all those impinging on a situation so that the general principles can be identified. The expanded model shown in Figure 1.2 highlights the interdependence of tourism businesses and this suggests that the quality of tourists' experiences depend on satisfactory services throughout their package. The failure of any one component to meet tourists' expectations can have detrimental effects on other companies, although at first glance their operations are independent.

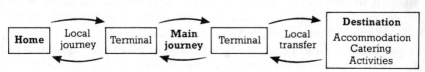

Figure 1.2 Expanded tourism model

The tourism system

In order to provide a framework for the examination of the complex relationships within the tourism industry, a systems method is adopted in this book. Kaspar (1986) has commended the systems approach in analyzing tourism as it brings a range of advantages, including the abandonment of one-dimensional thinking, and because it facilitates a multidisciplinary perspective reflecting the superordinate systems within which tourism phenomenon occur. These include economic, social, technological, political and ecological contexts to tourism management decisions.

Kaspar pointed out that a theoretical image of reality can be gained in three ways: by reductionistic, holistic or systemic approaches. Reductionism dissects a whole entity into separate, isolated units. That method places the focus on the elements of a system, rather than the interrelationships between them. Holism represents the contrary approach; it regards the whole as non-seperable and therefore non-analyzable. Kaspar quoted Kuhne's view that; 'these limitations are sufficient to abandon both approaches and to search for a perspective, which enables one to grasp the peculiarities of the whole and the specific properties of the parts at the same time'.

Business organizations are purposeful social systems, taking resources from their environment and using the skills of their employees to produce outputs to satisfy their clients and the organization's own objectives. Systems approaches can be applied to the tourism industry as a whole, or to its separate operating units, such as destinations, airlines, hotels, castles, theme parks or travel organizations and enterprises. A systems approach enables the goals, organization, resource and output decisions of management to be examined in order to understand the effects of their decisions on other people. Constraints such as competition and regulatory environments may also be studied to understand how levels of efficiency are affected in the industry (see Chapter 12).

A system is an ordered set of components; each component is affected by being part of the system: its behaviour is constrained by the needs and conditions of its setting and the entire system is affected if one component changes. Taking a view of a system is to recognize particular systems' boundaries; setting a clear boundary around the system under investigation emphasizes the inputs and outputs for investigation. Boundaries are fairly easy to define for smaller units of analysis, such as a specific tourism enterprise, but as the scale and complexity of the system under consideration increases the definition of appropriate boundaries to the investigation become less certain. Outside the boundary of any system are a range of other entities which influence its activities and which are affected by them: the system is itself part of the environment for other systems. The systems view of any organization suggests that it exists to carry out the activities and processes related to achieving its aims; that it controls its activities and communicates with the environment about them in order to obtain resources and attract support for its products.

Three stages are identified in models of system processes: Figure 1.3 shows how they may be applied to the tourism industry. Inputs are required in the form of equipment, skills, resources and clients' demands for an organization's

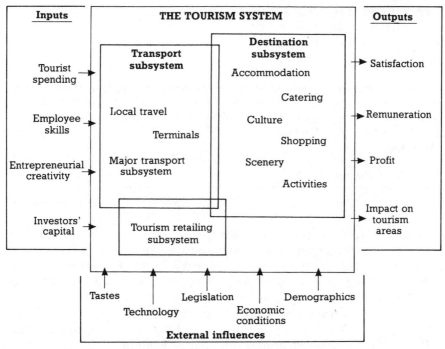

Figure 1.3 The tourism system

outputs. These include the services which it produces, the profit and work which it creates in so doing and the satisfaction which its clients obtain. The intermediate stage of systems analysis between inputs and outputs is concerned with the internal processes, whereby an organization transforms those inputs into outputs. The expanded tourism model shown in Figure 1.2 has revealed the complexity of tourism services in greater detail than the basic model, but their effects on the tourists, staff, residents and others should also be considered. Figure 1.3 provides a framework for consideration of these factors. The various components or elements of the system are interlinked, and the efficiency of the system operating within its boundary will be affected by changes to any of the elements of which it is composed.

Viewing tourism as a system gives the advantage of identifying people involved in it: the managers, staff, residents and tourists, and the systems model provides a framework to understand the effects on these stakeholders of the system's operation. The system inputs are the expectations and spending of tourists, the skills and attitudes of staff, and the resources and skills of management. The appropriateness and quality of the tourism system can be assessed by examining the outcomes for each stakeholder group — that is, the satisfaction experienced by clients of the system; the remuneration, work satisfaction and career development of staff; profit and growth of the system, which can be regarded as proprietors and managerial outcomes, and the benefits or problems which the tourism system creates locally which are the outcomes for residents. This suggests the need for an organization to monitor the external environment within which it operates. Georgiades and Phillimore (1975) have recommended that any organization should cultivate its environment in order to establish respect and rapport, specifying a number of concerns which are indicated in Table 1.1.

Table 1.1   Environmental considerations for successful systems management

1 Work with those who support change rather than resist it
2 Establish a team for mutual support; those near the top are less likely to support the status quo
3 Work with those who have sufficient control and authority to carry out change
4 Develop the support team

Adapted from Georgiades and Phillimore, 1975

The tourism system model focuses particular attention on the role of management in matching an organization's processes to the needs of the various groups with a stake in the tourism industry. It is the point of reference throughout the book: in particular, the case studies presented in Part Two of this book are best examined in terms of the structure outlined in the tourism system model. The scientific approach is concerned with the analysis of a situation by breaking it down into its component parts, whereas the systems approach is interested in the interactions of its components. When people are a significant part of the operation, a systems approach is particularly appropriate.

A further level of systems analysis focuses on the various subsidiary systems which contribute to an organization's overall functioning. For effective management two aspects need to be clearly understood: the effects on outputs of any change to its inputs and the ways in which its processes are organized and controlled. Control over the quality and consistency of a system's outputs requires regular sampling of its products and an effective feedback channel between the monitoring and decision-making subsystems within the organization.

Tourism services

A great deal of management theory, and increasing managerial effort, is directed towards improvements in the efficiency of organizations. A major focus of practitioner and academic interest is reliability in the performance and delivery of products or services. There is increasing recognition for the operational significance of the distinction between services and products. Many experts have pointed to the distinguishing characteristic of services showing how they depend on face to face delivery when service staff are in direct contact with the clients. In contrast, manufacturing of most products occurs 'offstage', remote from the public. Although managers may wish to specify precise standards for their services, just as a production manager in a factory setting would expect to, in reality each service transaction is itself a variable dependent on the performance of staff when in contact with the client. From this point of view, the service is a dynamic event during which client and staff may try to influence each other in many ways as they interact. The roles for management in service delivery systems are fundamentally concerned with designing and resourcing an appropriate delivery system.

> Examples of poor service are widespread, in survey after survey services top the list in terms of consumer dissatisfaction. . . . Faced with service problems, we tend to become somewhat paranoid. Customers are convinced that someone is treating them badly, managers think that recalcitrant individual employees are the source of the malfunction. Thinly veiled threats by customers and managers are often first attempts to remedy the problem, if they fail, confrontation may result. (Shostack, 1984)

The need for monitoring of recognized or agreed performance criteria is a key managerial role in any organization. The degree of work inspection and performance feedback required varies according to the predictability of tasks — rather more freedom and longer feedback periods being necessary to ensure effective individual responses in the complex and relatively unpredictable situations encountered by service industry staff. The purpose of monitoring is essentially marginal and remedial, either making changes to services as they occur, or attempting to prevent the reoccurrence of similar problems on future occasions. However an alternative strategy is emerging in which managerial attention is focused on organizational development programmes rather than remedial action after crises have occurred. The preferred approach becoming apparent in many organizations is to seek organization-wide consensus for improvement plans based on educational programmes underpinning organizational development exercises. The concept has also been extended to general sector training programmes; both applications are considered in the case studies presented later in this book.

Tourism marketing

The title of this book emphasizes the central role of marketing in the management of tourism. At the base of an enterprise's success is its ability to attract clients against competition from many providers, both of tourism and of other products or services, on which people can choose to spend their discretionary time and money.

Marketing theorists have pointed out that all purchases are made to satisfy needs. Any item purchased must be able to perform the function claimed of it and for which it was primarily acquired; this is the core of the product. Thus, the core of an airline's market offering is its capability of transporting its clients safely from airport A to airport B at the times agreed. However, it seems that consumers often have in mind a more complex concept — one which includes a wider range of benefits. As Kotler and Armstrong (1987) put it, 'to best satisfy customers, the producer has to offer an augmented product'. For airlines, additional features of their service may include attention to individual wishes, enhanced comfort, varied menus or faster procedures at their terminals. These additional features of products have been identified as the locus of new competition: 'The new competition is not between what companies produce in their factories, but between what they add . . . in the form of packaging, services, customer advice, financing . . . and other things that people value' (Levitt, 1969).

Success for any organization depends on its ability to identify and influence the flows of customers and ensuing revenue. Table 1.2 identifies the main customer flows for which all organizations must compete.

Table 1.2   Flows of customers

1   Additional customer entry into the market
2   Branch shifting
3   Customer market exit
4   Changes in purchase frequency
5   Changes in services standard preferences

Based on Fornell & Wernerfelt, 1987. Fifth element added by the present author

The key to an organization's marketing orientation is its understanding of how the individuals who are its potential clients make decisions to spend their resources of time, money and effort, and of the benefits they seek from so doing. Marketing's strategic role is to bring the organization around to an awareness of the needs of its customers and to develop ways of delivering its services effectively.

> The development of a new service is usually characterized by trial and error. Developers translate a subjective description of a need into an operational concept that may bear only a remote resemblance to the original idea. No one systematically quantifies the process or devises tests to ensure that the service is complete, rational and fulfils the original need objectively. No R and D departments, laboratories or service engineers define and oversee the design. There is no way to ensure quality or uniformity in the absence of a detailed design. What piecemeal quality controls exist address only parts of the service. (Shostack, 1984)

In their benchmark review of research on customer service management Lalonde and Zinszer (1976) identified three main targets for analysis, shown in Table 1.3.

Table 1.3   Service analysis phases

1   Pre-transaction analysis
2   The transaction itself
3   Post-transactional elements

Source: Lalonde and Zinszer 1976

Travel and tourism is purchased when individuals perceive that the benefits they will obtain can best satisfy their individual needs, but any decision to purchase is based on information about the service, and the way it is understood by each individual. The steps which a tourism supplier can take to attract potential consumers include the creation and placing of a desired image of the service (or the organization supplying it) with a target consumer audience. Ries and Trout (1986) have shown that positioning should be regarded as a communications issue, and discussed several examples of how the verbal and mental pictures which consumers have may be managed. The product or service is given and the objective is to manipulate consumers' perceptions of reality. The market position obtained for a service is, of course, also affected by each of the other marketing variables: pricing, distribution and the attributes of the service itself.

The visible manifestation of a competitive market, where the need is to offer benefits which distinguish one product from similar alternatives, is a strong branding strategy to establish identities. The objective is to make the brand the one which the consumer is most likely to purchase. What is important in branding is the way in which clients perceive the service offered, so effective brand management depends on market research. The position of a brand can be determined by techniques which examine the perceptual space occupied by a product in the minds of intended customers, for example in terms of price compared to comfort or to convenience (see Chapter 6). But a corollary of strong branding is that when a service provider has failed to satisfy a consumer in the past, it is unlikely that the consumer will repurchase that brand.

The second stage of Lalonde and Zinszer's model focused on the management of services. The challenges of managing tourism enterprizes are discussed throughout this book, but one complication has already been identified. Tourism is characterized by complex channel relationships in the creation and delivery of its services, and tourists' satisfaction often depends directly on the actions of staff employed by a variety of companies. This feature is largely hidden from tourists; their view may be summarized in a phrase as 'the one stop purchase of a complete holiday'. To take one component, a ticket issued for a journey bears the identifying symbols – logo, name and carrier codes of one airline, but even in the simplest analysis services for the traveller are supplied by two airports, one regulatory body and one airline. In many cases ticket sales, baggage handling, catering and certain passenger services may be provided by other sub-contractors, even by competing airlines, but inspection of customer correspondence files supports the view that passengers hold the airline, tour operator or retail travel agent responsible for every experience. Thus, tourism managers have another dimension to their work: managing other companies' staff towards the achievement of service standards which will meet the levels anticipated by their clients.

The final stage of Lalonde and Zinszer's analysis is concerned with the post purchase phase. Two outcomes from a tourism service are possible: either the tourist is satisfied (and then might be expected to return to the same supplier for future services) or he experiences disappointment with one or more aspects of a service which failed to match expectations. The consumer is then likely to complain to the tourism supplier. Complaining customer behaviour can be understood as attempts directly to change the firm's policies or the attitudes and behaviour of its staff, or to obtain compensation for the dissatisfaction. Similarly, many of the models of marketing behaviour include a feedback loop (or loops), a mechanism by which consumers are able to express their opinions of a current market offering. The function of feedback is to allow the producer to modify future output to obtain a closer match to clients' wishes.

Consequences of tourism

Croize (1982) has described the evolution of a major ski resort. When the snowfields around Val d'Isere were discovered around 1930 by the fringe of Parisian high society the village housed no more than 250 inhabitants and was completely lacking in public utilities. By 1987 the community had grown to 1600 residents, roughly 100 retail businesses, and 21 000 beds. The resort has 1500 salaried personnel, of which one-third are employed the year round.

It can be seen from this brief example that tourism has many effects on the areas which become major destinations. Beyond the measurable direct economic effects such as specialized employment and the income which it brings, are other economic influences that are harder to estimate. Tourism is a major entry point to the workforce for many first-time employees. It has significantly expanded opportunities for part-time and seasonal work, which is often particularly attractive to specific groups within the community, notably students, recently retired people or housewives. Furthermore, it offers a conducive environment for starting a small business, both in generating and destination areas and its services are a key element in the business environment for all companies.

Mass tourism imposes significant demands on an area for the supply of services with which tourists are familiar, such as comfortable accommodation, good water, sewage and electricity supplies and a wide variety of catering and entertainment services to suit their tastes. This tends to standardize sites around the world, resulting in uniform experiences and predefined roles for both visitors and hosts. In contrast, the benefits of planning tourism development in harmony with the local community have been emphasized by Krippendorf (1987), de Kadt (1976), and others who recommend that developments should reflect local traditions and lifestyles.

Another important aspect of international tourism has attracted increasing attention. Throughout previous history the people of one country had no clear image or understanding of other peoples, and lived in isolation behind national and even local borders, emerging mainly for war or trade. The other major reason for travelling was on pilgrimages to points of importance for their own culture, but which happened to be located outside its boundaries. This meant a long and difficult journey through alien, if not hostile cultures.

Mutual suspicion, hostility and conflict was often the result and international relations have remained the prerogative of governments, as indicated in the Preface and in Case Study D which discusses aspects of tourism to Tibet. However, the movement of large numbers of people builds social and economic linkages between different levels of society and between different countries. The official channel for inter-governmental relations has been described as Track One diplomacy by Davidson & Joseph (discussed in D'Amore 1988). To protect their countries, diplomats are trained to make worst case assumptions about their adversaries' intentions, thereby setting in motion a chain of mutual distrust, threats and hostility. Track Two diplomacy is unofficial, it takes place at the level of individual meeting individual and consequently it is non-structured and open minded. Individual Track Two diplomacy has the potential of being optimistic rather than pessimistic. The feature of tourism relevant to this analysis is that tourism spreads information about the people, cultures, and aspirations of one country directly to citizens of another. It can build bridges between nationalities through personal knowledge of the psychological and culture differences between races, religions and countries at different stages of social and economic development. Of itself though, tourism is neutral, causing neither conflict nor peace. The forms in which tourism occurs can, however, have consequences tending to increase contact and friendship between visitors and residents, or contributing to conflict between them.

These considerations increasingly underly the decisions taken by tourism managers and suggest a number of roles for local or national governmental agencies. The approach adopted by governments naturally reflects their political values, as well as the detailed context, and can range from participation on an entrepreneurial basis in competition with private organizations to the regulation of selected activities, or the various forms of financial and technical support available for the development of new tourism initiatives. These points are discussed in Chapter 12.

A frequent role is to coordinate planned development, often on a regional basis, and to phase the infrastructure investment required to support such developments. This implies a planning and regulatory function. Other issues of concern to governments are related to the management of the economy on a macro level where tourism's contribution to national income and the balance of payments may become the target for policy decisions. Increasingly the social effects of tourism are a direct issue for governments; both the text and the case studies draw attention to these issues.

Elements in the tourism system

The discussion in this chapter has ranged quite widely over the tourism industry and has also drawn attention to the effects of particular management decisions on the people who have a stake in tourism — whether as investors or managers, staff or tourists, or residents in destination areas. There are many tourism intermediaries, including tour operators, travel retailers and a variety of informational or promotional agencies such as National Tourist Organizations and the travel media. These act as channels distributing awareness of travel opportunities and providing easy means of booking complex travel arrangements, but the services which tourists seek benefits from are provided by travel principals such as hotels, airlines and attractions.

The two fundamental elements in every tourism service are transport and the attractions at the destination, while catering and accommodation also have a crucial role to play in the majority of travellers' decisions. As the many tourism

13

services required during a single journey are normally supplied by more than one organization it follows that attention must be paid to the management of relationships between organizations contributing elements to an integrated tourism delivery system.

The main area of tourist activity is the destination, but this is also home to a community and for many people living there tourism is a peripheral activity. Tourism brings many benefits to destination areas, notably employment and an increased rate of economic activity. However, there are many examples of resorts where tourism has become an intrusive and dominant factor in the daily experience of residents, through congestion, and the influence of very different lifestyles which temporary visitors bring, often most noticeable in incongruous out-of-scale resort architecture.

From the tourists' point of view, what is important is the satisfaction which they gain from their tourism purchase. There are several components to this, starting from the image of perceived benefits which tourism marketers seek to convey, and ending with a personal evaluation by each tourist of the satisfaction experienced against some benchmark of expectation. What they are evaluating is the service provided by the firms contributing elements to their tourism package and an analysis of service quality lies at the core of this book.

Conclusion

Tourism in its modern form is a very new phenomenon, and it offers people a range of benefits including the satisfaction of their curiosity about distant lifestyles, and a complete break from daily routine. As an industry, tourism is one of the fastest growing sectors in the world and yet it poses unique management challenges because of its service characteristics and its fragmented, complex nature.

A variety of theoretical approaches to the analysis of tourism and its effects have been identified, and a context has been set to the approach adopted in this book. The chapters which follow focus attention on selected aspects of the complex and dynamic tourism industry, and discuss how a range of problems may be identified and tackled. The cases which conclude the book integrate the many aspects discussed here, which concerned and forward-looking managers have to resolve in the reality of their every-day working decisions.

Suggested questions

1 What evidence is there of beneficial or adverse effects of tourism in an area with which you are familiar?

2 Which individual tourism organizations contributed elements to a tourism service you have recently experienced? Were you aware of any unevenness in the delivery of the service during various stages?

3 Analyse the tourism services which you discussed in answer to Questions 1 and 2, using the systems method to identify the stakeholders, the inputs, outputs and the main subsystems.

Recommended reading

Katz, G. and Kahn, R.L. *The Social Psychology of Organizations*, Wiley, Chichester, 1978
Mathieson, A. and Wall, G. *Tourism, Economic Physical and Social Impacts*, Longman, Harlow, 1982
Mill, R.C. and Morrison, A.H. *The Tourism System*, Prentice Hall, New Jersey, 1985
Young, G. *Tourism, Blessing or Blight*, Pelican, Harmondsworth, 1973

CHAPTER TWO

The Demand for Tourism

Introduction

Tourism is often regarded as a new industry, although of course people have always travelled for diverse reasons including trade or war, and as part of their culture. Nomadic traditions or pilgrimages, such as those recorded by Chaucer in *The Canterbury Tales,* stimulated regular, organized flows of large numbers of people. The scale of modern tourism is very much more significant, with travel undertaken for recreational, family or business purposes by millions of people every year, and a growing sector of the economy in virtually every country now specializes in servicing the needs of tourists. The demand for tourism varies from country to country and the tourist activity rate for each is based on a number of factors, including the varying ability to purchase travel resulting from economic conditions, or the tolerance of political regimes to international recreational journeys by their residents.

Vacations offer people a change from the daily pressures of urban living or industrial and office work routines, and their choice of location for a holiday is influenced by the relative attractions offered by the many leisure destinations available. The choice of any destination is also a consequence of tourists' increasing awareness of travel opportunities resulting from improved educational provision and modern mass media interest in foreign countries, their natural features and cultural traditions. But the great increase in travel recorded by Government statistical series since the mid-1950s also depended on technical and social shifts, such as the greatly increased ease of private mobility resulting from car ownership, and improved mass transport systems, particularly in air-travel. Another factor stimulating tourist activity has been the creative role of travel retailers and tour operators whose skill reduces the planning required by tourists; most noticeably through the development and marketing of inclusive tourism products and results in a price for the complete holiday package which is often less than the sum of its component elements if they had been purchased separately. The supply considerations are discussed in Chapter 3.

International patterns in tourism demand

The scale of tourism is enormous; a study commissioned by American Express reported that in 1987 some $2 trillion was spent on travel and tourism, and one in 16 of the world's workers were employed in the sector. In 1986 some 373 million international passenger arrivals were officially recorded at border crossings. Assuming that each traveller was counted twice, for by definition tourists return home, over 3 per cent of the world's population travelled abroad. Their expenditure on international tourism and travel accounted for 5 per cent of the total value of world exports. However, domestic tourism, defined as the activity of travellers staying within their own country, probably generated about three times as much business, although it accounted for 90 per cent of all tourist activity. Tables 2.1 and 2.2 provide some further details of the scale and significance of international tourism activity.

A visitor to any major destination quickly becomes aware of the international nature of tourism. Resorts in Spain attract people from all over Northern Europe; Hawaii is a popular destination for American, Japanese, Australian and other tourists; while in the major historic cities of the world, visitors for business and leisure originate from most countries of the world. Many factors determine a tourist's choice of destination. Three major factors are: the limited time available to individuals for travel, financial constraints on their choices, and thirdly the preferences of the individual or group for particular places and activities. An understanding of tourists' preferences and choices amongst services is a basic foundation for managers' decisions about the characteristics of the services they offer, and will be examined from several perspectives in the ensuing chapters.

Table 2.1   The value of tourism

A   By region of origin, 1987

	$ billion	Per cent of total
Europe	589	46
Americas	426	33
Asia and Pacific	243	19
Africa and Middle East	21	2
Total	1279	100

B   Capital investment in tourism developments, 1987

	$ billion	Per cent of total
Europe	161	58
Americas	41	15
Asia and Pacific	55	20
Africa and Middle East	18	7
Total	276	100

Source: American Express, 1989

Table 2.2   The five most active
tourism countries, 1987

A   Countries of tourist origin

	Value of spending $ million
US	356 181
Japan	193 208
West Germany	98 459
UK	75 805
France	65 901

B   Destination countries

	Value of earnings $ million
France	36 818
Spain	32 900
US	28 787
Italy	25 794
Austria	15 761

Source: American Express, 1989

Allocating time for tourism

The widespread availability of leisure time for individuals to use as they wish is a major characteristic of western industrialized nations and it seems that it has increased during the twentieth century, becoming more widespread and longer. Leisure is defined as time available to the individual after work commitments, and increased leisure has resulted from changes in society, such as earlier retirement, fewer hours spent at work each week or longer paid annual holiday entitlements, resulting in a reduction of the number of working days and weeks in the year. However, not all non-work time is available for tourism purposes as people have physiological needs for rest, meals and so on, and also want to spend time at home with their family. In the remaining time, people can pursue a wide range of activities — whether passively at home, e.g. watching television, or away from home, e.g. sports, social meetings and travel. Part of time at work may also be spent travelling for business purposes although, as mentioned earlier, commuting is excluded from definitions of tourism activity.

Tourism is the range of services which aim to satisfy needs when people travel away from home, for a day, overnight, or longer. Their needs may be recreational, developmental, active or passive, solitary or social in nature. The definitions of tourism discussed in Chapter 1 show that the concept embraces travel for business (but not commuting) as well as leisure. Table 2.3 provides a framework within which an individual's allocation of time for tourism can be understood.

Table 2.3   Allocating time for tourism

Major activity	Travel and tourism activity
Work	— Business day visits
	— Business overnight visits
	— Conference or convention travel
Leisure	— Day trips from home
	— Weekend breaks
	— Short vacations
	— Long vacations

Financial factors influencing tourists' decisions

The second factor influencing the demand for tourism is the cost of tourism services. Basic economic analysis indicates that, as the price of any good rises, the demand for it by consumers will fall. A rise in price of one good relative to all others means that the trade off which an individual makes to purchase it rather than other goods, has become more costly in terms of the amount of alternatives which the consumer has to forego from his limited budget. In the real world the situation is rendered more complex as income (or, more accurately, disposable income) also changes, while over a period of time the tastes and preferences of clients will develop in response to many pressures. Furthermore, some special categories of purchases do not conform to the stereotype. In particular, certain purchases seem to be more desirable because of their high price, at least to some consumers. The premium fare charged for travel by Concorde arguably falls into this category although specific benefits such as its speed and the exclusive style of service offered on board offer important advantages for many of its passengers. Thus British Airways developed a package which enables business travellers to make a return visit to New York from London in one day. The arrangement included the use of a conference room at the airport in New York, to maximize time for meetings.

A more difficult problem is that this opportunity cost analysis is normally applied to goods which are homogeneous in nature; that is, it considers consumers' responses when the prices change, but all other characteristics of the commodity are standardized and unaltered. In contrast, a theme developed in this book is the determined effort of tourism managers to provide their customers with services which are differentiated from competitors' and so it is apparent that simple comparisons between tourism services such as those based on price, are not valid.

From the tourists' point of view, financial constraints combine with the time considerations previously discussed to give a decision matrix, shown in Table 2.4. This suggests that short duration trips are constrained in both cost and distance, although they are likely to be taken fairly frequently. In contrast, a long-haul tour is likely to be undertaken less frequently as it will be both expensive

Table 2.4   Aspects of leisure tourism decisions

Length	Frequency	Cost	Distance
Day trip	High	Low	Local
Overnight	Moderate	Low	Short
Week	Low	Varies	Medium
Main holiday	Annual	High*	Not a constraint

*The cost of a main holiday is constrained by personal budget considerations, but is often treated as a priority expenditure to be saved for.

Sources: Based on Cohen 1972, Frechtling 1976 and Lawson & Baud Levey 1977

and will require a considerable period of time away from home. However, frequency, cost and duration are terms whose meaning differs for individual tourists according to their circumstances and preferences.

Leisure tourism is generally purchased from discretionary spending, but the opportunity costs associated with the decision are high. The median cost of inclusive overseas holiday packages purchased in Britain was about £300.00 during the last few years of the 1980s. But the typical transaction was for two or more people travelling together and overall cost of a holiday to the traveller also included additional items such as insurance, domestic airport transfers and 'pocket money'. It is therefore likely that total spending by a 'purchasing unit', that is, a couple or a family, was more then £1000. This amount was comparable with the price of two or three major items of household electronic equipment such as video recorders, or complete carpeting for a small house! Thus, it is not surprising that Boyer (1972) has cited lack of finance as one of the factors constraining holiday purchases. Other constraining factors are discussed later in this book and together can explain the different participation rates in international tourism between countries. Pearce (1987) has presented an interesting table on page 27 of *Tourism Today* which compares the travel propensities of populations in selected European countries. He has also highlighted the difficulties of making precise comparisons between countries.

Distribution of tourism activity

The uneven distribution of tourism activity between countries requires explanation. Tourists' decisions to visit a particular destination reflect many factors, e.g. the efficiency of its transport links or any strong historical, religious or cultural relationships between the two countries. For many partner countries there are several travel services, each offering particular disadvantages and benefits. The varying benefits of competing services can be analysed for cost, comfort, frequency, timing and accessibility, to both point of origin and ultimate destination, and the attractiveness of each for certain sectors of the market can be understood on this basis. On long journeys a sixth factor to consider is the opportunities to break the journey to visit secondary points of interest. These important considerations are discussed more fully in Chapter 9. The variety of factors which influence choice of location include climate, scenery; politics;

Table 2.5   Factors attracting tourism
flows

- Differences in climate
- Differences in scenery
- Different cultural traditions
- Cost advantages to the tourist
- Quality of transport links
- Availability of packaged holidays

economics; cultural or natural heritage, and the occurrence of special events such as festivals – these are summarized in Table 2.5.

In common with the basic tourism model discussed earlier (Figure 1.1), the simplest model of a travel flow consists of an origin point, a destination and a transportation link between them. The volume of travellers between an origin and a destination is determined by the population of each and the distance (or cost and ease of travel) between them. But the flow may be stronger in one direction, reflecting not only their differing demographics, but a greater propensity to travel in one country, or a wider choice of destinations attracting residents of the other. A low rate of tourism traffic between two points can be regarded as evidence of resistance factors on the route. Resistance can be a function of distance and cost, resulting in differing propensities to participate at the origin (Zipf, 1946) and these can be overcome by appropriate marketing and technical strategies.

In most partnerships one member is dominant. In the early days of modern tourism, the flow was normally generated by one country in the tourism partnership, such as British holiday-makers visiting Spanish coastal resorts, whereas the number of Spaniards vacationing in Britain was very much smaller. As tourism has developed, this simple model of tourists travelling from one country of origin to one destination is less common. Destinations seek to attract visitors from many nations, and travellers experience an ever widening choice of holiday destination countries and resorts. However, it still remains the case that destinations are dependent on the flow of tourists from a limited number of origin points, while from one origin a wide range of alternative destinations are available. Now that an increasing number of countries generate significant outbound traffic bidirectional demand for tourism is increasingly evident, but it remains the case that often a significant majority of tourism is from one country of origin to the other as destination. Figure 2.1 indicates these relationships schematically.

The importance of each origin country for any destination can be assessed relative to the overall demand on its tourism sector by overseas and domestic visitors. This can be done in terms of spending as well as visitor numbers, and the significance of the analysis, together with the patterns of geographic and seasonal dispersal of tourism around the destination, is discussed in Chapter 10. Another pattern of vacation travel is for tours which visit a series of resorts, or sometimes spend most of the time at one centre. This type of tour has been referred to as linear tourism (Holloway, 1986).

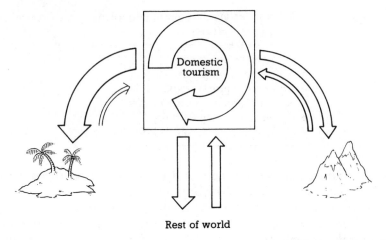

Width of arrows proportional to
value or volume of visitor flows

Figure 2.1 Tourism links between countries

Disruptions to tourism flows

Distinct patterns can be discerned in the flow of tourists around the world, but further analysis highlights a number of uncertainties in predicting future movements. In the few decades since mass tourism has become established there have been many localized interruptions to the general trends of steady relationships and increasing traffic. There are volatile factors in both the demand and supply of tourism services, with effects which may be very brief, or enduring. Table 2.6 distinguishes between some short and long term interruptions to established tourism patterns.

One example of disruptions to tourism flows cited in Table 2.6 is war. Civil strife or international conflict is the antithesis of tourism, which tends to bring people of different backgrounds together in harmonious ways which generate benefits for both visitors and residents, despite the potential serious difficulties

Table 2.6   Factors disrupting tourism flows

Duration	Examples of causes
Short term	Strikes and industrial disputes
	Storms, water shortages, etc.
	Transport accidents
Medium term	Fluctuating exchange rates
	Differential inflation rates
	Political unrest
Long term	War
	Harsh tax regimes
	Stern religious values
	New freedoms to travel (political or economic)

which are discussed in Chapter 11. War negates the attraction of travel to that region for leisure or pleasure, business is disrupted, and usually the public travel links between origin and destination are suspended. The damage to a war-torn country's infrastructure also means that physical recovery is likely to be slow after peace has been established; the opposite of this has been discussed in the Preface.

The image of a country or region can deter as well as attract tourists. Modern communications bring disaster, violence or stories of repression rapidly and vividly to everyone's attention, often as they occur. A war or terrorist acts can also have widespread effects on neighbouring tourism destinations. In the mid 1980s Europe experienced a series of terrorist incidents starting with the hijacking of a TWA aircraft to Beirut in June 1985, followed by the hijacking of a cruise liner, the *Achille Lauro,* the Egypt Air hijacking and terrorist attacks at Rome and Vienna airports. Many American tourists cancelled their holiday arrangements, business travel was curtailed and European travellers chose resorts in the Western Mediterranean, well away from the centre of trouble. Because of its location near the Middle East, Greece suffered more than any other country in the area even though very little terrorism took place in the country. Greece had been trying to attract US tourists, due to their propensity to stay in better hotels and their greater spending power than European visitors, although they formed a numerically small part of the overall market. The number of American tourists which had grown to nearly 620000 in 1985, dropped to 321000 during the problems of 1986, and even by 1988 had only partly recovered, to 444 000. It was reported that Europeans, who comprise the great bulk of visitors to Greece, returned relatively quickly.

Commenting on the effects of tourism in Europe from a North American tourism perspective, D'Amore (1987) pointed out that travel agencies and tour operators were among the first to feel the impact of terrorism on their business.

> One small group of agencies responded by announcing a European boycott since these countries did not appear to be doing enough to combat terrorism. In contrast, other agencies promoted special reductions in air fares and tours to . . . other European destinations . . . BA (British Airways) $6 million promotion campaign entitled 'Go for it, America' presented close to 5800 Americans in 15 cities with free flights to London . . . The massive promotional campaign also included prizes of a Rolls-Royce and a London town house . . . Prior to BA's American promotion bookings to London from the US were 30 per cent below normal. The BTA (British Tourist Authority) is now predicting a 15 per cent decrease for visitors for the year.

A comparison by other researchers of actual travel in June 1986 as a percentage of June 1985 gave the following results: England 66.6 per cent, West Germany 73.4 per cent and Greece 34.3 per cent (Brady and Widdows, 1988).

The demand or supply conditions of the market for tourism can be affected by a combination of factors. For example, there has been increasing pressure during the late 1980s for higher standards in holiday packages, a sentiment echoed by the resorts which had been targets for either rowdy behaviour by many visitors, or of severe pressure on hotel prices from tour operators. An unrelated set of problems was the frequent disruption to air travel which resulted from under-investment in ATC (air traffic control) equipment in the face of rising demand and industrial unrest, particularly amongst ATC staff in many European countries. The sporadic withdrawal of their labour caused lengthy airport delays, congestion and discomfort for many travellers (Travel Agent, 1989). These factors, the pressure for improved quality and ever increasing airport problems, provided the cue for the competitive strategies adopted by the major tour operators. Raitt (1990) has reported on a Tourism Society seminar at which senior managers discussed their views of the reasoning behind the aggregate reduction in holidays offered in the UK outbound market, from 11.6 million in 1989 to 9.28 million in 1990.

Communicating the attractions of destinations

In each major destination there are likely to be certain attractions which far outweigh the others. These often become a symbol for the destination. Examples include the Eiffel Tower, which instantly evokes thoughts of Paris, the minarets of Istanbul or the colourful submarine life of the Great Barrier Reef which is one of the dominant images of Australia. Typical indicators of the more enduring tourist images are to be found on the covers of national tourist organization or commercial tour operators' brochures. Thus, the British Tourist Authority often features traditional royal or military ceremonial on its posters. However, the longer the time tourists spend in a destination, or the more frequently they visit it, the more likely it is that remote and minority attractions will feature in their itineraries.

As a destination develops stronger links with its major originating countries the reasons why visitors are drawn to it are likely to become more diverse. It is essential for managers to gain an understanding of the benefits their actual and potential tourists seek and to monitor the way they experience tourism services in the destination. Inappropriate developments may reduce the attractiveness of the destination to certain groups of visitors, although without any investment it would rapidly become relatively less successful than competitors which had upgraded their facilities, and developed new markets.

It is important for destinations to promote as many of their attractions and activities as possible for two reasons. In the first place, a wider range of tourism services both reduces the localized impact of tourism in the main centres while spreading the employment benefits to outlying communities. Secondly, a diversified tourism base allows a destination to offer attractive benefits to varied interest groups. This can compensate for the increasing familiarity travellers have with established major sites, and allows the destination to develop a more effective marketing strategy based on segmentation, which is discussed further in Chapter 5. In addition to overseas originating visitors, destinations also provide services to local residents. Jackson and Schinkel (1981) have reported that local residents expressed a stronger preference than tourists for activities such as resting and relaxing, swimming, boating and canoeing in a particular setting, while tourists to the same area more frequently preferred activities such as sightseeing, hiking, photography, visiting and meeting people. This distinction suggests that different emphases are required when marketing a destination to tourists from different backgrounds and it raises the possibility of a conflict of interests and contrasting behaviours between tourists visiting one destination in search of very different benefits.

One of the fundamental precepts of marketing communications is that customers respond to the opportunities of which they are aware: the first step for tourism managers is to educate travellers about the range of opportunities available to them. But in the case of mass tourism destinations their success depends on easy access from the main tourism generating areas. Airlines can stimulate travel demand by providing information on what their destinations the intermediate stop-over points on scheduled routes have to offer. Thus marketing can benefit all major partners in a tourism service and so it often takes the form of a collaborative venture with local tourism enterprises or with destination representatives, as indicated in Case Studies F and J.

Seasonality in tourism demand

Nearly all destinations experience a seasonal pattern of demand: peaks and troughs in visitor arrivals and spending, with consequent variations in employment opportunities which are relatively predictable throughout the year.

The causes of these seasonal patterns differ. In some cases the country of origin generates seasonality as a result of some structural feature of its social institutions, for example through industrial or school holidays, or as a reaction against its climate. In other cases the destination itself has strong seasonality due to the characteristics of its climate, or the attraction to visitors of its traditional festivals. Figure 2.2 shows how marked is the seasonal pattern of tourism demand in Britain.

In either case the net effect of an existing pattern established between origin and destination is likely to change as entrepreneurs seek opportunities to exploit out of season tourism. A number of techniques discussed in later chapters, such as marginal costing and niche marketing, can be applied. It is often an objective of governments and enterprize managers to bolster the offseason trade to support more fully their investment in tourism plant and employment. Case Study F discusses one example.

The demand for business travel

Travel for business purposes is an integral part of human society; it arises from the unequal distribution of natural resources and climate differences between countries, and the resultant need to exchange specialized products. With the growth of a merchant class in Europe and the rapid accumulation of capital the stage was set to exploit the technologies of production and distribution which were to be developed in the industrial revolution, and with the further development of modern transport and communications systems, a shift to global

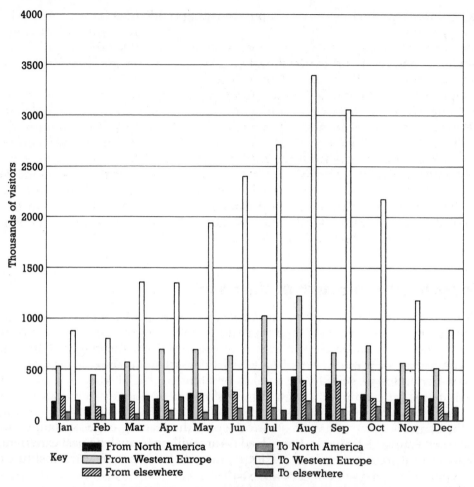

Figure 2.2 Seasonality in British tourism

business has been noted (Dicken, 1986). The recent growth in demand for business travel is strongly related to the changing structure of firms, the development of multisite firms and the movement to international rather than local manufacturing or markets. As gross national product increases, international trade is also likely to grow, and travel is required to visit multisite enterprises or to create and maintain distant contacts. Consequently, it can be argued that the business travel market sector is characterized by demand levels and patterns which depend on business conditions more than tourism managers' strategies.

The business market has different characteristics from the leisure sector. In general, business travellers spend more than holiday makers on a daily basis, as their demands for facilities and flexible arrangements are more expensive to service. They also need year-round travel, and the response by transport operators is to provide regular scheduled services. The significance of this market segment is further discussed in Chapters 2 and 9.

Recent trends in tourism demand

During the generation which has witnessed the development of the mass package tour, there has been a marked trend for the main holiday to be taken further from home. A number of factors can be identified which have contributed to this. Technical developments have played a significant role in the increased variety of tourism services and destinations offered. Airfares are tending to fall and so have become a smaller proportion of total holiday cost in real and relative terms, greater ease of travel has resulted from the more frequent schedules offered, and the point to point speed and ease of journeys is improving with regional departures from local airports direct to destinations. Against this positive trend a major influence against tourism is the increasing congestion and delay which characterizes international air transport, arising from security measures, under-investment and the rate of increase in demand which regularly exceeds projections, and the consequent under-provision of tourism infrastructure facilities.

The fundamental shift towards more leisure time during the twentieth century has already been identified as a major factor in the development of modern tourism. Social changes, including earlier retirement, shorter working hours during the week and longer holiday entitlements, combined with increased real and discretionary disposable income have made tourism accessible to many people. As demand has developed the nature of tourism has also changed, and the industry has responded with an increasingly diversified range of services to meet the demands of different market segments.

Mass tourism takes many forms, and one of the key challenges for the industry's managers is to anticipate what features of their services will appeal to future clients. Although their decisions form the leading edge of competition between suppliers, many industry leaders are willing to analyze past experience and to share predictions about the future in trade forums such as the Institute of Travel and Tourism, the Tourism Society, or the Chartered Institute of Marketing Travel Industry Group (CIMTIG). In America the Travel and Tourism Research Association performs a similar service for its members. CIMTIG is a group of senior tourism managers and academics who meet on a monthly basis, except in the peak summer season, to discuss and debate current issues of concern in tourism marketing. Table 2.7 indicates the main topics of

Table 2.7   CIMTIG discussion topics

- The over 50s market
- Marketing failures
- The hotel industry
- Marketing strategies
- Long haul tourism
- Winter holiday markets
- Humour in travel advertising
- Approaches to market segmentation
- Theme parks

discussion in the ten meetings of this group before this book went to press. Underlying the discussions were a number of themes; particularly the quality of tourism services, value for money, people's preferences for tourism compared to alternative purchases, staff recruitment, training and retention, the profitability of various tourism sectors, and the relationships between tourism businesses.

Conclusion

Demand for tourism is buoyant and dynamic. While this gives entrepreneurs many opportunities to enter an expanding market-place, it is also necessary for them to forecast future patterns of demand and predict the changing preferences of their customers so that appropriate services can be supplied to them.

International travel demand depends on three major sets of factors. Two related aspects explain the overall level of demand for tourism services; these are the social and economic conditions in countries of tourism origin, which together with the political climate largely explain the propensity for international travel from each country. Tourists enjoy choice between a wide range of destinations, and within any particular price band or duration of holiday the opportunities for vacationers are increasingly diverse. The distribution of tourists between destination nations is explained by another set of factors which include the historical, business and cultural links between them.

The volatile nature of international tourism, and the many factors which can affect any destination or country of origin suggests that enterprises will not want to be dependent on one source of business. The disruptive factors are very varied; they cannot be predicted and companies are unable to influence the events which have been discussed in this chapter. Taking a view of tourism as a system highlights the problem that the many small local tourism suppliers can take no effective action to cope with the sudden loss of a major source of trade and revenue, although companies based in originating countries may be able to retain their business volume by switching clients to alternative destinations.

Despite the foregoing discussion of intense and increasing tourism activity, it has to be noted that a very small minority of the world's population are tourists. Most of the world's tourists come from a relatively few countries, though the number is increasing. Typically these are the wealthy industrialized nations of Western Europe and North America. Recently the newly industrialized nations of Asia, first Japan and now Korea, have developed significant outbound flows and the range of transport and tourism enterprises to support their needs. However, it has been said that, 'On a world scale, fewer than 4 per cent of the world's population take international holidays and 80 per cent of international demand is generated by less than 20 countries' (Archer, 1989).

Questions

1 How do you account for the major characteristics of tourism demand in an area with which you are familiar?

2 Using published statistical sources such as those indicated below, redraw Figure 2.1 to show actual travel and tourism flows between a group of countries. How do you account for your findings?

3 Discuss the relevance of the concept of derived demand in relation to managing the market for business travel.

Recommended reading

Annual Year Book of Tourism Statistics, WTO, Madrid
The contribution of World Travel and Tourism to the Global Economy, American Express Travel Related Services, New York, 1989
The Tourism Industry, Bi-annual, The Tourism Society, London
Waters, S.R. *Travel Industry Year Book, The Big Picture,* Child and Waters, New York

CHAPTER THREE

The Supply and Distribution of Travel Services

Introduction

This chapter provides an account of the remarkable logistical achievement of the travel industry in enabling large numbers of people to visit distant destinations.

The origins of tourism

The early origins of mass tourism can be traced to 1841, when Thomas Cook claimed a place in modern history as innovator of the package tour holiday. He organized a train journey from Leicester to Loughborough, and as a sales incentive he added two brass bands, a gala, and tea with buns. The tour attracted 570 customers, paying a shilling each. Thomas Cook owned a print shop, so when he decided to run a weekend trip from Leicester to Liverpool four years later, he produced a brochure: 'A handbook of the trip to Liverpool'. Before the trip, he spent several days in Liverpool, assessing the merits of various hotels and restaurants, and organizing local excursions. As a result of the popularity of these trips, he decided to operate further excursions to more distant destinations. An advertisement at the time exactly defined Thomas Cook's view of the tour agent: 'The main object of the conducted tour apart from being able to calculate the exact cost before starting is to enhance the enjoyment by relieving the traveller of all the petty troubles and annoyances from a journey.' He believed in providing a full service to his clients, and devised an internationally acceptable form of payment for the services they required while travelling, which has evolved into the modern traveller's cheque system (Swinglehurst, 1982). Thomas Cook and Company continues to be a leading travel retailer and supplier of travel services, although at the time of writing it is part of a large banking group.

Other travel organizers became established about the same time in Europe and America, the core skills common to them being the packaging of travel, accommodation and excursion arrangements. A result of the packaging of travel opportunities was that tourists tended to go to the same places, meeting similar people and sharing complaints about the service they received abroad (Dulles, quoted in Gee *et al*, 1984).

Modern tourism

The predominant modern form of international leisure tourism is the air charter based inclusive holiday. This concept had its origin in the conditions in Europe following World War 2. During the war, many servicemen had fought or otherwise been engaged in foreign military campaigns, in Europe or further afield, and many had developed an appetite to return in peaceful times. After the war, specialized equipment developed for purposes of war, notably aircraft, became surplus to requirement and could be purchased relatively cheaply. In addition, the war had provided training and experience both in logistical skills, and for pilots. The first air inclusive tour is said to have been organized by Vladimir Raitz, who set up Horizon Holidays in September 1949. His first tour took place in May 1950, when 17 professional people travelled to Calvi, in Corsica, for a fortnight's holiday which was priced at £32.50. The group flew in a war surplus Dakota, and are reported to have stayed in old army tents (Davidson, 1989).

Since then tourism has established itself as one of the dominant economic and social activities of the late twentieth century. By the end of the 1980s British tour operators, retail travel agents, airlines and hotel groups and many other organizations were geared to produce and sell some 12 million overseas package tours annually. In Britain retail travel agencies and tour operators have developed mainly on their special ability to package and sell outbound tourism. Most are members of the 6000 strong Association of British Travel Agents (ABTA).

Tour operators and travel retailers are the main suppliers of overseas packaged holidays and as such they form the main channel of communication and distribution between destinations and potential visitors. They fulfil this role by developing advertising images, selecting illustrations for their brochures and other promotional literature, and by collecting and disseminating information about destinations to the trade and potential consumers. Many are now taking an interest in domestic opportunities for short breaks, special interests, and long stay or touring holidays in Britain. Other specialized UK holiday companies deal mainly with incoming travellers and are members of the British Incoming Tour Operators Association (BITOA).

The decision to supply tourism services

The tourism industry offers many opportunities for entry, both to entrepreneurs and staff. In part this results from the diversity and speed of development of the tourism industry, but it also reflects two related trends. The vision which drives the continuing development of tourism services offers scope for entrepreneurial initiatives, while the increasing scale of tourism operations is providing one of the main sources of new employment in many countries. The organizations supplying tourism services include public and private enterprises, and range from large to small in scale. Entrepreneurial opportunities to establish a business can be found in most sectors of tourism, but small scale companies are most common in catering, consultancy, attractions management and travel retailing or tour operating.

The smaller scale operations are generally established when their entrepreneurial founders see a coincidence of market openings with their own skills, interests or financial resources, or when they identify an opportunity to relocate to an attractive area with which they may already be familiar as tourists. Many are opened as a sideline initially. Start up enterprises may face a short life as their managers have limited experience, and they lack the resources if not the skills to significantly influence the flow of business. Typically they also lack the resources to survive any downturn in business such as those discussed in Chapter 2. A study of the formation and operation of tourism enterprises in Cornwall has discussed this.

Its authors found that a major feature of the tourist industry in Cornwall was its fragmentation into many small independent units. The area had traditionally been dependent on the domestic holiday market, and consequently it experienced marked seasonal peaks in July and August. The authors commented that these features play a significant part not only in determining the relative strength of the Cornish tourism industry, but also in the way it is able to respond to various policy and management strategies.

> The success of tourism depends ultimately on the efficiency with which local businesses respond to new situations ... In the hotel and guest house category a remarkable 60 per cent of establishments had been taken into new ownership between 1984 and 1985. Indeed, 28 per cent had only been in operation for two years at the time of the survey ... Family and personal savings were the two major sources of capital, and were instrumental in the setting up of 46 per cent of all establishments. This pattern of capital formation ... is suggestive of firms being controlled by relatively inexperienced business people who may have little or no conception of the need to draw up management strategies for their businesses. Twenty per cent were under the management of a founder owner and a further 62 per cent were managed by an owner purchaser. Most of the owners were between 41 and 45, although the accommodation sector owners were somewhat older on average ... The majority of owners had not received any education beyond secondary school level, although 35 per cent had some professional or vocational training, mostly related to former activities and not to do with managing a tourist business. Less than 8 per cent had held previous occupations relating to tourism, although 62 per cent had held last occupations in retailing or services. Sixty-seven per cent of establishment owners had previously been employees.
> (Shaw and Williams, 1987)

Other sectors of tourism, such as transport and related businesses, are mainly large scale operations, requiring sophisticated management techniques and substantial capital investment. They are often part of a group, sometimes devoted to tourism but operating an integrated range of services. Many larger organizations are involved in various sectors of tourism, a typical example being a tour operator which owns some of the hotels featured in its brochures, and has an airline which provides charter services for its parent and other tour companies. Alternatively the group of companies operates in many industrial sectors including certain tourism activities, and so its results are less dependent on the short term success of their tourism interests.

Organizational targets

Enterprises have financial performance targets to meet. Their proprietors expect returns from their investment which are comparable to the profits available from placing similar amounts of capital in other business ventures. Successful companies often have growth as an objective. Increasing size calls for changes in the structure and organization of the business; this often results in a reduction in the direct involvement of the original entrepreneurial team which had established the company. Additional staff have to be recruited, trained and rewarded. Marketing and product programmes have to be developed and financed, often using funds raised from external sources. As the business grows, control systems have to be established to monitor results and more stakeholders now have an interest in the detailed management of the organization. At the same time, as the initial market becomes more fully developed, new segments have to be identified and served, suggesting the likelihood of a further shift from the original business base or philosophy. Taken together the following outcomes are possible: competition leading to business failure, or improving services and expanded offerings, or consolidation by merger or take over.

Another outcome which certain organizations pursue is to maintain a given level of business, forsaking future growth, but this goal is difficult to sustain in the face of changing technologies, competition and consumer tastes. All of the companies operating similar types of service can experience development, consolidation or decline under the pressures of competition from new services, the introduction of new technologies, or changes in legislation, political and economic conditions, and consumer preferences.

Scale of tourism service operations

It is a basic tenet of economic theory that suppliers are willing to produce at greater levels of output as price in the market place rises. The interaction of changing price and volume decisions has been explained as a market regulating mechanism. However, few suppliers have a clear knowledge of their marginal costs of production at different levels of output, as each additional client is served. This point is discussed more fully in Chapters 6 and 9. In fact, most tourism suppliers are severely constrained by the scale of their equipment and the technical nature of their operation. A 100-room hotel could accommodate up to 200 people if all rooms were occupied by couples, or perhaps a total maximum of 400 adults and children. But, fire and safety considerations aside, that would be the ceiling on its capacity, and in reality, some rooms would be out of service at times undergoing refurbishment or improvement. Similarly, a 100-seat aircraft cannot fly with more than a hundred passengers, although in reality it may not even be able to carry a full load against adverse head winds on routes at the limit of its range.

These notional capacity limits do not form the basis of managers' costing decisions, as few operators expect to sell all the space they have available except at peak demand periods. Instead, fares and tariffs are based on normal levels of business which the company's experience indicates it is likely to achieve in typical business circumstances, and the prices are set so that all the costs incurred in operating the company will be recovered. If the volume of demand exceeds this target number, the additional profit from each extra seat or room sold is high since the additional costs of accommodating each additional client are relatively low: the overheads have already been recovered. However, if demand is greater than capacity business is lost and the obvious response to this signal is to obtain extra capacity by leasing, or in the long term by purchasing additional equipment. This creates new conditions, and the problem confronting managers is that total capacity has increased and so additional normal demand has to be stimulated. Instead of attracting, say, 60 hotel guests each night, the extended hotel has to attract 120 each night to earn sufficient to remain in business. At the end of the 1980s travel media reports indicated that approximately 1000 civil aircraft were on order, many of them twin aisle, extended range jets. Taking into account the need to withdraw ageing aircraft from operation, the question here is how the airline operators expect to generate sufficient extra demand to fill the increased seats which will become available. Chapter 9 deals with this in more detail.

Tour operations

Tour operators deal in holiday concepts. They select destinations, resorts, hotel or other accommodation, and package these elements with the other basic component of holidays, the travel. With so many tourism principals, relatively easy entry into the tour operating sector and changing demand conditions, tour operations is a complex business. The political and economic environments in which it exists are dynamic and often unpredictable as already indicated, consequently tour operating is often a risky but exciting business sector.

Tour operators market their holiday packages in the fullest sense: they take pricing decisions which they feel will attract the greatest volume of travellers or yield the best profit; they promote their holidays to customers and travel retailers through appropriate media; they produce and distribute detailed information in the form of holiday brochures by which clients can take buying decisions; they set up reservations systems to handle bookings and administrative systems to deal with suppliers and distributors; and they develop new holiday concepts for forthcoming seasons and work towards business goals of growth, market share and profit just as any other business does.

The tour operator's business revolves around booking blocks of hotel and travel space, and delivering large numbers of clients to those principals. The tour company bears the risks of researching and organizing a programme many months ahead of its sale, and also incurs the costs of brochure design, production and distribution, and the installation and staffing of a reservations system. A marketing communications programme is required to gain public and trade awareness for the tour programme, interest in them being a necessary precondition stimulating tourists' buying decisions. The tour operator can create interest in his programme through media communications campaigns and by educating the travel agents he deals with about the special characteristics and advantages of his packages, points which are further discussed in Chapter 5.

Marketing experience indicates that clients' views of a tour package are widening to include a range of additional benefits in their expectations of the overall holiday experience. These additional facilities can provide a basis for marketing the programmes and can be added to the holiday itself, or developed for clients before, or after their tour. Additional benefits of the package include pretour briefings, holiday risk insurance, assistance with airport check-in, home transfers, airport parking or predeparture accommodation. On tour, extra benefits include better flight scheduling, more comfort or uprated service standards, welcoming drinks or other tokens and full service at the destination. After the holiday a satisfaction questionnaire, with any follow up needed, may be offered.

Types of package tour

The simplest travel package has been described in Chapter 1 as consisting of two service elements – return travel and activities at the destination, although most airtours also include accommodation as a third element, and it is the type and quality of this element in the package system which is often the fundamental basis for differentiation from other similar packages. But most tour operators improve the basic travel package by including transfers at the destination, the services of representatives and through them opportunities for a variety of leisure, cultural sporting or entertainment activities. The precise mix of additional service elements helps the tour operator gain a unique position in clients' minds. Companies operating packaged tours are no different from other businesses in depending for their success on their appeal to sufficient clients. As more people travel, the range of destinations and the types of holiday offered become more varied. Increased spending power, increased awareness of holiday opportunities and the falling (relative) cost of holidays enable more people to exercise choice between an increasing number of holiday options, indicated in Table 3.1 (see also Figure 9.6).

35

Table 3.1   Package holiday concepts

Major feature	Variants
Transport	Air; scheduled, chartered
	Rail
	Coach
	Private arrangements
Accommodation	Hotel, various standards
	Self catering
	Camping
	Private arrangements
Organization	Guided
	Unaccompanied
	Single centre
	Multicentre
	Touring
Theme	None
	Sporting; participant or spectator
	Wildlife
	Culture
	Preformed group
	Conference

Mass market package holidays

Tour operators providing mass market holidays recognize the business opportunities from furnishing holidays satisfying large numbers of travellers. They work on the basis of regular programmes to well-known and developed resorts. Success comes from maximizing load factors on the travel portion, and through volume buying to negotiate very low rates with the accommodation suppliers they use. A high degree of organizational and managerial skill is required, with attention paid to marketing and sales, cash flow, channel member management and the sophisticated analysis of booking trends.

The design of holidays reflects research into market trends and the power of mass tour operators' volume buying. The holidays which tour operators offer typically have a wide public appeal and will be available from the majority of travel agencies on a routine basis. For a typical client there are no special considerations required in making a booking, and all salient information will be held in the brochure or on the central reservations computer which retail agents can readily access from remote locations for speedy confirmation. Prices for a particular holiday specification generally vary in a systematic way during the season, reflecting the tour operators' perceptions of fluctuating demand under such push influences as school holidays, or pull factors such as weather patterns in the destination.

Specialist tour operators

Other tour operators offer highly specialized opportunities for individuals to visit destinations of particular interest to them. Their brochures offer a collection of itineraries which may be very different from each other, emphasizing such activities as art, wildlife observation and expert guidance. The length and timing of each tour will reflect conditions at the destination: climate, festivals and so on, and each tour will be designed to maximize particular interests. Typically, such companies are led by enthusiasts who expect that clients will want to discuss the details of the itineraries they are considering at some length. Bookings are often accepted through the retail agency network, but many clients want independent advice. Managers spend some of their time leading tours, and more time travelling to investigate new opportunities. The people joining such groups are quite likely to share interests in common and as journeys to remote destinations often entail difficulties and sometimes discomfort, there may develop a group spirit which persists long after the tour, although lasting friendships can of course be forged on any type of journey or holiday.

An important aspect of specialist tour operating management is that the client may never meet a direct employee of the tour operator. Typically, the package will be purchased from a retail outlet, and local companies will be contracted to provide the services required on the tour. To a lesser degree, this situation can also occur with mass resort-based packaged holidays. When the added dimension of foreignness is considered it can be seen that there are many opportunities for variances in service standards. Indeed the opportunities for consistency are few, as distance makes tight monitoring cost ineffective, and the need to respond to local conditions requires a flexing of any given organizational style. When relations with local subcontracting agencies are considered it becomes apparent that consistent service delivery throughout one package is illusory as the many individual staff members with whom a client deals during the package are employed by separate companies, in varying cultures, and performing tasks ranging across a wide spectrum of skills. This point is developed further in Chapter 8.

The roles of travel retailers

Retailers are specialists in the skills of selling to their customers. As participants in the travel distribution channel they succeed by understanding how their customers behave, and by recognizing what travel services will appeal to them. Then their role is to persuade them to buy, to return to buy more, or more expensive, travel experiences. Effective travel retailers spend much of their time on cultivating this awareness and stimulating their customer base to purchase travel services. More effort may be invested in expanding the customer base by developing appeals to different target market segments, or alternatively, by narrowing the focus of their efforts towards satisfying more fully the specialized needs of selected segments, such as business travellers, those travelling to visit distant relatives, or people buying package tours.

Once a potential client enters a travel agency, the objective of staff is to close a sale during the interaction, and for clients to select a vacation offering their desired range of benefits. In order to achieve this, retailers need to invest in staff training at three levels. Technical training is required to enable staff to read the manuals, and cope with the requirements of the various principals' and tour operators' reservations systems; training in interpersonal skills can improve their techniques of dealing with individual customers, and product knowledge training is required so that staff can make relevant recommendations, appropriate for each client's needs. Their main role is helping individual customers to choose holidays which they will find personally satisfying.

Personal selling skills are at the heart of successful travel retailing. Two approaches have been distinguished in matching a client's needs to available services, referent and expertise bases. The salesperson acts as a referent by offering his or her clients a source of friendship and shared identity: the consumers perceive that they have similar needs and characteristics, and so what is offered by a referent salesperson is likely to have a direct influence on their decisions. It has also been shown that a sale is more likely to occur under these conditions. The second source of influence is the perceived expertise of the salesperson, that is, his confidence and knowledge of the services which he purveys. The effectiveness of one style rather than the other seems to depend on the product or service being sold, expertise being regarded as more important when a complicated product or service is on offer. Weitz (1981) has argued that expertise is the most appropriate mode of selling when the salesperson is credible as an expert, has the required technical knowledge, and in conditions where the customer regards the purchase as risky or complex, and when the salesperson and client are strangers. In most cases, a combination of referent and expertise styles is likely to prove effective, and consequently the salesperson should adopt a flexible approach to his customers, based on accurate diagnosis of their needs.

Hymas (1987) has discussed the special approaches to business travel retailing. He argued that

> this is an activity which comprises a number of distinct components. These can include relatively tangible items like the air ticket, hotel or car rental vouchers. But for the most part, they are intangible aspects of service delivery, consisting of features such as the prompt response of the reservations agent to the traveller's phone call, the accuracy of the travel information, the support which is delivered after the sale or the quality and reliability of the accounting arrangements.

He went on to describe the Travel Management Service (TMS) system or total travel management of a corporate client's entire travel related activities, drawing on his experience with the American Express 'Travel Cycle'. The cycle begins when the client corporation draws up a set of rules governing how arrangements should be made for employee travel, and continues with the detailed logistics of finding the best rates and fares. This stage also creates a management information stream. During the trip itself, clients need high quality travel services, a convenient and secure way to pay travel expenses, and the flexibility to make changes to their itineraries.

A further stage in the cycle following the trip itself is expense reporting, payment and reconciliation, and the cycle concludes with a review and analysis. Hymas pointed out that the familiar green American Express charge card is also sold as a corporate card, 'Corporations have been persuaded to issue it to certain classes of employees instead of giving them cash advances. This helps companies conserve cash and more closely monitor expenses'.

Tourism supply in Britain

Britain can be described as a mature tourism market place. It is ranked amongst the five most important tourist generating countries (see Table 2.2) and, as has been shown, Thomas Cook was in the forefront of establishing modern mass tourism. It is not surprising that its outbound businesses are leaders in development, technology and creativity. Britain is also a major tourist destination, attracting visitors who come from every part of the world for business, education or leisure purposes. The domestic demand for recreation and leisure in Britain is highly varied and a wide variety of attractions and activities throughout the country cater for local, regional and international tourists.

The UK tourist attractions industry

The traditional core of tourism activity in Britain is shown in Table 3.2.

Table 3.2   Tourist attractions in Britain, 1988
(3619 attractions)

	Million	
Total recorded visits	254	
Museums and art galleries	59	
Historic buildings	66	
Wildlife attractions	22	(estimated)
Churches	10	
Gardens	10	
Other attractions	98	

Source: Sightseeing in 1988, ETB, 1989

A study of tourist attractions managers' planning and policy intentions has revealed a range of objectives, summarized in Table 3.3. The attractions sampled in this study included historic houses and castles, some with gardens which were attractions in their own right, museums and zoos, theatres and churches. A quarter did not record attendance figures, the others claimed a total visitor count of 8 210 000, ranging from 81 000 to 2.5 million. Entrance to half of the attractions surveyed was free, the others charged between £2.50 and £6.50. The second part of Table 3.3 indicates how wide is the range of decisions which occupy the attention of tourist attractions managers.

Table 3.3   Tourist attraction management

A *The major stated objectives of the attraction managers over the next two to three years (not ranked)*
- Increase visitor figures
- Diversify the attraction
- Appeal to different audience
- Improve visitor services
- Achieve greater profit margins

B *Respondents were interested in the following products and services (not ranked)*
- Insurance
- Litter bins
- Display cabinets
- Lighting
- Guide books and related materials
- Security systems
- Ticketing
- Signing
- Maintenance services
- Souvenirs
- Catering equipment
- Toilet equipment
- Landscaping services
- Staff training

Source: Laws 1986, extracts from an unpublished consultancy report

Tourism trade channels

The diversified nature of the market, both in supply and demand for tourism which has been indicated in this chapter, leads to a need for distribution channels to overcome the gaps of distance and knowledge which make it difficult for most tourism principals to identify and recruit potential customers, who by definition seldom live nearby. A second aspect is the interrelation between several tourism principals. The business of tourism suppliers revolves around satisfying the wants of tourists, and that provides a strong rationale for looking beyond particular activities, such as the hotels and attractions existing in a destination area, and to see them as elements contributing to a tourism system.

It has been shown that organizations within the tourism industry trade with each other to provide a complete travel service for their clients to purchase. Various patterns of relationships are possible. Figure 3.1 shows the main ways in which tourism trade channels can be organized both to create and distribute tourism services. A number of functions can be identified for the channel including the construction of packaged holiday services by tour operators, the provision of information and reservations services by retail agents, and the provision of many specialized services by principals.

The characteristics of organizational buying behaviour differs in important ways from that of final consumers. Organizational buyers are more expert than private purchasers, and take a significant proportion of the supplier's capacity, often on a continuing basis. Organizational purchasing usually involves teams of several people from both the supplier and purchasing organization; this means that their role relationships and the structures of their respective organizations become factors in the final decisions taken.

Marketing to organizational clients entails an understanding of the factors within each buying organization that determine its decisions, so that effective marketing mix strategies can be developed. Organizational buying is complex; it is often a lengthy process, involving detailed considerations by teams of managers of cost and payment or delivery terms and, after the negotiations, formal approval by senior officers of both organizations is needed to seal the agreement. Since each partner has unique organizational characteristics which dictate the way it conducts business, but each is also an important supplier (or purchaser) different strategic marketing approaches may have to be adopted for

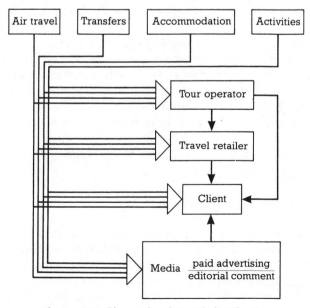

Figure 3.1 Channels of travel distribution

each organizational partner. Additionally, the buyer and seller are dependent on each other for services and flows of funds from the ultimate clients.

Conventional tourism marketing channels consist of independent firms operating to maximize their own profits (or satisfy a variety of other objectives). Alternative systems reflect the increased concentration of negotiating power or ownership of the system, in the most advanced cases the successive stages of production as well as distribution are owned by one company which operates an integrated business system. An intermediate stage is the coordination of most of the functions required to package, market and operate holidays by one company, which thus has the power to dominate the operations of the many small independent organizations on which it relies. Channel management tasks include the selection of dealers, setting up discount structures to reward and motivate channel members and the services required to distribute stock through the system so that it is available to potential users. In tourism retailing, this primarily means the brochures on which clients base their decisions, and which include the booking forms that function as a contract between clients and travel organizations.

A view of the channel as a system invites examination of the allocation between members of the functions it entails, and of the ability of any of its members to increase their profit by shifting costs elsewhere in the channel. For example, a National Tourist Organization might benefit from tour operator or airline advertising which feature it as a destination. In another case, a tour operator may require the travel retailers with which it trades to have staff trained in its systems and products so that the majority of client enquiries can be handled at the agency level, rather than by the tour operator's staff. Another example effectively brings the client into the channel; many car rental companies appear to expect their clients to act as car jockeys when collecting or returning vehicles, while competitors are happy to deliver cars to the booking office or to clients' hotels.

A further consideration is that the dominant member, for example a major tour operator, can offer extra inducements beyond what is normal business practice to entice retailers (or their staff) to sell a particular brand. Such extra incentives are typically linked to volume performance targets, considered further in Chapter 4. Thus, a distribution channel can be audited for efficiency. Other considerations revolve around understanding what customers want from the distribution system; this may differ according to each market and product segment as indicated in the earlier discussion of tour operators' styles.

Channel and direct sales

Travel principals, whether airlines, coach operators, hotels or attractions, have invested in capital assets and trained staff to provide the services from which the tour operator built a holiday package. In return for offering substantial discounts off standard prices they expect to receive a significant proportion of their customers from travel distribution system members. To varying degrees, they also deal directly with clients, but to do so they incur costs in providing their own information, booking and financial handling services. Travel agents pass tourists' deposits and final payments to the tour operator, who normally retains most of their funds until the service has been provided, when full payment is released to the principals. Before paying the principals, tour operators have substantial funds for a period and are able to place them on the money markets, thereby gaining a further contribution to their income and cash flow from the resultant interest which may be earned. Against this advantage, many payments are in foreign currencies, and so another type of risk falls on the tour operator sector as the exchange values of currencies shift frequently under a variety of unpredictable influences. To counter this potential threat to their profitability, many tour operators purchase foreign exchange on the futures market, speculating against such fluctuations.

In contrast to the pattern where clients purchase holiday services from intermediaries in the channel of distribution, such as travel agents or tour operators, most principals also deal directly with the public. Dealing direct with the customer means the operator's cash flow is improved, because payment is tendered to the operator rather than being routed through the agent, and of course the direct sale method also eliminates agents' commissions. As there is no need to maintain links with agents, that aspect of costs can also be reduced. A further saving results from tighter control of brochure distribution, thereby reducing wastage, and an allied improvement in the conversion-to-sales ratio. For many direct sell operators, another important gain is the more effective market segmentation which can be gained from analysis of detailed customer records. Thus it is possible to have relatively low start-up costs for direct sale tour operating, but market awareness of the new operation has to be generated and is likely to be expensive.

Against these benefits, the direct sale operator incurs additional costs. These range from postage and allied expenses to extra staffing required to deal with enquiries from interested people who may, or may not, purchase services from the operator. Therefore, additional office space is also required. Many companies provide both direct and agency sales but some choose not to distribute through retail networks at all. Their opportunities to reach potential clients are therefore more limited as they have no high street presence, and it is argued later in this book that many clients will not carry out extended search activities for services which are of only marginal importance to them; they are more likely to select a holiday from an alternative brochure which is readily available in a local retail outlet.

Communications

Two major strategies have been distinguished for marketing communication. In one case the service provider advertises to the client through public media such as newspapers, magazines, television and radio. The interest thus stimulated is felt by channel members as a pull through the distribution system when clients request specific brochures or information from travel agencies. This acts as a signal to the tour operator and principals, who respond by increasing the stocks of their brochures held by agents.

The alternative strategy is to promote a service to channel members, through public relations campaigns, educational visits, trade seminars, discounts or free offer schemes which reward the sales results achieved either by an agency or by individual staff members. Typically in the tourism industry, the push strategy described above is used to enhance the pull strategy with which it is run in parallel. In either case, the specialist travel publications and mass media have important roles to play. They act as vehicles for paid advertising and they have a role through editorial judgement and comment in communicating opinions on travel products which they have elected to sample. These methods are considered in Chapter 5, and in the case studies dealing with the marketing communications strategies of Hawaii, England and Texas.

Quality in an integrated tourism system

The discussion so far has emphasized the relationships between companies which underlie the provision of leisure tourism services. This should be seen against the background of evolving tastes, values and expectations which motivate tourists' decisions and act as the benchmark for the satisfaction they experience. The following quotation highlights this point, which is developed further in later chapters.

> Resorts such as Torremolinos, Benidorm and Magaluf – which at the beginning of it all seemed unattainably exotic – are being seen increasingly as cheap, tacky and simply not good enough. People believe there should be more to a holiday than sitting on the sand sipping sangria. There's a demand to do things. Aspirations have changed. Twenty years ago the hotels were of superior quality to peoples' homes, but today the cheaper resorts are no longer like this. (Davidson, 1989)

Conclusion

This chapter has described the disparate nature of tourism businesses and emphasized the contribution they all make to a tourism system. However, it has to be noted that the factors critical to the success of one, for example an hotel, may be irrelevant in other tourism sectors.

In a typical case, tourists purchase a holiday from a local travel agent by selecting between the many alternative tour operators' brochures. The retailer acts as an agent for the tour operator, earning a commission on the cost of the holiday, and being rewarded with higher commission rates by tour operators for whom he sells above a target volume or value of packages. The travel agent performs clerical functions for the operator but in addition advises his clients on their holiday choice – a time-consuming, labour-intensive and skilled activity.

Since the client typically buys a holiday package which includes travel and accommodation, the quality of his experience – the satisfaction he gains from the journey or the stay – is an integral aspect of his satisfaction with the holiday. Uncomfortable accommodation will reflect poorly on the tour operator from whom it was purchased by the client, even though the operator has no direct influence over the day-to-day operation of the hotel.

Questions

1 What do particular organizations contribute to a specific package holiday?

2 Draw up a checklist for a start-up tourism entrepreneur, highlighting decisions which should be taken regarding business objectives and methods appropriate to his scale and sector of operation.

3 Compare the package holidays which are available to an established destination. What are the main points of competition between the tour operators? What features would you recommend for a new brand serving this market?

Recommended reading

Carter, J. *Chandler's Travels,* Quiller Press, London, 1985

Gee CY Choy, D.J.L. and Makens, J.C. *The Travel Industry,* AVI Publishing Co., Westport, 1984

Hodgson, A. (ed.) *The Travel and Tourism Industries, Strategies for the Future,* Pergamon Press, Oxford, 1987

Holloway, C. *The Business of Tourism,* Pitman, London, 1986

Swinglehurst, E. *Cooks Tours, The Story of Popular Travel,* Blackwell, Oxford, 1978

Witt, S.F. and Moutinho, L. *Tourism Marketing and Management Handbook,* Prentice Hall, London, 1986

CHAPTER FOUR

Understanding Tourists' Decisions

Introduction

Success in managing any business venture depends on understanding the needs, preferences and behaviour of clients, whether actual or potential. This understanding provides the basis on which managers can plan a range of services, offering a set of benefits which are attractive to specific groups of clients. A detailed understanding of clients' differing needs enables the tourism organization to distinguish its services for particular groups of clients according to their separate interests, and to direct its marketing communications to specified target audiences. The routine operation and management of services also benefits from increased sensitivity to clients' varied motives, expectations and behaviour.

This chapter reviews a range of descriptive and analytical research models useful to marketers and demonstrates how the developing range of typologies describing tourists' motivations provides practical benefits in understanding the different segments in tourist markets.

The need to understand tourists' decision making

Tourism enterprises share with firms in all other industries the need to understand what their clients want, and to be aware of overall dimensions and trends in their industry. All face the central business challenge of selling and they compete with companies offering similar services. Often their competitors face similar internal costs of operation. Their potential clients inhabit similar social and economic settings, and competitors have equal access to them. Their business rivals may readily gain an understanding of clients' many common values and aspirations. For most of their clients, a decision to spend a proportion of the individual or family discretionary income (or savings) on tourism experiences inevitably means foregoing alternative purchases.

Seen against this competitive background, the recognition that the market is made up of a variety of individuals is both helpful and frustrating for managers. Few consumer businesses are able to invest the resources needed to identify and know their individual clients' preferences, and yet they need to take a more specialized view of potential clients than is afforded by traditional economic understanding. Marketing behavioural models disaggregate the homogenous price responsive behaviour described in macro-economic theory, and offer alternative perspectives on clients' behaviour. This can help a service provider to segment the market, the many potential individual clients can be seen as members of reasonably sized groupings in which people have sufficient features in common to enable a company to develop a coherent range of services to satisfy their varying needs. A segmentation strategy also enables the company to reach each group with advertising communications appropriate to its members.

As the capacity of computer reservations systems to store data improves, and the speed with which the data base can be interrogated increases, it is becoming feasible to retrieve valuable information on clients' past preferences economically and speedily, to assist in their bookings. Relevant information includes seating or meal preferences on scheduled airline services, or a client's preferences for features such as automatic transmission or cruise control in reserving a rental car.

The insights into their customers' behaviour which managers need can be gained by systematic observation, directed research into customers' experiences or analysis of their correspondence praising or criticizing their personal experiences of a service. The benefits to be gained from an appreciation of differing customer needs and behaviour are not limited to the marketing function. In operating any tourism enterprises, whether resorts, tours or flights, retail outlets or airports, insights into human behaviour can help managers avoid situations which might cause dissatisfaction, or to minimize the consequences which result from the inevitable problems of running service operations.

Companies adopting a market segmentation strategy tend to deal with subgroups of clients, and need to know how to reach them through the media, how to make advertising messages attractive to each group and how to design, sell and operate tourism services satisfying a specific group of clients. An increasing variety of tourist typologies offering differing perspectives are available as the outcomes of both commercial and academic research.

Demographic typologies

One of the main ways of classifying people who may be in the market for products or services is in broad terms, typically including basic biographic data such as their age and sex, their social status or class and their income level. It is clear that economic welfare, and particularly peoples' discretionary spending power, plays a significant role in their decisions about whether to travel, and then where and how to do so.

Since the family is such a fundamental feature of social and economic life, this is also a consideration in the determinants of travel behaviour. The various stages of a family's life cycle are a major predictor of its members' leisure travel behaviour (although it is not significant in the majority of business travel decisions). The first stage is that of the bachelor, defined as young, single people not living at home. At this stage individuals have few financial burdens, and tend to be fashion followers, oriented towards recreational activities including vacations. After marriage and the arrival of children to fill the family nest, opportunities to travel decline, until, with the passage of time, the empty nest stage is reached. These are older married couples with no children living at home. Their financial position tends to be very secure and their interest in vacation travel can be satisfied. However, as they get older, they participate less in the travel market (Wells and Guber, 1966). The insights to be gained from this approach depend on understanding the extent to which these categories apply in particular social and cultural contexts, and also on the demographics of a particular market.

The basic approaches of life cycle, occupation and income have been combined in one study, known as SAGACITY. The concept underlying this is that behaviour and aspirations change as people move through four major stages in their life. These are dependent, pre-family, family, and late life-cycle stages. In each of these stages people are classified according to their occupational status as white collar, that is ABC1, or blue collar, C2DE. However, the family and late stages of the life cycle are further subdivided into better-off or worse-off groups, giving a total of twelve SAGACITY segments (Crimp, 1985).

Other widely used discriminators of purchasing behaviour rely on the characteristics of individuals' social status or age, but seem to be less effective predictors of travel behaviour: people of all ages, from any social background and most economic conditions may be found enjoying all conceivable tourist destinations and activities.

Broad tourist classifications

Broad client descriptions are helpful in macro-analysis where the industry's overall dimensions and trends are important data inputs to policy decisions at local or national levels, or in assessing both the viability and impacts of major investment proposals. The aggregate numbers of tourists moving between points of origin and various destinations, the directions of tourism flows, length of visitors' stay and the purpose of their visits are basic data for governments and the major tourism enterprises.

The technical definition developed in 1963 by the United Nations Conference on Travel and Tourism distinguished three major groups of international tourist. Tourists were classified as 'temporary visitors' staying in the country visited for at least 24 hours either for leisure or for business purposes. Those two groupings were distinguished from 'excursionists' who stayed in the destination country for less than 24 hours. Excursionists are unlikely to require accommodation, although they will make demands on the other components of the tourism experience including transport, catering and activities, depending on their particular interests.

Important though macro-economic definitions are for governments, and for an understanding of the size and trends in the industry, the demands of businesses for insightful bases to their decision making are not met by such broad approaches. Another macro-level approach distinguishing between three major motivations for travelling does provide a useful starting point for tourism managers. The three groups are 'Visiting Friends and Relatives' (commonly abbreviated to VFR), 'Business' and 'Leisure'. This simple typology remains fundamental to much theoretical and practical work; it offers a convenient shorthand to describe major segments in the market for tourism, and is helpful in predicting the preferences and behaviour of each major segment. It clarifies the opportunities to be gained by businesses responding to each segment, although in itself this typology is unable to predict how to manage their tourism experiences.

For example, Makens and Marquardt (1977) found that a high proportion of American airline passengers travelling in premium class were using tickets purchased from company funds. This finding is significant for an airline considering how to develop an appropriate marketing communications programme for its premium fare (business or first class) services. It might, for instance, be considered necessary to commission further research to identify what special needs businesses are endeavouring to satisfy when buying premium fare air travel for their staff. Another focus for study is the purchasing decision processes of companies. In some companies the individual managers who need to travel have authority, or they may delegate it to their secretaries. In others a company travel expert is responsible for buying tickets while others establish agreements with preferred retail agents, or have a permanent business house implant which sometimes follows policies laid down by its own head office.

The basic approach of sorting travellers into the three general groups of VFR, Business and Leisure has been extended by recent writers who argue that there are several segments to the demand for mass tourism. These are shown in Table 4.1.

Recognition that there are detailed differences in the reasons why people decide to travel, and that consequently their needs while travelling and their budgets will vary, enables a tourism organization to develop suitable services for each market segment to which it wishes to appeal. Additionally it can focus its

Table 4.1   Segments in the mass travel market

---

1 'Relaxation and physical recreation' including nature lovers and beach-oriented people
2 'Sightseeing and culture', including the wandering tourist who may adopt either a 'nodal mode', based at one touring centre, or prefer a 'linear tour', moving from hotel to hotel
3 'Visiting friends or relatives'
4 'Special interests' including study, sport, health, religion and conventions

---

Based on Holloway, 1986

marketing communications more effectively by approaching each group through appropriate media channels and with messages relevant to that group of clients. Such marketing strategies are considered in later chapters.

Each of the typologies already discussed has a role in describing and understanding overall tourist decisions about destinations and duration of travel, but rather more disaggregated models are required for pro-active, situation-specific tourism management.

Psychographic segmentation approaches

As society develops, the ways in which people spend their non-work time also changes. The balance between time devoted to the major life-spaces of family commitments, work, and leisure also shifts, as indicated in Chapter 2. The significance of this is that peoples' activities, interests and opinions (collectively referred to as 'AIO') are recognized as important factors in their decisions about how to spend their money and time, and are generally a good indicator of the sort of experiences which they will find satisfying. As their interests change, it can be predicted that their preferences for particular tourism activities will also alter – effective marketing planning and market or product development depends on predicting accurately how people's activities, interests and opinions will change.

Segmentation offers a way of gaining a richer, more detailed understanding of travellers' needs and of ways to attract their attention through images or messages which are particularly relevant to those individuals. The procedural issue is how to select segments for research. Age, income, occupation and family structure have already been identified as suitable bases for such studies, but psychographic profiling offers deeper and more insightful approaches. A psychographic study builds up a picture of people's beliefs and attitudes by analysing the responses of a sample of interviewees to a series of questions probing relevant aspects of their personality, attitudes, beliefs and values. The questionnaire also focuses on their buying behaviour and usage of products and services, in specific circumstances, or in relation to selected brands. The procedure results in quantified categories of consumers, and provides a practical basis for marketing programmes. One of the benefits, as noted by Wells (1975) is that 'psychographic information can put flesh on demographic bones.' It is most often encountered as a series of verbal descriptions which instantly evoke each market category.

One example is VALS (Values and lifestyles), which was developed in America and classifies the population into four general consumer groups, with a further subdivision into a total of nine subgroups. Table 4.2 shows how the method may be applied. The system is useful in identifying differences in consumer patterns of behaviour. Mitchell (1981) has described VALS as 'a comprehensive conceptual framework describing people's values and lifestyles in such a way that it would help explain why people act as they do, both as consumers and as social beings'. Similarly, Kotler has defined the concept of

Table 4.2   A VALS approach to tourism market segmentation

Type	Characteristics
Survivors	People in this VALS lifestyle type typically have shied away from activities which require high levels of physical energy and they recorded the lowest participation in most travel related categories
Belongers	The central concern of people in this lifestyle type is to be accepted by others. More vacations are taken by all other VALS types combined than by belongers. When they did travel, there was a strong likelihood that the trip would be by automobile
Achievers	Members of this lifestyle type exist in a world where success leadership and power are of central concern. They exhibit better than average participation in several business and pleasure activities. In pleasure travel they are higher than average in hotel/motel stays, use of rental cars and use of travel agencies
Societally conscious	People in this group emphasize social concerns and place less emphasis on materialism. They mirror the achievers in their travel participating in higher than average amounts of travel by air, stays in hotels/motels, use of rental cars and use of travel agencies

Based on Blazey, 1989

lifestyles as 'a person's pattern of living as expressed in his or her activities, interests and opinions' (Kotler, 1983).

However, stereotypes can be misleading. A survey of American women under the age of 35 showed that 90 per cent did not aspire to being lifetime home-makers, contrary to popular belief. Three-quarters of the interviewees planned to combine home-making with a paid job throughout their working life. Commenting on this study, Asseal (1986) suggested that this trend is indicative of a shift from family to individual goals, 'There is greater willingness to spend on leisure products, entertainment and services. Parents are more willing to enjoy themselves now – to travel, dine out, buy luxury products – rather than to save for their children's future'.

Management decisions about the specific attributes to offer in their services are based on beliefs about the satisfactions which tourists are seeking. These beliefs may reflect managers' experience, personal values and assumptions, or they may be derived from research. Insight can be gained through questionnaires designed to elicit information from a sample of clients on their activities, interests and opinions. However the resulting classifications may be ephemeral as tastes change with time and few individuals would feel themselves entirely in tune with any such artificial group's values, even if they recognize some validity in the analysis.

Managers may gain several advantages from psychographic research; it is useful in identifying new targets for particular services, and gives insights helping to identify market segments as a basis to position products through advertising. Furthermore, an understanding of the interconnections between people's habits and interests forms a basis for the development of media guidelines to underpin advertising campaigns.

Many market research studies of tourists' reasons for selecting particular tours, activities, or destinations also include a series of demographic questions and a set of attitude statements. These are used to explore the common characteristics of sub-groups of tourists and the perceived attractiveness of a service or a resort. However, Pearce (1987) has identified shortcomings and limitations in the questionnaire formats employed in such studies.

The realization that an individual's interests, discretionary spending power and a wide range of his perspectives change as he matures has important implications. Recognition of the individual as a member of a family itself moving through a series of stages further enhances a sophisticated awareness of appropriate advertising appeals and the design of satisfying tourism experiences. Programmes can be developed for people of a particular age group having much in common, such as the elderly or unattached youths. Others are intended for family groups and structured in ways which allow parents freedom from routine family chores together with opportunities to mix with people from similar backgrounds. The advertising for such holidays will typically feature individuals or groups apparently similar to the target audience in important characteristics and enjoying situations which it is hoped will appeal to the potential clients.

Operational tourism typologies

McIntosh and Goeldner (1984) have argued that the anticipation of pleasure is a major motivator in travel purchases. They specified four travel motivators: the reduction of tension through physical activities; the desire to know more about other countries; the desire to meet new people and escape from routine; and fourthly, the desire for recognition, attention and appreciation.

This analysis of tourists' motives suggests that there could be conflicting interests amongst the patrons of any destination which offers a variety of tourism experiences. Alerted by this typology to an awareness of the varying motives and expectations of their clients, a destination's managers might be prompted to conduct an audit of its attractions, and the activities available there, as the first step in researching customer perceptions. Gaining an understanding of how its potential visitors see the resort might suggest to its managers that their advertising should emphasize the opportunities it affords for physical activities, or alternatively for social opportunities to mix with other people in order to attract one preferred client segment. Similarly, an airline might decide that its advertising messages would gain wider audience attention by emphasizing the caring, personal approach of its inflight service style, or a tour operator might consider adapting its itineraries in ways which afford increased opportunities to learn more about the countries visited and to get close to the local people.

Sunlust and wanderlust

Two classical tourist motivators are the desire to travel, and the pleasures of sun, sand and sea. Gray (1970) has suggested that 'sunlusters' are likely to travel to one country, but once there they polarize into 'relaxing' and 'energetic' tourists. The research was based on American samples, and consequently emphasized the attractions to American sunlusters of their domestic resorts. In contrast Gray considered that people tended to satisfy 'wanderlust' by travelling abroad, usually on a multi-country trip.

The differentiated sunluster model distinguishing between relaxation-seeking and energetic tourists suggests that it may be inappropriate to promote a beach holiday resort both to clients seeking quiet opportunities to improve their tan and to those others who want a wide variety of water and beach sports activities. The immediate consequence might be clashing interests and in the longer term dissatisfied clients are likely to choose alternative resorts for their future holidays.

Escape-reward models

Iso-Ahola (1980) has argued that the drive to escape personal problems or routine situations interacts with the pull of anticipated pleasures from new encounters. The range of personal rewards people hope to gain from travel experiences suggested by Iso-Ahola include relaxation, ego enhancement, learning about other cultures and increased social interaction. Similarly Crompton (1979) identified novelty and education as the two cultural interests of his 39 interviewees and a break from routine as their basic motivator for leisure travel. He established an agenda of psychological motives for travel, often 'hidden' from the tourist, as shown in Table 4.3.

As Crompton pointed out, his findings, though based on a small sample and qualitative, underline the complexity of travel motives. These models present leisure travel as a psychological response to personal disequilibrium. By taking a break from routine and enjoying alternative scenery, climates and cultures people are able to overcome the frustrations or dissatisfactions of their regular work or domestic life.

Cohen and Taylor (1976) considered that escape motivations can best be

Table 4.3   Psychological motives for travel

- Escape from mundane surroundings
- Exploration and evaluation of one's self
- Relaxation
- Prestige
- Reduced constraints on behaviour
- Opportunities to get closer to relatives
- Social interaction

Source: Crompton, 1979

understood as a search for individual identity, while Dann (1978) has demonstrated that visitors to Barbados seeking self-enhancement had relatively low-status positions in their home society. They were from lower socio-economic backgrounds and were often women on their first visit to Barbados. They participated in staged local folk events and wanted to visit all the tourist sites on the island. In contrast the anomic visitors were married, from above-average socio-economic groups, and on a repeat visit. They stayed in the more expensive hotels, were interested in relaxation, or sport and good meals. They sought sophisticated entertainment.

The lesson from such studies for Barbados' tourism managers appears to be to develop two different campaigns to bring the differing appeals of Barbados to the attention of its two major American visitor groups identified in the study by Dann. Within Barbados, each of the two groups of visitors will be seeking different satisfactions from the hotels and activities they patronize.

Institutional preferences

Cohen (1974) has developed a classification of tourists according to the extent to which they prefer their experiences to be organized by others. According to this typology, 'drifters' search for exotic environments while 'explorers' prefer to make their own arrangements, but 'institutionalized' tourists travel to popular destinations both individually and in organized groups. At their destination the institutionally-oriented tourists are likely to be insulated from the realities of local life, finding familiar standards of comfort and associating mainly with other tourists. They prefer to purchase a complete holiday package, to stay in luxury (or at least, in comfortable purpose-built hotels), to eat familiar foods and to benefit from the support of a tour operator's representative while away from home. Readers may find the case study of tourism in Tibet interesting in this respect.

The distinction discussed above is significant for tourism managers. It is the drifters and explorers who first identify potential tourist destinations. As local entrepreneurs recognize the business opportunities which the early tourists bring the nature of the destination begins to change and tour operators in the originating countries feel able to introduce the new destination to their clients. These developments may attract the more institutionalized tourists but alienate the sensitivities of the drifters or explorers. The regular arrival of packaged tourists will speed the development of the destination area as more infrastructure is required and as total tourist spending increases. Later chapters discuss the possible sequence of events and the consequences for the various groups involved.

Fundamental marketing distinctions for managers

An important distinction for managers is that between people who are clients of an enterprise and those who are not. Within the latter, the major groupings of potential interest to the organization's marketers are those who may become clients in the future, those who have been clients in the past and those who are unlikely to become clients.

A second fundamental distinction for tourism managers was drawn by Valene Smith (1978). By pointing to the interaction between 'hosts' and 'guests' she has drawn attention to the significant fact that tourism services are created by people working in the tourism industry, while concurrently others enjoy its benefits as tourist consumers. Clients' enjoyment of tourism services and any subsequent repurchase of particular tourism experiences, depends on the quality of performance by client-contact employees with the appropriate range of skills to deliver satisfactory service standards. In this sense, tourism employees may be regarded as hosts and their skills are important variables in the effective management of tourism, the significance of which is discussed further in later chapters. The concept of host has another connotation, the broader meaning which encompasses all residents in a tourist destination area. The significance of this point is developed in Chapter 11.

Market research

The benefits of market research have already been identified in connection with segmentation of markets. Analysis of its trading records provides a useful insight into the past buying behaviour of a company's customers. It is possible to identify seasonal or weekly trends in bookings, and to identify the relative and changing popularity of its range of services. From the point of view of understanding customers' decision making an understanding of their past buying behaviour can point to the most promising services to develop for future success, and can help a company avoid repeating mistakes.

It is also possible for managers to identify segments of the market for whom a company could develop new services, and to gain insights into what tourists might find satisfying by applying market research methods. Businesses which recognize the utility of understanding their clients' behaviour can develop a management information system linked to bookings procedures which can yield much useful information. A computerized reservations system can be adapted to generate such data with minimal additional effort. Another application of market research is in advertising, where the effectiveness of campaigns can be assessed by tracking the responses obtained from various media, first in terms of enquiries and then of conversions, that is sales, to gain additional insights into customers' media habits.

Many large tourism principals prefer to deal with clients through the retail agency network, for reasons critically discussed in later chapters, but they still need to communicate with clients to remind them of the benefits of their particular services and to gain awareness amongst new clients. Close scrutiny of their past records will reveal much about the characteristics of those people who tended to become its clients. Precise categorization can be coupled to an analysis of nationwide data, such as the census, to establish what segments of the population to target for mailshots to their homes to reinforce the appeal of the general advertising placed on the media. An effective extension of this approach is to develop a series of programmes which appeal to those different groups, and to approach them directly. It depends for its success on several factors, apart from the holiday service offered, the range of critical factors includes the timing of the offer, the way in which it is communicated and packaged, how it compares to competing options for discretionary spending and critically, the salience to each group of the benefits communicated to them. The more closely their past behaviour and responses and their present attitudes and needs are understood the more accurately the tourism experiences offered to them can be developed and explained.

It is not only final consumers whose behaviour is significant in the success of a company. Prior to the British Airways take-over of its assets British Caledonian had been experiencing difficult trading conditions. Research showed its managers that they could not identify the IATA agents who had produced the best results, nor could they communicate directly with the sales staff who influenced passengers' decisions about which airline to fly on. They developed a database of the individual qualified staff members in each IATA agency in Britain, and learned about the mailing preferences of each travel agency. For example some required mail to be addressed to the manager, in others the individual staff member was responsible for his own workload. The understanding which BCal managers gained from this exercise enabled them to bring special offers and the introduction of new services to the attention of the appropriate people in each agency and by offering attractive incentives for sales results which staff had a realistic expectation of achieving, sales levels were boosted.

Typology research and management practice

Goodrich (1979) has described a study commissioned by American Express and discussed its application to marketing. Nine hundred questionnaires were mailed to American Express clients resident in New York State, generating a 26 per cent response rate. Information was gathered about respondents' frequency of visits to nine destinations popular with Americans. They were asked to rate each destination on 11 tourist attracting attributes on a seven point scale. Their ratings were factor-analyzed, and a series of 'benefit bundles' sought by the main groups of travellers were identified, as shown in Table 4.4.

In response, American Express developed a new range of advertising appeals to broadcast a much wider variety of tourist benefits specific to the destination. American Express brochures too were reformulated to depict broader based bundles of benefits. More fundamentally, the holiday packages were developed to emphasize the particular benefit groupings which had been identified.

A further important benefit to American Express of the research highlighted by Goodrich was that retail sales staff became more sensitive to the interests of individual clients and so were better able to provide a professional service in satisfying their wants by asking more probing questions during a sales transaction. They were more able to match the characteristics of particular destinations to their individual clients. Consequently, it was more likely that

Table 4.4   Benefit bundle analysis

Type	Characteristics
Passive-entertainment types	Middle aged, their interests are urbane and passive, and include shopping, relaxation, good cuisine, entertainment and climate. A pleasant attitude by local people is important
Sports types	Male dominated and sports oriented, they value good accommodation, a range of sports facilities and relaxation away from the children
Outdoor types	Middle aged, they are interested in scenic beauty, historical and cultural aspects of the vacation are important

Adapted from Goodrich, 1980

clients would be satisfied with the travel experiences they had purchased from American Express, and more likely to return to the company for future travel purchases.

Conclusion

The managerial advantages to be gained from understanding tourists' motivations and propensities to travel can hardly be over-emphasized. But, however convenient it is to categorize travellers, individuals do not fall neatly into the patterns proposed in behavioural models or typological classifications, and managers should be aware of the limitations as well as the advantages of these approaches.

Nor is it realistic to believe that an accurate description by tourists of their reason(s) for travel gained at the time of purchase will necessarily remain constant throughout the travel experience; it may change during a trip, and clearly varies over a period of time. Indeed there are often several motivators underlying a decision to purchase travel.

An essential prerequisite in marketing to tourists is to understand the degree of freedom they have in their choices. Salient factors include their choice of destination, mode of travel, budget and travel timings, their departure and return flexibility and duration of stay. Understanding their clients allows services to be differentiated and markets to be segmented in ways which will enhance a company's marketing efforts. A thorough understanding of the varying freedoms enjoyed by each market segment underpins the rationale for approaches, such as differential service-class pricing linked to ticket rule flexibility found in many transport operations. This is discussed in later chapters.

Modern computer technology has significantly decreased the cost of interrogating relevant databases: these include the data generated from a company's own trading records and the national aggregated data available commercially as well as government sources such as the census material. In common with the products of other industries, successful tourism experiences offer benefits significant to the clients and the challenge for managers is to develop methods of communicating those advantages to all potential clients. Given the complex and dynamic range of influences on travel decisions discussed in this chapter, the design marketing and operation of travel and tourism services should be related to the clearly understood needs of each client group.

Questions

1 Suggest relevant classifications for marketing purposes of tourists currently using a service with which you are familiar. How might these be researched further?

2 Contrast the market research needs of a major tourism supplier such as an international hotel group with those of a small operation, such as an independently owned guest house.

3 Conduct a pilot survey of the leisure habits of a convenient sample of people. How do you account for the findings?

Recommended reading

Chisnall, P.M. *Marketing, a Behavioural Analysis*, McGraw Hill, Maidenhead, 1985
Crimp, M. *The Marketing Research Process*, Prentice Hall, London, 1985
MacCannell, D. *The Tourist, a New Theory of the Leisure Class*, Macmillan, London, 1976
Pearce, P.L. *The Social Psychology of Tourist Behaviour*, Pergamon Press, 1982

CHAPTER FIVE

Influencing Tourists' Decision Making

Introduction

Traditionally, and necessarily, the thrust of a company's marketing effort is competitive, as managers invest a proportion of its resources to establish a position in the market, protect its market share, or to take a competitor's clients. The tourism industry is characterized by many suppliers competing for an increasing number of clients, and is typical of an industry at an early stage of its development. Under these conditions the strategic options open to an organization are based mainly on pricing differences, or on tailoring their services to selected groups of customers as each supplier's marketing actions are concerned primarily with influencing potential tourists to purchase its services. Thus, as the industry develops, consumers benefit from a wider choice of products, offered at affordable prices. However, although there is a great potential for growth, it is not certain that the industry will continue to expand overall, nor that a particular sector or region can anticipate an endless stream of business.

The philosophy underlying marketing campaigns is to change the market conditions within which a supplier operates. Therefore, a preliminary management decision is to define the demand conditions in which it wishes to operate. The objective may be to increase total demand, or reduce the sensitivity of clients to changes in price, or to create conditions in which it is harder for competitors to enter the market.

Several specific tasks for tourism advertising can be distinguished. The primary objective is to sell a specific destination, or brand of accommodation, carrier or retailer. Secondary tasks for advertising include shifting demand into the slack season, or encouraging early booking, or influencing choice towards a higher, more expensive standard of service. The first two reflect the inability of tourism suppliers to store their inventory, while the latter exploits the marginal costs of operating services, and is discussed later.

Stages of demand

The central task for marketing managers is to manage demand. In the first instance this means stimulating an interest in the organization and its offerings, and then influencing customers towards purchasing its services. Table 5.1 indicates how the tasks of marketing evolve as a demand for a company's services develops. Marketing expertise provides specialized inputs to managerial decisions dealing with the service offered, its pricing, distribution and advertising.

Table 5.1   Managerial responses to the stages of demand

Stage	Response
None	The public has no knowledge of the company or its services. The task is to research the market and present information to the public, giving them reasons to buy. Prices must be determined and channels of distribution must be established
Normal	The organization is supplying its services at near-full capacity. The task is to monitor customers and competitors, and to remind the public about the advantages of the brand
Irregular	Patterns of demand are inconsistent with supply, either in terms of season, location or standards of service (e.g. class). As the existing patterns of demand tend to reflect conditions in society it will be costly to shift
Full	All capacity is taken. The problem for a service firm is to maintain the quality as increasing numbers of clients use its services
Unwholesome	Overuse of facilities, or inappropriate tourist behaviour causes problems to staff, residents or other clients. The problems may be countered by advice and information, or high prices may be set in an attempt to exclude troublesome clients, if they are considered to be sensitive to rising prices

Adapted from Kotler 1973

The purchasing decisions of customers, whether past, present or future, are crucial to any company. Existing customers generate flows of both revenue and information about current customer perceptions, attitudes and preferences. The needs and preferences of potential customers have to be anticipated in developing tourism packages and contracting for the services of which they are composed, and a major source of understanding what will attract clients is the historic data which the company or the industry has generated from its past trading experience. As was indicated in the previous chapter, this will be held in company records and customer correspondence files, although it is seldom organized in a form which readily yields these insights. Market research is also needed to gain a detailed understanding of customers' evolving attitudes and expectations.

Consumer decisions

The key to an organization's marketing orientation lies in its understanding of how its potential clients make decisions to spend their resources of time, money and effort, and of the benefits they seek from so doing. Without this philosophy, managers focus their attention mainly on the operation of their services from a technical perspective, with a potential loss of sensitivity to their clients' real and changing concerns and perceptions. The decisions which people take, both in purchasing and using services, can be seen from several perspectives. In many respects the decision to purchase a holiday is a similar process to any other consumption choice, but there are certain specialized factors, shown in Table 5.2.

Table 5.2 Specialized factors in tourists' purchasing decisions

1 Tourists obtain no financial return on their investment (except in the case of business travel)
2 Travel, or holiday purchases typically account for a high proportion of disposable income
3 The majority of travel purchases are planned rather than spontaneous
4 Savings often have to be planned for a travel purchase
5 Tourists visit the site of production. Distance may be regarded as a utility

Source: Mathieson and Wall, 1982

The traditional view of consumer behaviour has been that people made choices having gathered and evaluated all the available information about the relative costs and characteristics of alternative products. The next stage of this argument was that they ranked benefits or disadvantages to reach a decision based on marginal utility, thus their choice amongst alternative products was determined by economic rationality. The modern approach recognizes that in seeking out information, or the views of other people they trust, individuals are undertaking risk reduction behaviour. The better the information on which a purchasing decision was based, the more likely it is that the features of the service will prove acceptable to the client.

Table 5.3 The decision process for tourism purchases

Decision	Process
Desire for travel	Collect and evaluate information
Select holiday type	Decide on destination, tour operator, price range; duration; travel companions
Prepare for holiday	Purchase clothing, photographic materials, guide books
Experience holiday	Evaluate satisfaction against expectation

Based on Mathieson and Wall, 1982, Schwaninger, 1989, van Raaij, 1986

Attitude formation and change

It is evident that a group of people who face similar choices may make different decisions; people are impulsive and irrational, and have deep feelings about certain things, leading to behaviour which does not fully conform to these information-processing models. A person's individual view of the world reflects two major factors, his experience of it, and his personality. Personality can be described as the series of traits which are reflected in individual behaviour and is what makes people different from one another. Each trait which contributes to an individual's personality is held both to varying extents and with varying degrees of stability. Typical approaches to classifying personality traits identify dimensions such as reserved or outgoing; less or more intelligent; timid or venturesome. It is the combination of one's rating on each of these traits, derived from analysis of responses to a set of questions which is the external evidence of an individual personality. One widely recognized method of classifying personality is Cattell's 16-personality factor inventory.

Consumer choice also reflects the interplay between cultural, social and individual factors at a personal level. One explanation is that information or experience has no meaning until an individual has interpreted it. The mental process by which this occurs is known as cognition. It is generally thought that people form an interlinked framework of attitudes about their experiences. An attitude about a certain thing is that person's evaluation of it and the significance for managers of an attitude is that it predicts the individual's actions towards some object. The technical consumer behaviour literature suggests that there are three components of an attitude; cognition and affect leading to connation. This means that an individual's beliefs and knowledge about a particular object lead him or her to act in a certain way towards it.

Attitudes develop in response to a person's changing situation, as he ages, as his career and family circumstances develop and according to how important to him various external stimuli may be. One of these is the information received from other people, perhaps derived directly from comments by friends, family and colleagues, or through modern media. These important sources include print, radio and television, and take two forms: paid advertising or editorial comment. Advertisements are directly under the control of managers, in contrast to the unknown views contained in private, informal communications from friends and acquaintances. Communications theory indicates that the quality of both the information and its source affect its ability to influence any target individual; the information is communicated and received with varying degrees of both accuracy and enthusiasm. It is gathered systematically and deliberately in those cases where the person considers the purchase important, or information may be received casually, for example in conversation or while passively watching television when the purchase is less significant to a person. Consumer recommendations are powerful influences, as most discussions are held with people who are known and trusted, and this rapport lends high credibility to the source. Furthermore any conversation is a two-way process in which clarification of statements can be sought. Finally, recommendation offers a form of vicarious trial, in which one person can learn from other people's experiences before committing his own resources (Reynolds and Daden, 1971).

However, attitudes do not exist in isolation, rather it seems that the attitudes of one person about related things are linked. The more connections there are, and the more consistent these attitudes are, the more central they are said to be to a person's value system. Attitudes which are central to a person are more difficult to alter, but can be more readily reinforced by further information, or the views of other people which are consistent with those they already hold. On another level, Fishbein and Ajzen (1975) have argued that a person's attitude towards some action or object (that is the strength of his feelings about it) is a combination of the strengths of his beliefs about the action and the consequences of the action.

Group decision making

Attempts to influence another person's attitudes and behaviour have varying success depending on the relative status of the communicator and his credibility to the person. The opinion about things which other people hold are also factors in the attitude which an individual develops. The more he interacts regularly with certain people such as friends, work colleagues or family, and the more important to him those people may be, the more likely it is that they will influence his attitudes and the actions he takes. This effect is further reinforced because people have a tendency to join and remain in groups where the other members' interests are compatible with their own.

Many holiday decisions are taken by groups of friends, or by families. The extent to which the members of any group participate in the discussion leading to choice, and the ways in which they are able to influence each other have been analysed, particularly in the context of household decisions. Groups of people such as families reach a joint decision by one of two major processes: consensus, when the members agree about their goals, or accommodation when disagreement is a factor, but the strength of the family unit leads to acceptance of a compromise. In either case, the members play roles in the negotiation, based variously on their expertise, experience or their negotiating skills and status in the group. Consensual decisions are reached through problem solving strategies, while accommodation is gained either by persuasion or bargaining, when various benefits are traded (Davis, cited in Wilkie, 1986).

Another relevant study considered by Wilkie was that by Bonfield in which four types of decision were identified: it was more likely that the wife would be dominant in buying household and children's consumption items, while the husband was dominant in the purchase of garden machinery or items for the car. An intermediate case was the selection of gifts, which was found to be a decision for either partner depending on the situation, while the family holiday was largely a matter for joint discussion.

Satisfaction with tourism services

One of the themes explored in marketing literature is the significance of trials – a means by which the consumer gains more detailed information about the product or service and its compatibility to his own needs and preferences. Theories dealing with this aspect of consumer behaviour argue that post trial evaluation is crucial in leading to the consumer's consequent behaviour with respect to that particular brand. It will be shown later in this book that the satisfaction which a tourist experiences is often a determining factor in subsequent purchases, and forms the basis of recommendations (or cautions) to friends and colleagues.

Consumer decision taking represents a choice between alternative allocations of time and funds, in the expectation of differing satisfactions with varying degrees of importance to that individual. Such choices can cause anxiety about the correctness of the decision taken. One way of reducing the potential risk of making a wrong decision is to seek information beforehand, and similarly, after the decision it is typical behaviour to welcome information supporting the decision taken while paying less attention to data which challenges the validity of the decision. A mechanism which enables this to happen is selective perception, that is, people tend to screen out data which is considered less relevant or acceptable, while they concentrate on information and views which contribute to and support their cognitive structures, the view of the world which they hold. Another risk reduction strategy is to avoid situations which in the past have been seen as an incorrect choice. Cognitive dissonance is the term used to describe this concept (Festinger, 1975), its relevance to tourism management is discussed further in Chapter 6.

Purchase and subsequent use of goods or services can have two outcomes: satisfaction, or post decision dissonance. The consumer evaluates whether (or not) the prepurchase expectations of satisfaction which he held were met. The vendor's hope is that a client will conclude from the evidence of using a product that the decision was correct, and consequently that the purchase will be repeated. Dissatisfaction with a service may trigger further action, perhaps in the form of complaints to the company. The outcome may reassure the client that his choice of tour had been correct, and the dissatisfaction he experienced was dealt with effectively, or it may lead to brand switching in future purchases.

Tourists' images of tourism experiences

This book has already identified two of the most powerful tools available to marketers, the branding of services to achieve a strong identity and segmentation of the general market into groups of these methodologies is the creation and management of the way services are perceived by consumers. Marketing communications, particularly advertising and public relations, convey information to clients on which they can form an intention to purchase a service. Additionally, an image is created and conveyed to provide a powerful evocation of the benefits to be gained from purchasing a brand. Information on what is available to tourists is critical in their decisions but when a tourism service experience does not match their expectations dissatisfaction is likely to result. The larger the difference between image and reality, that is between expectation and experience, the more likely is the tourist to be dissatisfied.

Market segmentation has to be managed concurrent with product branding and differentiation. Branding, a technique which will be examined in the next chapter, recognizes that tourists evaluate and buy services based on perceptions and images that are unique to each competing tourism supplier. Companies can claim a position in peoples' minds for their services by emphasizing selected attributes, such as the benefits which a particular organization offers to customers, or by drawing contrasts with competitors. Typically, campaigns are based on a hybrid of these appeals. What is important is the way in which clients perceive the service offered, so effective brand management depends on market research.

The image which a person has of any product is highly subjective and therefore it is not easily quantifiable. Kassarjian and Robertson (1973) have explained various ways of determining the mental position of a brand. These include research techniques by which the subject assigns a numerical score along a continuum ranging from positive to negative. Mental images can also be understood using open-ended questions and in-depth interviews. A series of projective techniques can be used including word association, sentence completion, picture interpretation, or 'balloon tests'. Additionally, the position of a brand can be determined by techniques which map the perceptual space occupied by a product, for example in terms of price compared to comfort.

The perceived characteristics of a range of competing destinations, hotels or airlines can be plotted on a map. Embacher and Buttle (1989) have discussed the application of this technique to Austria's image. 'Image has a number of meanings. These include artificial imitation of the apparent form of an object, e.g. a picture, form identity or design, and an idea or conception. Image is therefore comprised of the ideas or conceptions held individually or collectively of the destination under investigation . . . Image may comprise both cognitive and evaluative components.' The elements for their study were elicited through a number of questions relating to recent vacations, and countries regarded as either ideal or undesirable destinations. 'Austria was perceived as having a number of strengths and weaknesses. The strengths included attractive landscape, many natural attractions, fresh air, familiar culture (comfortable foreignness) accessibility by car, cleanliness, suitable environment for children, . . . Perceived weaknesses were lack of beach facilities, an inadequate variety of activities particularly for children . . . and cost.'

Marketing communications

Advertising is one of the major tools of marketing communication, as Rothschild (1987) has demonstrated, and is always a central feature in the marketing mix for any organization: it is concerned with communicating awareness of a company and its products, stimulating an interest and desire for them amongst a selected

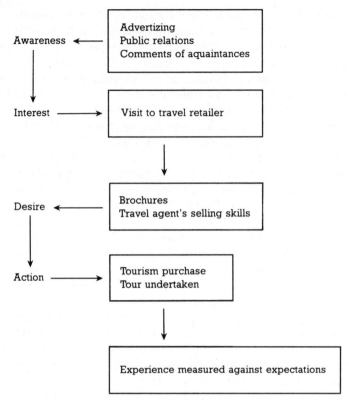

Figure 5.1 Marketing communications for tourism

audience by emphasizing to clients the benefits thought likely to appeal to them. Its major purpose is to stimulate the action of purchasing. The marketing communication process has been summarized by the AIDA model and its many variants setting out the steps to consumer action. Figure 5.1 shows its application to tourism.

The general AIDA model emphasizes the point that a potential client cannot express his preference for a specific product until he has been made aware of it. Figure 5.1 indicates that awareness can be created through deliberate marketing communications strategies such as advertising or public relations. Casual conversation can also bring awareness of a destination or service to a potential client. A visit to a travel agency will enable the client to obtain more detailed information from the agency staff, or a principal's brochure. If this stage of communications is managed effectively, awareness and interest will blend into desire and the final stage is action – that is, the purchase of a travel service. In this phase the acid test of customer satisfaction is applied, as he evaluates the satisfaction he experienced against what he had anticipated. Consequently, the model is iterative, e.g. the client's future decisions are based on his past experience, as well as the continuing influence of formal and informal marketing communications.

It has been calculated that individuals see and hear perhaps as many as 4000 messages attempting to influence, persuade or to provide information every day. Very few of these advertisements are consciously registered, and so one challenge facing marketers is to gain the attention of their target audience amongst the stylishness and creativity of modern marketing communications which is a feature of Western life. Two approaches are required: the creative appeal to both visual and textual advertising content has to be decided, and the media channels selected which are most likely to be seen by potential customers.

Nor is it an effective use of limited advertising budgets to present advertising messages to every person in the community, for most products appeal to certain groups and the resources of a company are best targeted towards those most likely to purchase its services. A variety of methods are available for the effective targeting of messages. The basic step is to define the characteristics of the audience and to understand their media habits so that correct placement can be made. A number of studies such as Target Group Index, a syndicated service operated by the British Market Research Bureau are available in major markets to help in these decisions and most media owners have carried out research into the characteristics and habits of their readers or viewers (Crimp, 1985). These methods are based on interviews and cross-tabulated analysis which links their media preferences to product and brand behaviour. The power and extent of particular segments in each market category can also be gauged from accompanying socio-economic and demographic tables, which can be compared to nationwide census data and linked to postal codes for direct or database marketing applications.

Advertising

A distinction is often drawn between informative and persuasive advertising. Informative advertising supplies consumers with detailed information about alternative choices so that they can choose the price range, quality and type of experience from those on offer which most appeals to them. As it improves consumers' knowledge of a particular category of services, informative advertising contributes to the effective operation of competitive markets by enhancing competition and improving the allocation of resources throughout society. Economic theory argues that this arises from rational choices by consumers, and the producer's responses to these collective signals, but it has already been suggested that the concept of rationality does not fully explain what happens in complex market situations.

Persuasive advertising tries to influence consumers' tastes towards some preference of the advertiser. The argument against persuasive advertising is that it acts by developing an image of a product or producer rather than by building substantive knowledge as a base for decisions at the consumer level and therefore it may be considered wasteful or inaccurate. In reality, most advertising is a mix of these two traditional types.

In selecting appropriate messages to transmit in advertising campaigns, both the goals of the particular campaign and the value satisfactions being offered have to be considered carefully. The creative task then is to communicate the bundle of benefits to people who are likely to want those benefits and in ways which will generate sales. The temptation for tourism managers confronted by the intangible nature of services is to promise clients a high degree of satisfaction and high standards of service delivery, for example in terms of on-time performance or comfort. In practice these standards may be very difficult to achieve. This makes it even more important to resist the temptation to oversell, e.g. raising the expectations of visitors for personal service, style and so on beyond levels which can realistically be delivered.

Advertising budget decisions

The view that advertising is a management function designed to reach corporate goals implies that the firm has decisions to take about the purpose and scale of its advertising expenditure in a period as well as the allocation of that budget between different media. The setting of budgets for advertising can follow several patterns reflecting differences in management philosophies. A common approach is to allocate an advertising budget based on the previous year's spending (adjusted in various ways in recognition of inflation or new marketing tasks). In another approach, the advertising department is allocated a standard percentage of revenue. Such methods are easy to administer and provide a degree of certainty in the setting of future advertising tactics. However, these methods ignore the realities of the marketplace. The decisions of competitors and the specific tasks for marketing to perform are the context for a schedule of costs which should then form the basis of negotiation for the limited resources available to all departments within an organization. An implication of this task-based budgeting technique is that a restricted budget may lead to reassessment, and a reduction of targets set in the organizational plan.

In addition to promoting a specific service, advertising is also used to gain awareness and support for the organization. The goal of advertising a particular travel product is to sell enough of it to satisfy business objectives, whereas the purpose of corporate advertising is to create a favourable climate for all the company's activities. Corporate advertising is not directly concerned with sales targets for specific products or markets, so it is less easy to monitor the effectiveness of spending on corporate awareness promotions. An important extension of advertising theory regards it as an investment rather than a time or volume related expense similar to costs of production or overheads. The investment view argues that goodwill, or at least awareness, is built up by a successful campaign and persists for several periods of time. Thus, effective marketing communications can increase the value of the firm and when the internal rate of return expected from advertising exceeds the market interest rate, it is rational for the enterprise to invest in advertising.

Measurement for control purposes is an integral aspect of marketing, but the effects of advertising are difficult to quantify. A major problem in assessing a campaign is that the results are not immediate; a message broadcast today may influence decisions for purchases where the client will travel many months in the future. Although it is pointless to advertise for more business when the organization is already operating at full capacity, the flow of tourists cannot be rapidly turned off, or turned on. It is therefore common to regulate fluctuating demand levels by tactical price variations to distinguish between peak and slack seasons. This point is discussed in Chapter 6.

Public relations

One of the most potent, but still underrated tools available to marketing managers, is the range of activities collectively known as public relations (PR). The premises on which PR is based have been described in the following terms: 'That in a modern democracy every organization, from the national government to the corner store, survives ultimately only by public consent, and that the consent of the public cannot exist in a communications vacuum' (Tymson and Sherman, 1987).

In the case of tourism, several targets can be identified for PR communications. These include the public, as a principal needs to make them aware of the benefits of specific destinations or types of holiday or transport, and the members of the channel of tourism creation and distribution whose active support the principal has to recruit in order to gain sales. Other important communications targets for public relations campaigns include national and local government officials, residents of tourist destinations, potential investors and the staff of tourism companies.

Public relations can perform a variety of functions for principals, depending on specific conditions. Publicity is useful in establishing awareness of services or destinations, and can rebuild confidence in a destination or company after some service setback such as a strike, storm or accident. It can be used to draw attention to the results of a deliberate policy of service improvement such as the repositioning of a company. Overall, the purpose of public relations is to gain a favourable impression of the organization amongst its various stakeholders, including clients, staff, shareholders or suppliers and politicians. Depending on the objectives and targets set for public relations, a range of decisions has to be taken about selecting appropriate messages and media. Achieving the objectives is dependent on an understanding of what the audience will respond to favourably and therefore entails a detailed knowledge of what the organization is doing and has achieved, so that interesting stories can be released in a format which the audience will find acceptable. The case study of Texas' promotion to the UK travel trade and public consumers provides more detailed examples of public relations methods.

A simple measure of public relations activity is the amount of media coverage, in column inches or seconds of airtime which has been gained in a period. Some organizations like to assess this in value terms by calculating the cost of buying an equivalent space of paid advertising. Often this is weighted by a factor of several times as it is believed that the editorial coverage which results from successful PR campaigns is far more valuable and credible than paid advertising. On this basis, a PR campaign can yield very substantial returns. However, more sophisticated measures of achievement are available: changes in product awareness, more positive attitudes towards the company, or sales and profit impact can be evaluated by measuring these factors ahead of a campaign, and again after it, although the connection between PR and profit results is unlikely to be direct.

Brochure design and use

Once a person's interest in a destination, activity or tour has been aroused by PR and advertising, the next step is for him or her to obtain more information about the service. The major sources of information for tourists are brochures published by attractions, hotels, destinations and tour operators. Taking the latter as an example, the usual source from which the prospective client obtains the tour operator's brochure is a local retail travel agency. The agency staff normally engage the client in a dialogue during which further information will be given (or requested) leading to the client's decision to purchase. This technical information may be backed up by guide books or guide videos (purchased, or borrowed from a library and perused at home, often with other members of the travel group or family), or by contacting the national tourist organization, airline, etc. Competing agents' brochures are likely to be scrutinized to confirm the selection before a commitment is made, and TV, magazine and other information will be considered. Brochures serve to provide information for clients, enable them to make specific reservations and form the basis for a contract between them.

It follows, as Conroy (1987) has pointed out, that 'brochures are an important and effective way for tour operators and travel principals to communicate information about both the company and specific products. Not only must the look of the brochure attract the right market, it must also supply answers to potential clients' questions'. She argued that an appreciation of balance, emphasis, proportion and rhythm on the printed page contribute to the success of a brochure and that underlying this was an understanding of the effects of white space on readers' attention as their eyes scan across a printed page. Another consideration for effective brochure management is the set of factors which lead retailers to stock and display in the racks certain brands rather than others.

Purchasing behaviour

An understanding of how consumers actually make their buying decisions is fundamental for companies competing in the marketplace. Decisions are routine for many purchases, and consumers have little interest in the product beyond its ability to meet a need they have. Examples include household detergents and low price confectionery. Here, the task is to build a strong brand awareness so that a named variety becomes their preference when they shop. For other products, consumers take a real interest and experience a high degree of involvement. In these cases, their brand decisions are characterized by active reasoning processes.

It has been suggested that customers' purchasing behaviour may be considered to be distributed along a continuum from 'routinized response behaviour to extensive problem solving' (Howard, 1977). The search behaviour of customers whose interest in tourism is high is likely to be extended and, as the model developed in this section suggests, such tourists are likely to base their decision on the enhanced aspects of the service.

Engel Blackwell and Miniard (1986) have distinguished between three levels of consumer decision process: extended problem solving; limited problem solving, and routine problem solving. Extended problem solving behaviour occurs under three conditions; when a purchase is very significant to an individual, product alternatives are difficult to distinguish, and there is sufficient time to evaluate the alternatives. These conditions lead to active reasoning in the form of extensive information searching for a match to some ideal which the consumer has in mind. Perceptions of what is ideal vary by individual and are influenced by many factors including the norms of other people whom he regards as important, and his beliefs about that type of product. The consumer's beliefs about products are derived from past experience of using them, from marketing communications and from what others have said about their experiences.

The consumer is likely to be highly involved when a service has functional or symbolic significance to him, or because it implies financial or emotional risk, or if it is identified with the behavioural norms of an important reference group. High involvement implies a careful choice based on experience and information. Consumer involvement has been defined in the following terms: 'a state of energy (arousal) that a person experiences in regard to a consumption-related activity' (Cohen, 1982). Cohen considered that involvement is high when customers are enjoying a service. He also pointed out how it occurs within specific settings, differing for an individual between various situations.

In many markets the generic service such as a holiday package to a Mediterranean resort is available in several versions branded by various tour operators. In such cases the first contradictory evidence that the holiday maker receives about his chosen brand results in a feeling that an alternative brand should have been chosen. Indeed, variety seeking is a recognized behaviour of consumers in markets where there are perceived to be significant differences in brands, although it is thought to be more common amongst low involvement customers. High involvement customers will have investigated many brands' characteristics and selected a supplier on the basis of criteria which are important to them. High involvement customers are less likely to switch to alternative suppliers and may be more tolerant of minor service failures, in part because of a deeper understanding of the service delivery system.

Consumers are likely to be highly involved in the decision when the product has the characteristics shown in Table 5.4, which accord with many tourism purchases.

This theory suggests that in high involvement decision situations a consumer will compare brands in a detailed and systematic manner. In high involvement

Table 5.4   Product characteristics in high
involvement purchasing behaviour

- High priced
- Associated with performance risks
- Complex
- A speciality good
- Associated with that consumer's ego

communications the mode of influence is through persuasion. Such advertising tends to deal directly with desired product benefits, but often more information is sought and further brands are evaluated. An integral part of the process is that each consumer establishes his own criteria on which those brands will be judged. Similarly, after purchase the consumer will evaluate the chosen brand's performance. Satisfaction will reinforce the consumer's judgement and that brand is more likely to be repurchased in the future. If dissatisfaction occurs the consumer will reassess his choice, and repurchase of that brand is much less likely to occur. However, as his interest has been engaged, and since he is probably experienced in using this class of services, it seems that the high involvement consumer may be relatively tolerant of errors, particularly when the organization takes effective steps to remedy any problems which occur.

Much of the argument in marketing literature, and many of the actions of marketing managers, assume that customers are very interested in their product, when in reality they are often not. Low involvement decision making occurs where the consumer does not consider the product particularly important to his belief system and does not strongly identify with the product.

In contrast to the rational, information processing model of high involvement behaviour, the consumer who has low involvement with a particular product is likely to be a passive recipient of information about it. When a purchasing need or desire arises, one brand is likely to be purchased rather than others on the basis of some token familiarity; repetitive advertising can have this effect and give managers an advantage.

The consumer will however be relatively neutral towards any brand as it (and the product) has no strong association with any of his important beliefs. The role of communications in the case of low involvement consumers is to create awareness and familiarity. Thus, relatively few points need to be made, and opportunities can be taken for symbolic associations to strengthen identification of the brand. Low involvement products offer solutions to consumers' problems rather than optimizing the benefits. Services are purchased on the basis of price or convenience since the consumer has no basis for distinguishing between the benefits of various brands. In low involvement conditions promotional incentives may induce repeat purchases if they are maintained long enough for the consumer to gain familiarity with the brand, and if he is satisfied with its use. After the habit is established, it should be possible to withdraw the additional benefits slowly. Widespread channels are important for low involvement products as the consumer will not be willing to search for a particular brand, and as loyalty is not established, he will brand switch rather than devote time and energy to obtaining a specific brand.

Branding has been shown to be an important marketing tool in many sectors of tourism, and the strength of links between branding and consumer choice at various levels of involvement can now be considered. Asseal (1987) has suggested that the degree of consumer involvement is the critical factor in both consumer behaviour and in setting marketing strategy, as Table 5.5 indicates, this leads to four levels of consumer involvement, with four distinct managerial strategies.

The concept of involvement is consumer related rather than product related. It follows that the features of a service which its managers believe distinguish it from competitors' should be defined in terms of the consumers' evaluation of the importance of each service attribute. The varying extent of consumer involvement

| | | Consumer involvement | |
		High	Low
Differences between brands	Significant	A Complex decisions or brand loyalty	C Variety seeking: random choice or experimental
	Few	B Dissonance reduction or attribution	D Inertia: random choice or spurious loyalty

Source: Asseal, 1987

The differing managerial approaches to the four quadrants in this table are discussed below.

A Complex decision making, and brand loyalty requires high consumer involvement and sufficient differences between brands to sustain their involvement. Consumers form beliefs about the brands, evaluate them and choose.

B Dissonance reduction assumes a high level of involvement, but the consumer considers few brands. Since there is no formal basis for deciding on one brand rather than others, doubt is likely to arise after the purchase. The consumer may have second thoughts after choosing, but seek positive information to affirm the choice and to reduce any dissonance experienced. He may ignore negative information about the brand, also thereby reducing dissonance. Thus, information search and brand evaluation can occur after a purchase.

C Variety seeking; a low level of involvement but differences between brands are recognized. However, low involvement with the product restricts brand evaluation. In such conditions consumers switch to other brands to try something new. Given low involvement, a consumer is less likely to be very dissatisfied, but strong branding and promotion may be effective in attracting attention and getting to the stage of trial behaviour.

D Inertia assumes that few differences exist between brands. Consumers will either choose an available brand at random under these conditions or will become familiar with one brand and a spurious brand loyalty can be developed. This is passive information processing and buying behaviour and it suggests that marketing based on differentiating low involvement products as separate brands is ineffective as the customer does not care about those differences.

Figure 5.2 Consumer involvement and choice between brands

can be measured on an individual level, and can be used as a basis for segmented approaches to a general market.

Conclusion

Marketing theory has traditionally taken as its focus the exchange of clients' money for vendors' goods and services. The discussion is often in terms of people responding to economic and other signals in attempting to satisfy their felt needs by selecting rationally amongst a wide range of alternative goods and services. One of the central themes in this book is the ways in which tourists' experiences of satisfaction can be influenced during the extended delivery of a complex service. The point made in this chapter is that in many cases managers' attempts to attract tourists rely on heightening their expectations of service standards or satisfaction and that this strategy has potential risks for both the consumer and the company.

Blackman (1985) has pointed out that customers often do not know how to tell when they would be satisfied by a service, and managers do not know how to structure the service process to satisfy customers. Yet this satisfaction is crucial to both customers and service providers. Chapter 7 considers these points in more detail.

Marketing communications convey the initial expectation of a service through the marketing images it broadcasts in attempting to develop a favourable attitude resulting in a purchase. An image is conjured up from information interpreted through the personal and behavioural characteristics of the tourist: 'Image is an expression of all objective knowledge impressions, prejudices, imaginations and emotional thoughts an individual or group have of a particular object or place' (Lawson and Baud Levey, 1977). However, attitudes reflect past experience, and a dissatisfying purchase will lead to a strong negative attitude towards the supplier, with the probable result that the tourist will turn elsewhere for future purchases.

Questions

1 Contrast the advertising media and imagery employed by two tourism services of interest to you. How do you account for any differences?

2 What evidence is there to support (or challenge) the distinction between high and low involvement categories of tourists discussed in this chapter? What is the significance to tourism managers of such a distinction?

3 Investigate the sources of information which have been employed in purchasing services by a group of people who you are able to question. Evaluate your findings.

Recommended reading

Middleton, V.T.C. *Marketing in Travel and Tourism,* Heinemann, Oxford, 1988

Ogilvy, D. *Confessions of an Advertising Man,* Pan Books, London, 1987

Ries, A. and Trout, J. *Positioning, the Battle for your Mind,* Warner Books, NY, 1986

Rothschild, M.L. *Marketing Communications,* D.C. Heath & Co., Lexington, Mass., 1987

CHAPTER SIX

Strategic Tourism Marketing

Introduction

The functional view of marketing identifies four variables which marketing managers can control – price, product, place and promotion. In tourism these tasks involve setting a price or prices for the services offered, developing the service so that it appeals more strongly to the target market groups, setting up appropriate channels of distribution so that clients can purchase their travel services without difficulty, and fourthly, creating awareness and interest through advertising and public relations strategies. Beyond these four marketing mix decisions, marketing's special contribution is to focus managers' attention and the organization's resources and skills on the achievement of its goals by satisfying clients' needs. Underlying the discussion in the previous chapter of the methods which marketing adopts to influence potential clients is an understanding of their consumers' decision making and of the particular operational strengths of each organization. Thus, marketing expertise has a significant contribution to make to an organization's strategic decisions.

The traditional view of competitors is that they are those firms in the same industry supplying similar products. However, as tourism becomes an established, more mature industry, a broader context to tourists' decision making becomes important. People's decisions to spend a greater or lesser proportion of their disposable income on travel rather than on other product categories are influenced by the total impact of the sector's marketing efforts. In times of growing demand, when the response to competition was based on building a volume of business through price reductions to fill a temporary oversupply of hotel and travel capacity, in order to keep the unit costs of operation at an affordable level the quality of tourists' experiences was sometimes sacrificed to stimulate volume. Low margins for operators and travel principals meant that the services they offered were set at minimum standards and low prices attracted clients who had not previously been able to participate in such markets.

Although low standards of accommodation may have been regarded as an acceptable part of the early mass tourism experience, clients learned to discriminate between the services on offer, both by observing other tourists enjoying superior service standards in a resort or hotel and as comfort further declined under the pressure of the ever increasing numbers of tourists. The case studies dealing with tourism to China touch on these points. Increasingly, airports and other services are unable to cope effectively with the growing numbers of travellers and any delay to flight schedules has repercussions on many people. Tight pricing at resorts meant that customers on inclusive packages found they were offered lower standards of service compared to other travellers, and the frequent shifts in relative currency values were passed on as last minute surcharges. The overall result was a decline in the growth rate of the tourism sector (although terrorism, recession and the temptation of the expanding range of alternative purchases are relevant considerations). One response was a search for alternative ways of packaging and presenting tourism products.

Contribution of marketing to organizations' strategic decisions

Marketing insights and methods also play a central role in setting organizational resources to work towards achieving predetermined targets of turnover, growth, volume of business and so on. Organizational targets, and the steps to reach them, are usually specified in a business plan which shows how the organization intends to satisfy its objectives. These are set out in a formal statement of its mission, the way in which it relates to society and reflects intelligence about emerging trends in the company's environment and a detailed understanding of the company's operational strengths. The business plan provides a framework for the decisions of the management team, and of their respective departments. An example has been discussed by Zalloco (1989):

> Each year American Airlines develops a System Marketing Plan that summarizes the marketing programme for the upcoming year. Some of the plan's key components include: planning assumptions in areas such as economic growth, and how they will affect travel and tourism markets; forecasts of market potential and revenues by market segment; marketing objectives and strategies to be employed; and action programmes including quality and reliability, ticketing, reservations, service levels, and special vacation packages.

Marketing's traditional role is to generate the flow of income from sales by stimulating and then satisfying customer interest, as discussed in Chapter 5. To achieve this marketers require support from other management functions; including financial resources, staffing and training. Marketing is directly concerned with understanding consumers' needs and identifying ways for the company to satisfy them profitably. Clearly, these are the same factors which are the focus for the company's mission statement and its goals, as indicated in the case study dealing with the management turnaround at British Airways. This line of reasoning suggests that marketing's role is more important than that of other managerial functions and this appears to be particularly critical for service organizations such as tourism, where consumer satisfaction is immediately dependent on the performance of the company.

The generally accepted approach to marketing planning is to begin with an audit to diagnose the current business situation. A typical marketing audit reviews the company's products in comparison with competitors' volumes, appeal to market sectors and their contribution to the organization's revenue and costs. The understanding gained will be applied in the major decision taking forum of the organization to construct the business plan over the next period, typically from one to five years. Several steps have been identified in marketing planning, which is considered to be an iterative process in the sense that the plan constantly evolves in the light of experience and evolving circumstances. Both the internal operation of the organization and circumstances in the market can lead to revision of planned targets. The traditional starting point for a marketing plan is diagnosis – that is the analysis of an organization's current market performance, its consumers' behaviour and attitudes and its competitors' strengths – as well as other factors which could be significant, such as changes to relevant legislation, or new conditions in the economy. Diagnosis provides a detailed platform for prognosis, the forecasting of future trends for each of the market sectors of interest to the organization.

The next stage involves taking an objective assessment of the strengths, weaknesses, opportunities and threats facing the organization and its various services. Formal planning integrates this detailed work with the objectives of the organization, and in the constraints of its marketing budget a programme of marketing mix decisions is drawn up to specify the steps required to meet the objectives of profit, growth and so on. The final, and key aspect of the planning process is a control system through which the implementation of the plan is monitored and results evaluated as a basis for further planning. However, Leppard and MacDonald (1987) have recently argued against the formalistic planning approach, suggesting that the planning process and its outcomes instead reflect the political realities of an organization's internal politics and dynamics.

In February 1987 the English Tourist Board published two related documents setting out its strategies for the development and the marketing of tourism in England (Table 6.1). Together, these two plans were intended to set the framework for tourism investment and promotion over the next five years. They emphasize the importance of 'partnership between private and public sectors to stimulate increased investment and create both wealth and jobs'. The stated intention was to generate £3 billion to £4 billion investment, and to create some 250000 jobs. 'A successful tourism marketing plan requires coordination and integration among the different levels of government and the private sector' (ETB, 1987).

As a basis for the company's planning, further understanding of the organization's place within its market can be gained from a detailed consideration of the strengths and weaknesses of its current operations, and from scanning the various environmental influences for threats or opportunities. This leads to a formal SWOT analysis; Table 6.2 draws from a published example.

Table 6.1   Key objectives of the ETB marketing strategy

1   To support the marketing of enterprises with a proven record of success and to encourage ventures with clear and demonstrable potential for success
2   To concentrate resources on markets which will offer the greatest potential returns
3   To help the industry make better use of its actual and potential assets
4   To encourage more effective use of England's existing tourism capacity by matching it with demand
5   To engender a positive attitude to English holidays through more creative marketing
6   To improve the quality of presentation of holiday ingredients to the customer
7   To ensure that reliable information about tourism products and opportunities is readily and attractively presented to the consumer
8   To achieve a better use of resources within the industry
9   To provide a national framework for quality control of accommodation, attractions and other tourism products, in order to foster consumer reassurance and to encourage investment and upgrading by the industry
10   To encourage and foster higher standards in all aspects of marketing and customer relations
11   To develop appropriate products in conjunction with the regional boards and BTA to maintain and enhance Britain's appeal in overseas markets
12   To increase the understanding among opinion formers and the general public of tourism's wider benefits to England's social and economic fabric

Source: A vision for England, ETB, 1987

Table 6.2   SWOT analysis of a site for a proposed tourism development

Strengths	Near motorway; large population within one hour; grants available; land available for development
Weaknesses	Unattractive environment at present; difficult access to site for construction; limited range of visitor accommodation; poor image of the region in market-place; no overall development plan for the area; limited local managerial expertise in tourism
Opportunities	Commercial opportunity to maximise leisure spending in the area; good catering; potential for package arrangements with complimentary local attractions; grant may be available for improvements to visitor accommodation
Threats	Rail link uncertain; competitive plans for tourist attractions to be developed locally; poor customer care reputation of existing neighbouring attractions; industrial plans for the area; low spending existing local clientele

Based on Pearleman, 1989

Strategic gaps

The company's business targets form the basis for the development of marketing strategies; in nearly every case there will be a gap between present performance and the future sales, revenue or growth targets set in the business plan (see

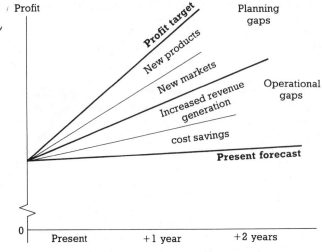

Figure 6.1 Strategic gaps

Figure 6.1). The marketing plan is largely concerned with the various steps needed to bridge that gap. Most organizations offer a range of products or services, and attract a variety of clients. The marketing plan will deal with each major group in turn, identifying appropriate ways of distributing them to clients, adapting products, setting their prices and creating promotional campaigns to achieve targets. Marketing expertise contributes in two ways, by assessing prospects for each product category, and setting strategies to satisfy each market segment which the company has decided to serve. Given the uncertainties of future events, and the margin for error in forecasting, a sound business plan will also specify interim performance measures by which progress may be judged. Actual results at each stage act as feedback by which the later targets are modified in the light of experience, according to whether business has slipped or improved from the levels planned for.

Tourism service development

It has been suggested that a key role for marketing expertise is its contribution to managerial decisions about the future product range and characteristics offered by the company. Development of both products and markets is necessary to service future markets. Without the continuing refinement of existing tourism services such as holiday packages, the customers to whom an enterprise sells at present are likely to be attracted away in the future by the improved or more sharply priced offers of competitors. Improvements to existing holiday packages can include greater ranges of destinations or accommodation, increased opportunities for activities, price reductions or more relaxed schedules; Chapter 9 deals with service developments in the airline sector. Entrepreneurs may also identify opportunities to develop a new range of holiday concepts in addition to their established business.

New tourism products are introduced in response to changing tastes, fashion

MARKET

	Existing	New
Existing	Air packages to major resorts	Special interest resort holidays
New	Self drive with major resort stay	Inbound heritage tours

SERVICE

Figure 6.2 Categories of tourism development

and style. They represent a risk to the company, which has to invest time and resources in researching them, establishing the supplier network, promoting them and staffing the reservations and administration function. Figure 6.2 draws on Ansoff (1968) who argued that the decisions to be taken in regard to products fall into one of four broad categories. New offers may prove attractive to some of their existing customers, or they may choose to advertise to potential clients they had not previously serviced: for example, elderly people, sports fans or people more likely to use a local airport than travel to one serving the capital. Another option is to offer the existing range of holiday products to a new group of clients.

These major choices amongst development strategies can be categorized in terms of risk: the greater the experience of dealing with a particular type of client such as young adventurers, or in selling particular types of holiday such as skiing, which a company has, the more likely a new service drawing on these skills is to succeed. However, it can be deduced from the diagram that it is most risky to sell a type of holiday which is new to the company to a segment of the market which the company has no experience of dealing with.

Finance is required to support any product or market development programme. Development costs include the expense and time spent travelling to research potential new destinations and in selecting accommodation or carriers for the new programme. Another expense is incurred in setting up the reservations system (although there may be excess capacity on the installed system), producing the brochure and education for public and trade channel members about the new offering through public relations and advertising. Licences may have to be negotiated, or deposits placed for the various trading bonds required by trade bodies, or by legislation.

The major sources of finance for development available to companies are the proprietors' investment (equity), profit earned from operations and retained for this purpose, and borrowings or loans from financial intermediaries such as banks. In special circumstances, public funds may be loaned or granted to stimulate the sector. Often this occurs in regions where tourism is regarded as

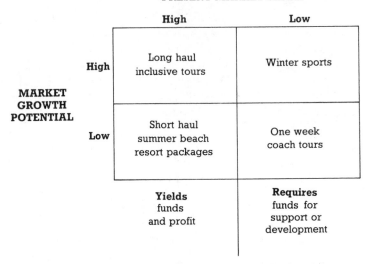

Figure 6.3 Internal sources of funds for service development

the main way of bringing employment and revenue to an area (see Chapter 12). Established, or diversified companies can support development programmes from other activities through cross subsidies. They are able to allocate some of the profit flowing from successful ranges already on the market.

Once a company has established a successful holiday offering its challenge is twofold: to manage the development of the concept, and to decide on the role which that product should play within the company. Most successful businesses have a portfolio of products: some at the research stage, some which are very successful, others which are declining in popularity for a variety of reasons, and some which have just been launched onto the market but which are not yet generating profits. Figure 6.3 presents a hypothetical example which shows how the development and launch costs of new services can be found from the net revenue earned by established holiday packages which are ploughed back to ensure the company's growth and survival.

A key way to build a competitive position is through service differentiation which creates a clear image of the service organization in the eyes of customers and can lead to distinctive positioning in the market. Similarly, management's technical decisions often have marketing implications; customers may interpret a change in the way a service is delivered as a change in the service itself and then may question the extent to which it meets their needs.

Market segmentation

An understanding of customers' perception of tourism products provides a basis for specialized marketing techniques whereby the features of essentially similar products which distinguish one producer from another are used to convey an appeal to chosen sections of the market. The technique of segmentation has been defined as 'The process of dividing a potential market into distinct subsets of consumers, and selecting one or more segments as a target to be reached with a distinct marketing mix' (Wilkie, 1987). Segmentation is an effective marketing tool, but to be selected for management attention and action it has been suggested that the segment must have three characteristics; it must be measurable, easy to reach through advertising and distribution systems, and it should offer a sustainable flow of business for long enough to repay the costs of developing it (Woodside and Sherrell, 1977).

The technique depends on identifying the characteristics of visitors seeking particular sets of benefits from their tourism purchases. Several steps are required to gain an understanding of how consumers choose between similar services; firstly a limited number of relevant and objective attributes are chosen by preliminary research as the basis for product profiles. A group of people are assembled who may be current clients of the company, or who have demographic or other characteristics of interest in the research. The list of product attributes previously developed is then ranked by each respondent before coding and analysis. The relative importance of different attributes for different contexts is determined in this way, and their managerial and marketing implications can be examined. One feature of interest in this approach to segmentation by product-related decisions is that any service has many attributes. It is often necessary to compromise in one area, such as airline seat width, against another service feature such as the width of aisles in the plane with consequent detrimental effects on the style and quality of the service.

A permanent problem in segmentation research of this type is whether to focus on actual behaviour or clients' expressed preferences. Pragmatically observed behaviour can be assumed to be rational if it is consistent and so it can be modelled. However, the basis of rational choice for one consumer may be irrelevant to another selecting between the same range of products. Price may be critical for one person, habit may dictate the preferences of a second, while convenience is a choice criterion which dominates other consumers.

An effective segmentation method is based on research to identify the characteristics and needs of regular customers. Any organization attracts people who use its services more, or less regularly. Heavy users bring regular business to the company, and the patterns of their demand are often relatively predictable, making a reliable base for decisions on the volume, frequency and standard of services to offer. Twedt (1964) has identified three demographic variables which distinguish the heavy airline travel segment – in particular: education, occupation and income. He argued that they are about equal in their ability to discriminate, though the research indicated that the heavy airline travel segment is becoming more upscale in education, occupation and income through time.

Tourism branding

Branding is a feature of modern marketing methods; it offers the consumer a way of distinguishing between alternative products with similar core attributes. The method depends on strong labelling for instant recognition, heavy promotion to keep the brand name of the service at the front of peoples' minds and consistent quality or performance throughout the production run. It offers companies an established position within the broad product category, and is a technique which can be used by both travel principals and retailers.

Branding is at the centre of much modern marketing effort. A strong identity is felt to give opportuntities and benefits to the company. From a promotional point of view the task of marketing is to establish strong market awareness for the brand, so that it becomes the first choice of the consumer. Branding builds on the core features of a product or service, offering additional benefits which distinguish one product from similar alternatives. The stronger the brand, the less readily will a consumer accept an alternative.

The task is to make the brand one of those which the consumer is most likely to purchase. However, it is also possible that a particular brand may have failed to satisfy a consumer in the past, in which case it is unlikely that he will repurchase it. Those two groups of brands have been described as evoked and inept sets. Evoked sets have been described as 'the collection of brands the buyer actually considers in his decision process' (Howard, 1963). The second category is those brands about which the consumer has so little knowledge that he is unlikely to consider them. Inept brands are those which the consumer has rejected from his purchase consideration, either because he has had unpleasant experiences or because he has received negative feedback from other sources and this category represents a general failure in their management. Inept brands represent a failure on the part of marketing, in contrast to the successful marketing awareness gained for evoked brands. Branding can be implemented through the consistent use of a corporate symbol or trade name. The case study of the Hilton International acquisition by Ladbroke Group PLC discusses the branding and image decisions taken subsequently.

Many tourism organizations have adopted a branding strategy which enables them to offer particular services to different segments of the market. In some cases they adopted a common name with a secondary identifier for each segment, thereby retaining the market awareness of their major brand for all business sectors. Okoroaka (1989), has studied the hotel group Radisson, and reported that originally it operated full service hotels, located in business areas to target all segments of the business market. Later, Radisson introduced additional brands: Radisson Inns were located in secondary areas to serve a broad business market; Radisson Resorts offered recreational provision and scenic locations for leisure travellers, Radisson Plaza Hotels offered full facilities in city centres for executives and Radisson Suites catered for the extended stay business market, and were mainly located in office districts.

Advertising and competition

It is very probable that the share of a market between existing firms will be changed as a consequence of successful advertising campaigns initiated by one of them. Successful companies attract customers from their competitors and so will gain a larger share of the market. The increased business may be a larger proportion of customers newly attracted to the market, or there may be no overall increase in demand, just people switching away from other firms. This increasing concentration in the industry will tend to speed up as the successful firm benefits from economies of scale, and as managers continue to gain in experience.

Advertising is one of the most important ways of differentiating services and therefore it creates and then reinforces significant barriers against companies entering a market. Any newcomer has to buy exposure to overcome established companies' awareness and brand loyalty. The entrant would incur penetration costs to establish a position in the market, by promoting its image as well as its services. This expense does not fall on the established firms which therefore will enjoy a lower unit cost of servicing sales. Economies of scale can be gained by the regular, heavy advertiser so that the unit cost of reaching a desired target audience falls as more advertising is placed. In addition the commissioning costs of message and copy production are incurred only once, so that a large advertiser may choose either to reduce the unit cost per target of the advertising production, or to increase the spending on production, thereby hoping to increase impact through creativity or by a series of messages.

Pricing strategies for tourism services

The price at which a service is offered has two functions for the consumer and of course it is critical to the service provider. Price acts as a primary signal of quality and accessibility for consumers. When comparing with similar purchases their relative prices act as an indicator of what to expect from each; the more expensive service is presumed to offer more, or specialized benefits. Secondly, the price set for any good or service is a filter – too high a price excludes the service from consideration by many people, within the constraints of their individual disposable income and budget priorities and their expectations of the benefits a particular service will bestow on them.

The company's main source of income to cover costs of production is revenue from sales. Since revenue is a function of both price charged and the volume of sales achieved, management has a set of related decisions to take. It was shown in Chapter 2 that economic theory indicates the strong likelihood that sales volume will decrease as price is raised. The rate of change in volume purchased as prices are raised (or lowered) is known as the price elasticity of demand. Elastic demand is indicated by a shallow slope to the demand curve, and highly elastic demand means that there will be a significant change in the number of clients for a given adjustment in price. In addition to an understanding of consumers' reactions to price changes, managers also need a detailed knowledge of the changing costs as they adjust the volume of service which the organization offers.

A characteristic of many tourism industries is that they have fixed capacity and high fixed costs, but the direct cost of serving each customer is relatively small. The objective of pricing tactics is to match demand to supply, generating revenue to cover costs and to ensure profit over a time period. Other objectives of pricing

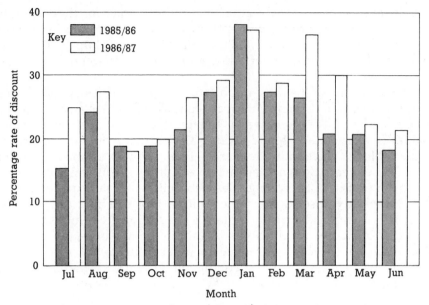

Figure 6.4 Average discount by month in London Hotels

Source: Laws 1988, based on Pannell Kerr Forster Associates

decisions include the nurturing of new routes, expansion, and so on. This suggests that a large organization may apply different pricing principles around its network at any one time. Marginal costing approaches are often adopted to sell remaining capacity after full-tariff sectors of the market have been served. The method depends on careful segmentation of the market according to the willingness and ability of each sector to pay. A study of hotel pricing in Britain by Pannell Kerr Forster Associates identified a wide range of discounts from rack rates. Table 6.3 indicates the range of rates at a small provincial hotel, while Figure 6.4 contrasts the average discounts in 1985/86 and 1986/87 in London hotels.

Variances from standard price may reflect the relative power of market intermediaries, such as group organizers, who generate significant volumes of repeat business on a regular basis, or it may be a response to seasonal (or weekly) patterns of demand. At times of known low demand discounted business can still bring in sufficient revenue to make a contribution to company running expenses over the costs of providing the service. At the other end of the price spectrum, premium rates offer extra value elements for which people will pay more. To meet profitability goals the marketer must respond to individual market segments and understand the variable costs per unit as enhanced service is likely to cost extra. Offpeak economy demand may be stimulated by reallocating all its overheads, but the full company overhead must be covered within the pricing matrix, shown in Figure 6.5.

Another supply characteristic of tourism is the inability to store services. Once a plane door has been closed a seat on that flight can never be sold again, and so there is a temptation to accept any reasonable fare after the costs of the flight operation have been met. A low fare sold at the last moment before departure

Table 6.3   Hotel discounts: Notional average daily rates for a 50-room provincial hotel*

Market segment	Room type	Annual market mix %	Annual rooms let	Annual average discount %	Average daily room rate £
Commercial/	Twin	26.0	299	10.0	39.52
Corporate	Single		2701	10.0	35.22
Conference	Twin	33.0	380	15.0	37.32
	Single		3427	15.0	33.26
FIT	Twin	21.0	726	5.0	41.71
	Single		1697	5.0	37.17
Leisure/	Twin	12.0	1110	35.0	28.54
Function	Single		277	35.0	25.43
Tour	Twin	8.0	832	60.0	17.56
	Single		91	60.0	15.65
Totals		**100.0%**	**11 540**	**18.0%**	**£33.21**

*Based on an annual room occupancy of 62.0 per cent, and rack rate of £39.13 Single, £43.91 Double net of VAT

Source: Laws 1988, based on Pannell Kerr Forster Associates

would be reasonable if it were set high enough to recover the actual costs involved in ticketing, the relatively small additional fuel costs incurred by the extra weight carried, and the baggage handling and catering expenses. In addition, a contribution to the company's cash position would be sought. Price

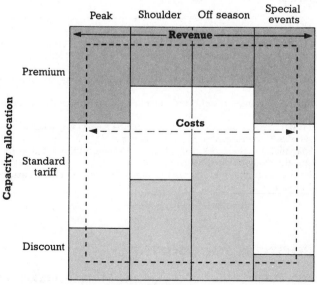

Figure 6.5 Cost recovery and pricing strategies

reductions are an attractive revenue enhancing tactic, as it is impossible to store tourism services for sale at a later date, in the way which goods can be kept in inventory. Reducing the price of travel just ahead of departure encourages passengers who would not otherwise have travelled. However, against this it is possible that people will learn the rules of late booking, and change their buying behaviour accordingly. Managers' and tourists' perspectives on price discounting can be understood in terms of the varying degrees of risk, indicated in Figure 6.6.

Effectively, passengers trade off less certainty in their travel arrangements against the price reduction while the company gains some additional revenue from capacity which it would not otherwise have sold. Discounting might achieve greater volume, but the tactic may not increase total revenue significantly since the gain from every additional holiday sold at a discount will drop. An alternative strategic approach which is popular with many clients is to offer certain extras with the normal package. Enhancing the benefits which clients obtain by including merchandising options such as flight bags, cameras or umbrellas, or offering extra nights or upgraded accommodation and so on, increases the attractiveness of the core benefits purchased. However, a possible consequence of this strategy is that it may lead to expectations of continuing improvements in the packaging of holidays.

Interval between booking and departure

		Long		Short
Standard		1		2
Price charged				
Discounted		3		4

The four cells can be understood from the discussion which follows:

1 **Customers** are likely to obtain their preferred holiday, or can search at leisure for an acceptable alternative. Company obtains full revenue.
2 **Customers** who are still undecided may be unable to find available capacity which meets their requirements.
  Companies risk capacity remaining unsold, and potential customers being tempted by competitors' discounted offers.
3 **Customers** do not expect below-standard prices, and may be suspicious of discounted offers.
  Companies have no reason to discount in normal circumstances.
4 **Customers** who delay their purchase risk their preferences being sold out, but in return for flexibility in their requirements they may obtain a bargain.
  Companies can obtain a contribution to their overheads by selling remaining capacity at any price above the costs of providing the service.

Figure 6.6 Discounting and risk

Planning horizons for tourism

New tourism services take time to develop and bring to market. The span varies from a few hours' work to set up a simple day excursion, to many years to develop major capital equipment, such as new aircraft types or hotel and resort developments. Clearly, as the interval between research and implementation of a service yielding cash flow lengthens, the risks of the venture increase. The degree of risk also increases with the number and variety of organizations on which the development project depends.

Achieving a company-wide customer orientation

Satisfactory service experiences call for a systematic approach to quality control. This suggests both that the organization should be designed around good service delivery, and that its management should focus on quality issues, designing the system from that perspective. Garvin (1988) has shown how this has been applied by manufacturers:

> At the best plants audit problems triggered an educational process in which the line workers were brought to the audit area to review units and discuss ways of avoiding future problems . . . despite the diversity (in their backgrounds, attitudes and so on) the common goal was to increase employees' sensitivity to quality and to avoid repeated mistakes.

Similarly, it has been shown that in the best service firms

> a consistent pattern to the managerial process is evidenced. One sees a pronounced emphasis on controllable details, continuous investment in training, a concern with the customer's view and reward systems that place value on service quality. In poor service firms however, one sees an internal rather than external orientation, a production orientation, a view of the customer as a transactions generator, a lack of attention to details affecting the customer, and a low priority placed on 'soft' service quality values.
>
> (Shostack, 1985)

These topics, and the contribution which a service marketing approach can make to successful tourism management, are developed in Chapters 7 and 8.

Conclusion

Marketing theory has traditionally taken as its focus the exchange of clients' money for vendors' goods and services. The discussion has often been in terms of people responding to economic and other signals in attempting to satisfy their felt needs by selecting rationally amongst the range of suitable products at a point in time. The emphasis in this book is on the ways in which passengers' experiences of satisfaction are influenced by managerial decisions during the extended delivery of a complex service and reflects Czepiel and his co-editors' (1986) definition of the three tasks of marketing; design to meet consumers' needs; attracting clients; and the monitoring and control of results.

Consumer satisfaction with a service is a function of the appropriateness of its design, and the quality of delivery by every member of staff in the service system. The discussion in this book shows how tourism's appeals to customers go beyond the physical aspects of the service. Rather than component parts assembled in a particular form, tourism marketing stresses the set of attributes offering the buyer satisfaction of his wants and needs. It then becomes the objective of the organization's management and staff, and the basis of its survival and prosperity, to deliver the benefits which marketing has promised to its clients. Appropriate tour package design and administration and carefully researched destination development linked to successfully communicated travel brands, can bring the advantage of an overall increase in tourist activity and spending. Chapter 7 introduces the analysis of tourism service management.

Questions

1 Identify tourism organizations which offer their services at several price levels and discuss the advantages of this approach.

2 How do various tourism organizations manage their product portfolios?

3 Conduct a SWOT analysis of tourism in your area and draft a marketing plan for the local tourism authority. What assumptions have you had to make and what further information would be required to draw up a full marketing plan?

Recommended reading

Hawkins, D. E., Shafer, E.L. and Rovelstadt, J.M. (eds.) *Tourism Marketing and Management Issues*, George Washington University Press, Washington DC, 1980

McDonald, M.H.B. *Marketing Plans*, Heinemann, London, 1986

Wilkie, W.L. *Consumer Behaviour*, Wiley, New York, 1986

CHAPTER SEVEN

Managing Tourism Services

Introduction

This chapter reviews the growing body of literature dealing with the management of service industries. It examines the major characteristics of this sector, and provides a basis for the discussion of tourists' satisfaction which forms the subject of Chapter 8.

Tourism is part of the expanding service sector of the economy (Akehurst, 1989) and consequently this chapter examines the distinctive challenges of operating service enterprises. The service sector is very broad, and includes many other industries such as banking or hairdressing. Each is a specialized activity, requiring a specialist set of skills from its managers and workers. Customers have differing expectations of satisfaction from each type of service. However, the developing literature on service industries indicates that there are many significant similarities shared by all industries in this sector. This chapter presents readers with a summary of the most important perspectives to emerge from this interesting area of study.

Special characteristics of services

Specialists analysing services often draw a distinction from the production of goods, emphasizing that jobs are carried out directly for clients and pointing out that a service cannot be stored for future sale, nor can it be measured or sampled. The following definitions bring the many strands together clearly: 'A service is any task performed for another, or the provision of any facility or product or activity for another's use, not ownership which arises from an exchange transaction. It is intangible and incapable of being stored or transported' (Uhl and Upah, 1983). Table 7.1 illustrates an idealized approach to service management.

Table 7.1   Idealized approach to service management

---

1 Orchestrate the encounter
     Access buyers' needs, expectations, knowledge of evaluative criteria
     Process technical expertise, manage interactions, elicit customer participation
     Output satisfying service purchase experience
2 Quality assessment using established expectations as the basis for judgement
3 Educate buyers about the unique characteristics of the service
4 Emphasize organizational image and communicate the image attributes of the firm
     and its service
5 Encourage satisfied customers to communicate to others
6 Recognize contact personnel's role
7 Involve customers during the design process

Source: George and Kelly, 1983

Service and manufactured sector distinctions

Four factors distinguish the management and enjoyment of services from approaches in the manufactured product sector; examples are provided to illustrate these points. The first difference is that each customer gets a unique service. In a restaurant one scoop of ice cream will differ in some respects from all other such servings; it may vary slightly in size, texture or the style with which it is presented to the customer. Secondly the individual customer's attitude towards his meal will contrast with other people's. The range of influences on an individual's mood are many and include varying degrees of haste, hunger, and the individual's relationship to the people around him. The third distinguishing feature is that the waiter or waitress who serves the ice cream is actually an important part of the experience of the service. Consequently the managers of a service enterprise who wish to develop a quality control system must address two issues: technical aspects of the service, such as the composition and preparation of a meal, and secondly the service staff whose abilities and attitudes are both significant factors in clients' overall experience.

The operational significance of the distinction between services and products is increasingly recognized as the basis for specialized managerial skills and approaches. Services depend on face-to-face delivery when staff are in direct contact with their clients. In contrast to the production of goods where the detailed characteristics of each item are the outcome of managerial decisions, each service transaction is itself a variable dependent on the interaction of staff and client. The inseparability of its production and consumption means that each service interaction is in some respects unique. For example, the American company Federal Express has defined its service as 'all actions and reactions that customers perceive they have purchased' (Lovelock, 1984).

From the point of view of tourism managers, a fourth factor may be added to the three distinctions between services and products just outlined. In addition to the unique character of each service transaction, the differing attitudes of clients, and the role of staff in service transactions, many of the essential component services for tourism are provided by other companies. It was pointed out earlier in this book that in extreme cases a package holiday client may never meet an employee of the tour operator. He purchases a holiday package from an independent retail outlet. The airport, airline, hotel and the ground handling arrangements are all serviced by employees of those companies. The tour operator coordinated all those services, marketed them and accepted the client's booking, then made reservations from its allocation with each supplier contributing to the package. The client on a mass package holiday is often met by a resort or hotel representative of the tour operator, but in some cases they are actually staff of local handling agencies. Under legislative changes emanating from the European Community, and the increasing pressure of consumerism, it seems probable that tour operators will become responsible and liable to their clients for every component of a holiday which they package.

The nature of service experiences

The foregoing discussion suggests that the twin foci of concern for service managers are the underlying technology of their business, and the human interactions required to deliver satisfactory experiences to their clients. These twin responsibilities have been referred to as Type A (technical) and Type B (service) aspects of the service experience in an earlier study by this author (Laws, 1986). In common with other services, tourism is put to the test in the interaction between client and the staff providing each aspect of the package, whether this is check-in at the airport, the hotel or excursions. Thus, there are many occasions when clients match what they experience to the standards of service which they had expected to enjoy.

Many tourism services are technologically complex, and few customers are able to judge the technical quality of the service experience, but they do make assessments of the skills and attitudes of staff. This implies that service quality is difficult to manage, and that the method common in manufacturing, that of prescribing specific attributes for products, cannot be applied to tourism. Chapter 8 discusses approaches to the management of quality in tourism.

Many factors impinge on customer satisfaction, some under the control of managers, others remote from their influence. Table 7.2 identifies factors which are typically under the control of managers.

Table 7.2   Quality factors under management control

• Access	• Reliability
• Communications	• Responsiveness
• Competence	• Security
• Courtesy	• Tangibles
• Credibility	• Understanding the customer

Source: Zeithaml, Berry and Parasuraman, 1988

93

However, Zeithaml and his co-authors went on to point out that three other factors are beyond management control, and these are shown in Table 7.3.

This emphasizes the significance of the client's role in the success of service delivery. The customer reaches a judgement about the quality of service actually experienced when measured against the perceived service, based on the ten determinants listed in Table 7.2. Tourists often express overall satisfaction or dissatisfaction with their holiday package or airline journey, but more detailed analysis shows that every service is actually experienced by the client as a series of episodes during which the connected stages of the service unfold. Each of these episodes are judged. Jan Carlzon, Chairman of SAS (Scandinavian Airlines) has called these episodes moments of truth.

> SAS is not a collection of material assets but the quality of contact between an individual customer and the SAS employees who serve the customer directly . . . Last year, each of our ten million customers came in contact with approximately five SAS employees, and this contact lasted an average of 15 seconds each time. Thus, SAS is 'created' 50 million times a year, 15 seconds at a time. These 'moments of truth' are the moments that ultimately determine whether SAS will succeed or fail as a company. (Carlzon, 1987)

The significance is that it is important for managers to listen to customers to find out what their moments of truth are and how well they consider such episodes are managed.

Table 7.3   Quality factors beyond management control

- The customer's attitude, influenced by word of mouth recommendation
- The customer's personal needs
- Any past experience he may have had with that company

Source: Zeithaml, Berry and Parasuraman, 1988

At any one time, people requesting a particular tourism service may have very different attitudes towards it. An airline steward or stewardess serving lunch shortly after take off may be faced with passengers having a variety of needs and attitudes. One passenger may have a strong dietary preference which may (or may not) have been notified to the airline. That special meal may not have been boarded. Another passenger may have made a long overnight flight to connect with this sector and his need may be for a light snack, or simply to sleep. Yet another passenger may be very anxious, either about flying, or as a result of events in his personal life. The majority of passengers will be content to choose from the options on their menu cards, but towards the end of the meal service some choices will be out of stock. Similarly, two airlines may have different approaches to aspects of their in-flight service. Beverage service is an example which can cause another set of problems. While complimentary wine is offered by some airlines to passengers in economy class, others ask passengers to pay for their drinks. Nine situations likely to cause problems for staff have been identified, and are shown in Table 7.4.

Table 7.4   Potential problems for service staff

1   Unreasonable demands
2   Demands against policy
3   Unacceptable treatment of employees
4   Drunkenness
5   Breaking social norms
6   Special needs customers – psychological, language or medical difficulties
7   Unavailable service
8   Unacceptably slow performance
9   Unacceptable service

Source: Nyquist et al, 1985

Tourism is seen in this book as a service system within which the company, its staff and customers interact in technical and social processes. While the outcome for the customer is satisfaction or dissatisfaction, the significance of consequences for staff and the company are also considerable. Dissatisfied customers are likely to cause stressful working conditions for staff, both those from whom they received poor service and others they encounter. Dissatisfied customers can damage the company in several ways; their future business is likely to be lost to the company. Those who complain impose costs on the organization which will have to devote resources to investigation and response. Others will discuss their bad experiences with friends, relatives or colleagues, possibly influencing them against future purchases from this company.

The interactive aspects of service encounters are significant at a more fundamental level: interactions with other people are basic human activities, and occupy a large part of our time. Staff may spend their entire working day in repeating service encounters and poor service encounters reduce the quality of their work satisfaction. The point stressed in this chapter is that quality of the psychological outcomes to both clients and staff are partly dependent on managerial decisions about the design of service delivery.

Much of the service management literature is concerned with situations in which one client is served by one contact person representing the company; technically this service situation is known as an interaction dyad. Typical studies focus on interaction at the point of sale (Evans, 1963; Olshavsky, 1973). However, in tourism the presence of other people may sometimes become a significant factor in clients' experiences. Such transactions are performed in a public setting and often the service affects more than one client, while most people tend to take notice of different levels of service offered to those around them.

Mini-encounters and part-encounters

Taking one type of tourism service as an example, an airline journey is experienced by passengers as a series of events which have varying effects on their satisfaction. The term 'part-encounter' has been introduced in this book to refer to an event which is a component in the overall service. Such face-to-face service encounters should be distinguished from other events which Blackman (1985) called mini-encounters, such as the firm's advertising where the firm impacts on a client's consciousness.

A part-encounter contributes to the client's overall satisfaction with the service purchased, but each is a separate event during the overall service episode. Although many components can be identified in these events (including technological factors and the presence of other passengers) the interaction with staff is always a factor. The outcome of these part-encounters may boost or depress customer satisfaction, but the intangible nature of services previously discussed makes it hard for the client to judge what to expect, or to know how to assess what was received.

> In most service encounters, there are few or no natural clues to utility, either before the service occurs or after it is accomplished. Often, the customer does not know how to tell when she or he would be satisfied, and managers do not know how to structure the service process to satisfy customers. Yet this satisfaction is crucial to both customers and service providers. (Blackman, 1985)

Queuing for tourism services

A common feature of the modern traveller's experience is waiting in line for various services such as a flight. Even before the plane takes off a typical journey by air can involve a series of part encounters and queuing for the many purposes shown in Table 7.5.

Table 7.5   Part encounters before take-off

1	Buying a ticket for the flight
2	Buying a ticket to travel to the departure airport
3	Queuing to check in
4	Queuing for security checks
5	Emigration control
6	Making duty free purchases
7	Boarding the plane

Research suggests that the way people are treated while queuing significantly affects their overall perceptions of the quality of service provided later in the flight. Most studies have been concerned with objective matters such as queue discipline, or service speed, there has been less discussion of the experience of waiting. Waiting can be demoralizing and it often engenders a feeling of powerlessness, particularly when the reasons for a delay are not clear, or there is uncertainty over the outcomes. Often, it is also necessary to queue after a flight has landed, but once the flight is over any extra waiting is aggravating because there is no more value to be received (Maister, 1986).

Service blueprinting

It is a managerial prerogative and responsibility to allocate appropriate resources to the various tasks of an organization and to set up human and technical systems for effective task performance. The customers' understanding of what is appropriate and effective should be taken into consideration at the design stage of service management. Shostack has pointed out that the design of the service dictates the job characteristics for staff and should 'support a positive encounter quality' (Shostack, 1985). Several methods exist to model service organization and delivery systems; for example Chase and Tansik (1983) have highlighted the points at which a customer interacts with the organization, distinguishing between 'front and back office' activities schematically.

Blueprinting is the process of defining the range of resources required for the performance of services, and of coordinating the various components which contribute to more complex services such as package holidays, as indicated in Figure 7.6. The method can be regarded as a tool for depicting and analysing all of the processes involved in delivering services to the consumer.

> The basic requirements of a service blueprint are three. First, since processes take place in time, the blueprint must . . . show time dimensions in diagrammatic form. Secondly blueprinting must identify all main functions of the service . . . All input and output of functions must be shown. Like systems design, the blueprint must identify and handle errors, bottle-necks, recycling steps, etc. Finally, usually after research, the blueprint must precisely define the tolerance of the model, i.e. . . . the degree of variance from the blueprint's standards which can be allowed in execution without affecting the consumer's perception of overall quality and timeliness. (Shostack, 1981)

Quality is an issue at both the service delivery and the service design stage. Management has to understand the factors which its clients consider significant in boosting or depressing the satisfaction they experience and use these as the criteria for service specification. Against that, the quality of services delivered can be assessed and future standards for tourism services can be adjusted in the light of experience. 'Market research is needed if products are to offer the dimensions of quality that are of greatest interest to consumers and if they are to target a defensible quality niche' (Garvin, 1988).

Blueprinting has provided an effective method for the investigation of specific situations and studies show that in many instances tourists see little of the work involved in delivering the service. George and Gibson (1988) have discussed the implications of this finding.

> The line of visibility is the part of the blueprint used to separate those processes which are visible to the consumer from those which are not . . . The percentage of the blueprint which lies above the line of visibility varies according to each service, but in general the majority of the blueprint is below the line of visibility. Shostack likens what lies above the line of visibility to the tip of an iceberg. She believes that particular attention must be paid to the processes which are below the line, even though customers are totally unaware of them . . . all processes must be carefully designed to maximize the desired effect on the consumer.

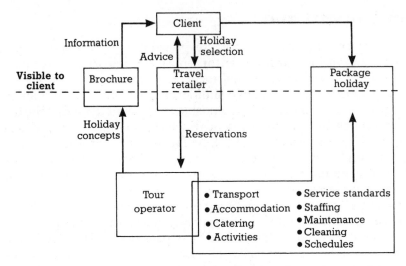

Figure 7.1 Blueprint of a package tour

Two further points which George and Gibson made in their paper are relevant here. They argued that the blueprinting method is effective in identifying the aspects of a service which are most susceptible to failure.

> Failpoints are the part of a service blueprint which identify those processes of the service which are most likely to go wrong and function other than intended . . . Failpoints can be internal and invisible to the customer, or visible . . .

Secondly, they argued that blueprinting is a system model which emphasizes the interrelationships between its components.

> Blueprint facilitates a system-wide perspective of the entire service process allowing greater understanding of institutional quality . . . It makes the service tangible and can provide employees with a picture of the service process which includes the key quality determinants . . . No longer is the service delivery system considered a series of discrete events. Instead it can now be visualized as an interconnected whole . . . It can model the actual versus the desired qualities of the service delivery system . . .

If its design works against a service it is likely that clients will experience dissatisfaction. A range of problems result as staff will be less able to deliver the performance standards expected of them.

> In a blueprint one can trace through all the components of the underlying design and see how they culminate in the various encounter points during which the customer interacts with the service . . . Each item that is visible to the customer represents an encounter point, during which the service will occur. (Shostack, 1985)

The role of staff in service experiences

The foregoing discussion of service delivery and design has emphasized the role of contact staff in the experience of clients and supports the view that it is the service encounter which should be the focus of analysis. In any encounter a range of behaviours are possible for both customers and staff, although this is constrained by several factors, including their expectations about the process and the outcome of the service. These expectations have variously been termed a template, or a script (McCallum and Harrison, 1985). The suggestion is that individuals have a repertoire of scripts, from which they select one most closely matching the type of service interaction they anticipate. The script chosen and then acted out is the basis for that person's judgements about the outcomes experienced. This analysis points to one reason why tourists may hold differing views of what to expect from a service. Customers with wider experience may be expected to have a repertoire of more differentiated, more specialized scripts.

From the point of view of staff, specialized service transactions occur frequently. In such a situation they quickly learn that certain behaviours are more costly in terms of effort, or time than other options, and consequently a sterotyped style of service tends to be offered. But the style of the provider's behaviour may influence the tourist's own behaviour, reflecting or reacting against the role model offered. Furthermore, the response to a client's difficulty is often for the member of staff involved to summon the assistance of colleagues. The increased complexity of the resultant interaction tends to increase uncertainty and to raise the apprehension of passengers.

The greater familiarity which staff have with service delivery routines, combined with their specialized role knowledge and skills and their position as representatives of the company, establishes a status for them in the encounter. However, status relationships in services are often specific to the type of encounter. Airline cabin crew spend much of their time serving meals but they also enforce safety regulations. The relative power of client and staff, in terms of their expertise, personal control, degree of urgency and so on, influence the way a service interaction episode evolves. Within the framework of the service design, this aspect of their relationship largely determines the outcomes for each. Airline staff have a significant power differential over passengers based on their greater technical knowledge of the service delivery technology surrounding flights. This is enhanced by the brand differences between carriers, reflected in their differing service styles, with the result that passengers experienced on one airline, type of service or class may have misperceptions of another airline's practices.

The tendency for service enterprises to provide uniforms for their contact staff has several features of interest. It serves to enhance the company's brand image, and to make staff immediately distinct, and therefore accessible, in crowded areas. As Blackman (1985) noted,

> Putting each service technician into a uniform helps create an image or 'package' of sameness common to other technicians in the company. This common package fosters a brand image to help assure a purchaser that the service will be essentially similar each

time he uses it. By giving purchasers visual cues common to all interactions with the
company, the service provider gives purchasers a way of accurately predicting the
utility and equality of service.

But Hollander (1985) has introduced another dimension to the consideration
of uniformed service staff, 'uniforms . . . confer authority on some wearers and
impose it on others'.

Given the importance of staff attitudes and behaviour, Mills (1985) has
pointed to the significance of how people control their emotions and reactions in
work related encounters: 'Very little empirical work has been undertaken to
determine how employees in organizations control themselves. The results from
limited work would seem to suggest that self-management is related to
(organizational) structure.'

This point of view indicates the importance to management of gaining the full
support of staff at all levels for a customer-oriented service delivery. The case
study of BA's approach to the management of its passengers' experiences shows
how this had been achieved in one airline. 'Since service encounters are the
consumer's main source of information for conclusions regarding quality and
service differentiation, no marketer can afford to leave the service encounter to
chance' (Shostack, 1985). Similarly, Adams (1976) pointed out that 'Employees
of service organizations are often as close to their customers psychologically and
physically as to other employees. They are the organization's most immediate
interface with the customer'. This line of reasoning has led Shostack to argue
that service encounters can be controlled and enhanced.

Service standardization

One strategy which service managers can adopt in their search for consistent
service is to eliminate employee discretion and judgement whenever possible
(Saaser, Olsen and Wycoff, 1978). This approach relies on the specification of
tasks to a standard of performance expected by management and provides them
with a basis for measuring the effectiveness of staff performing services.

Performance criteria are often specified for service delivery systems in terms
of how quickly staff (or equipment) should perform specific tasks. Some tourism
sector companies have adopted this approach; airlines publicize the proportion
of their 'on-time' arrivals, or aim to open the plane's doors within two minutes of
'engines-off'. Other companies expect staff to answer telephone enquiries within
ten seconds. American Express is reported to have developed 180 such
measures of timeliness, accuracy and responsiveness (American Express, 1982).
Locke and his co-authors (1981) recommended that any such goals must have
the characteristics of being specific, accepted, covering important job dimensions,
be reviewed, with appropriate feedback, be measurable, challenging but
attainable.

Many tourist boards have a classification scheme for hotels in their area. Its
purpose from the travellers' point of view is to help them locate a hotel in an area
which offers suitable standards of accommodation and meets their budget.

Nightingale (1985) has commented critically on the philosophy of the Crowne criteria which had recently been introduced by the English Tourist Board (ETB).

> A single bed should be of a minimum size of 6' 3" by 3', but they do not make any comment that it should be comfortable. The bathroom requirement is one for every ten resident guests but little mention is made about its cleanliness or the availability of hot water. There is evidence, however, that customers do not evaluate the quality of their stay in a hotel on this basis. They are more likely to consider such factors as the availability of a service, the smoothness or speed of response to a request, ease of use, pleasant and relaxing surroundings, spaciousness, value for money, the provision of reasonable facilities and adequate choice.

Examples such as this disprove the claims made in product-attribute quality control models that a simple link exists between measurable product attributes and the subjective perceptions of customers.

Increased standardization implies a reduction in the discretion allowed to individual employees, although this contradicts their need to assess each client as an individual, with needs which may vary during the various part encounters of which a service is composed. Efficiency goals may clarify performance targets for staff, but can conflict with the customer's expectation of warm and friendly service. A particular problem for companies operating from many branches, or in several countries, is that strong advertising messages concerning a company's special service style means that consumers will expect similar standards from each branch, so management often cannot allow operating units significant autonomy.

A study of 101 successful service firms in America concluded that they had several factors in common, and this is summarized in Table 7.6.

Table 7.6   Features of successful service firms

- Managers are obsessive about listening to and responding to changing customer wants, needs and expectations
- They create and communicate a well-defined, customer-inspired service strategy
- They develop and maintain customer-friendly service delivery systems
- They hire, inspire and develop customer-oriented frontline people

Source: Zemke and Schaaf, 1989

Conclusion

This chapter has indicated that a specialized understanding of service management is required to ensure satisfactory outcomes for tourists, staff and the organization.

Problems in the service delivery system may be caused by technical failures or human error in the encounter, either through incorrect task performance on the part of the server, or because the customer acted incorrectly at some stage in the service. These have been classified as Type A (technical) and Type B (service) aspects of services (Laws, 1986). In production management, allowance is made for breakage, etc. Much of it can be flagged by quality control before it reaches the customer. If any product fails after purchase, repair facilities can be provided under warranty, and the anticipated costs of such repairs can be factored into the product's price. But service failures are more difficult to anticipate, understand and respond to, and the following chapter will examine the ways in which quality in tourism services can be managed.

Questions

1 Identify the individual part encounters in the delivery of a service you have experienced recently, distinguishing between technical and service aspects.

2 Discuss the analysis of service delivery given in this chapter, supporting or criticizing the view that the quality of service encounters is a variable dependent on the interaction of staff and clients.

3 Sketch and discuss a blueprint for a service with which you are familiar. Discuss any improvements you might wish to make, pointing to difficulties in implementing them.

Recommended reading

Czepiel, J.A., Solomon, M.R. and Surprenant C.F. (eds) *The Service Encounter, Managing Employee/Customer Interaction in Service Businesses,* Lexington books, Mass, 1985

Moores, B. (ed.) *Are They Being Served?* Phillip Allan, Doddington, 1986

Zemke, R. and Schaaf, D. *The Service Edge, 101 Companies That Profit From Customer Care,* NAL Books, New York, 1989

CHAPTER EIGHT

The Management of Tourists' Satisfaction

Introduction

In this chapter attention is focused on the ways in which managerial decisions can affect the satisfaction which tourists experience. Underlying this chapter is the view shared by many theoreticians and practising managers, that dissatisfied clients will turn for future purchases to alternative suppliers. Thus, the survival of any firm which fails to satisfy its clients' expectations is in doubt; virtually all managerial theorists recognize that ensuring the survival of an organization is the primary responsibility of its management.

Sir Colin Marshall, Chief Executive of British Airways, put the challenge in the following terms at a conference in 1986.

> Why not merely run an airline which is so good that it never has any problems? May I assure you that we are in a service business, and service businesses deal with people. There is never one perfect set of answers for dealing with people problems, otherwise they would not be people. What makes service businesses so interesting and so complex is that their prime stake in trade is people relations, and we are expected to handle those relations in the hurly burly of commerce, not in the quiet professionalism of a therapist's room.

Quality control in manufacturing and service industries

The issues distinguishing service organizations such as tourism from businesses which manufacture products for sale were discussed in Chapter 7. These include the process nature of services, the interaction between staff and clients, and the factors determining clients' expectations of service standards.

Two important issues for tourism managers are the problem of defining quality levels for their services, and explaining unequivocally to clients what benefits and experiences they can expect to enjoy. In contrast, the specification of standards for industrial products seems somewhat less controversial, and communicating them to clients is more straightforward. Industry is a term which evokes images of mechanized, large volume production to satisfy a mass demand, the finished good such as a car tyre is an undifferentiated product, which is identical for every client. The tyres intended to fit a particular type of car are equally suitable for every other car with similar characteristics. Tyres with virtually identical specifications in terms of size, construction and performance ratings are manufactured by several companies. Drivers expect every tyre to conform very closely to the specifications given by its manufacturer.

Managers responsible for factory processes can achieve this high degree of uniformity for their products by a series of controls at critical stages of production. The formula for the tread, the strength and weight of the carcass, the temperatures at which the tyre is cured, and many other details are each carefully monitored. At any stage in the process of production a batch may be sent back to be reworked, or scrapped if defects outside of predetermined parameters are detected. After manufacture, each batch of tyres is subjected to other tests including weight, dimensions and balance, before it is released to the trade for distribution and sale to customers. Approved distributors have specialized fitting equipment, and staff trained to use it quickly and effectively.

The rigorous approach outlined above can be contrasted with quality control in tourism, where quality is taken to mean the delivery of services which customers find satisfying. Customer satisfaction can be seen as the outcome of managerial decisions about service delivery and the technology employed. That is to say, quality is a variable dependent on technological and service management decisions. By examining the factors influencing passengers' changing satisfaction the appropriateness of the technical design of systems can be explored, and with an understanding of the meaning to customers of their experiences, managers can develop a competitive position for their company.

It has been suggested that customers' understanding of the total quality of a service is composed of three factors: corporate image; technical quality and functional quality (Gronross, 1980). Such a view emphasizes the range of difficulties facing service managers attempting to develop and implement effective quality control programmes, and highlights the role of consumer judgement in evaluating those services. Following their experience of a service, and evaluation of it, any future decision will range from a repeat purchase of the same brand when the traveller is satisfied, to a change in purchase behaviour in

Table 8.1 Definitions of quality

---

1 *Technology driven and product oriented definitions,* such as Crosby (1984) who defined quality as conformance to requirements based on company specifications
   (This equates to consumerist gap Type A technical management)
2 *Fitness for use definitions,* that is market-driven and customer-oriented, focusing on customer utility and satisfaction (Juran, 1982)
   (This equates to Type B service management tasks)

Source: Gummesson, 1988

favour of a competing brand or an entirely different product following dissatisfaction. It therefore becomes critical for managers to understand their customers' perceptions of services.

Two main approaches to the meaning of quality have been distinguished, based on their technology or service delivery emphasis. Table 8.1 shows their equivalence to the Type A and Type B technical and service management tasks identified in Chapter 7.

Satisfaction and dissatisfaction

An important model focused attention on the reactions of consumers to satisfying or dissatisfying purchases (Hunt, 1977). Customers' experiences with any purchase give rise to outcomes for them varying from dissatisfaction to satisfaction. These outcomes are emotional responses, reflecting a divergence from the standards of service which clients had anticipated, as the following abbreviated quotations indicate: 'The seeds of consumer satisfaction are planted during the prepurchase phase of the consumer decision process' (Wilkie, 1986). It is against this individual benchmark that tourists measure the quality of their service experiences. 'Satisfaction is defined as a postconsumption evaluation that the chosen alternative is consistent with prior beliefs and expectations (with respect to it). Dissatisfaction, of course, is the outcome when this confirmation does not take place' (Engel, Blackwell and Miniard, 1986).

Dissatisfaction has also been defined as a state of cognitive or affective discomfort. The consumer has allocated some of his resources, spending money and time, and built up an anticipation of satisfaction, but if his judgement of the service he received is that it was not up to his standard, he will experience cognitive dissonance (Festinger, 1957). It was explained in an earlier chapter that disappointment with any situation causing serious discomfort results in efforts to correct the situation, or a determination to avoid it in the future. 'The disconfirmation paradigm maintains that satisfaction is related to the size and direction of the disconfirmation experience where that is related to the person's original expectations' (Churchill and Surprenant, 1982).

Tourism service processes

Another feature distinguishing the service sector from the market for goods is the process nature of service transactions: clients themselves contribute to the production, as has been pointed out. 'The process is the product. We say 'airline' when we mean 'airtransportation'. The use of nouns obscures the fundamental nature of services, which are processes, not objects' (Mcluhan, 1964). Other researchers have argued that consumers develop a script, a picture of the process which resides in their memory and against which they measure current experiences (Abelson, 1976). This point is critical in understanding the challenges of managing tourism quality as each consumer chooses the stimuli that are important to him, and develops a personal template of an ideal service

Table 8.2   Understanding the enjoyment of services

---

1 Service quality is more difficult for the consumer to evaluate than the quality of goods
2 Service quality perceptions result from a comparison of consumer expectations with actual service performance
3 Quality evaluations are not made solely on the outcome of a service; they also involve evaluations of the process of service delivery

---

Source: Lewis and Booms, 1983

encounter as the basis for his judgements. Table 8.2 provides an overview of how services are enjoyed. (The additional complexity, that an individual's base for evaluating services may vary over time and according to circumstances, is also worthy of note.)

Outcomes of tourist satisfaction and dissatisfaction

Garvin (1988) has shown how Taguchi had focused attention on 'the loss function of quality, the costs imposed on society by shipping a product which does not conform to specification'. Similarly, although on first consideration travellers' dissatisfaction is a private matter, it can be argued that part of the burden may be regarded as a social cost. Delay imposes costs on travellers; the resultant stress and discomfort may lead to ill-health and could impose consequent health-care costs on the individuals or society. Further, dissatisfied travellers exhibit complaining behaviour which turns the attention of others to their discomfort, thus imposing both costs and lost revenue opportunities on the service provider.

The World Tourist Organisation (1985) reported on the wider effects of tourists' satisfaction: 'The satisfaction of tourists has direct effects on the satisfaction of hotel staff . . . an unsatisfied customer is a lost customer . . . Losing a customer is often felt as a hard blow for a firm'. The report pointed out that it is often difficult for staff to known whether the customer is satisfied, as his wants, and his perception of quality is different form the professional's perspective of good service. The WTO recommended that the image given by the firm to sharpen the customers' perception must stick to reality: 'an advertisement cannot sell a dream at any price for fear of deceiving the customer. Displeasure will often result in complaint'.

It was shown in Chapter 7 that a common managerial strategy for service quality control is to specify performance criteria. However, the differing expectations which travellers have can cause problems to staff even when the service criteria specified by the company have been delivered. 'Customer expectations and requests that exceed the firm's ability to perform account for 74 per cent of the reported communications difficulties. This implies that . . . even if the system is working at optimal efficiency, employees can expect to face a large number of communications difficulties' (Nyquist et al, 1985).

Consumerist gap analysis of travellers' satisfaction

An acid test for a company is the level of satisfaction which its clients experience from its services: the success of a company depends on its ability to attract sufficient clients, and in a competitive industry its continuing survival depends on their satisfaction with the service they receive.

The psychological framework within which clients evaluate a product or service has been shown to result in two outcomes. The quality of service experienced is often satisfactory, but in other cases clients are dissatisfied with the service they receive, and uncomfortable experience results in cognitive dissonance. The discussion of cognitive dissonance in this book has demonstrated that people try to reduce the features of a situation which cause them discomfort, and they will avoid situations which have made them uncomfortable in the past. Clients' experience of a service may be measured along a continuum ranging from 'very satisfied' to 'very dissatisfied'. This continuum forms the vertical axis of the consumerist gap diagram shown in Figure 8.1.

In the consumerist gap model, A_0 represents the level of service which clients anticipated at the time of purchase, but the satisfaction they experience during the delivery of a service can be higher, or lower, than anticipated. The assumption is that the company passes its acid test of consumer satisfaction when an individual's anticipated level of service as measured by E_0 is indeed experienced, and $E_0 = A_0$. This occurs at the outset of a service, and it is a measure of managerial success (the acid test) to return satisfaction to this level after any problems.

When service standards are higher than anticipated, consumers are very satisfied, and at level E_w positive outcomes include compliments to staff and

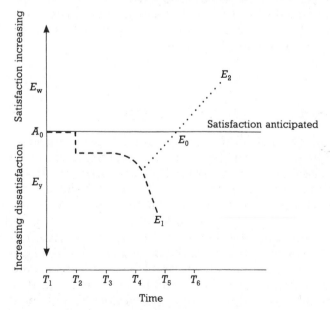

Figure 8.1 The consumerist gap model

favourable personal recommendations of the company to friends or colleagues by clients. The opposite extreme, when the service standards fail to meet the clients' expectations, is characterized by their increasing discomfort, frustration and ill-will. This situation can result from unscheduled interruptions to a journey, caused by technical failures, or from unsatisfactory performance of service events. In the consumerist gap model such problems are recorded at E_y, when individual clients experience so much discomfort that they complain, but if the crisis worsens dissatisfaction spreads amongst more clients, and becomes more extreme.

The horizontal axis of the model is calibrated in time units during which the interruption episode evolves as the company seeks technical solutions to restore normal service. Initially, satisfaction is at the level anticipated at $E_0 = A_0$, and the service proceeds smoothly. But if an interruption occurs, satisfaction falls below the anticipated level. In the model this occurs at time T_2, and a gap in consumer satisfaction is opened. The depth of the gap reflects the degree of dissatisfaction which the consumer has experienced.

The sequence and intensity of the company's responses to any technical (Type A) problems during a service affect clients' satisfaction. It takes some time to marshall the resources needed to overcome failure and this takes the model to T_3, when the company begins to correct the problem. At the same time service responses (Type B) are needed to restore customers' confidence or overcome their anxieties and discomfort. If these responses are inappropriate, by T_4 their dissatisfaction will have deepened. However, with effective action the model shows that technical (Type A) problems have been overcome and the normal service is resumed by T_5. The final level of satisfaction depends on how clients' needs were met by Type B responses during the interruption episode. Appropriate Type B responses can bridge the consumerist gap, even building greater customer satisfaction than had been anticipated. These are shown in path E_2. In contrast, path E_1 tracks the result of inappropriate actions which deepen the dissatisfaction experienced by clients.

Service gaps

A variety of problems may occur in any tourism service; tourists' perceptions of quality and their satisfaction with a service are influenced by these problems which can be classified as a set of service gaps shown in Table 8.3.

A common theme in both the service gap model and the consumerist gap model is the significance of the service standard level which tourists anticipate when purchasing a service. A_0 in the consumerist gap model reflects the expectations of satisfaction by clients, and several factors determine its value. In other models discussed in this book the benchmark nature of point A_0 has also been highlighted. From a managerial point of view it then becomes important to understand how anticipation is formed and how it can be influenced. The main tool is communications, especially but not only through paid mass media advertising. The problem is that idealized imagery is the common denominator,

Table 8.3   Potential service gaps

1 Differences between consumer expectations and management perceptions of consumer expectations
2 Differences between management perceptions of consumer expectations and service quality specifications
3 Differences between service quality specifications and the service actually delivered
4 Differences between service delivery and what is communicated about the service to consumers
5 Differences between consumer expectations and perceptions of the quality of the service received; depending on the size and direction of the other four gaps

Source: Parasuraman; Zeithmal and Berry, 1985

and most companies competing in a sector stress certain aspects of their service, using stylized models and settings.

An example of this is airline advertising. Passengers are often shown seated, or reclining in relaxed comfort in spacious cabins. They are attended by elegant and calm stewardesses (more rarely by stewards), and are featured enjoying delicious, carefully presented meals and fine wines. The reality is often very different. The point is that marketing communications are educating passengers to expect a level of service which it is beyond the ability of a carrier to deliver in all but the most favourable conditions. These might occur when there were no strikes, no mechanical failures, the cabin crew were on their peak performance, the plane was less than full, and all passengers were relaxed.

Responding to tourists' complaints

The consumerist gap model presented earlier in this chapter showed that two outcomes are possible for tourists; satisfaction or dissatisfaction. Management discovers its failure to provide satisfaction by two feedback mechanisms: exit and voice. Voice occurs when a consumer expresses dissatisfaction directly to the firm, either at the time, or subsequently. Exit is a corrective market mechanism which should affect the firm's decision-making. Successful firms both listen to their customers and are sensitive to exit (Hirschman, 1970).

Many theoretical models of marketing behaviour include a feedback loop (or loops), a mechanism by which consumers are able to express their opinions of a current market offering. The function is to allow the producer to modify future output to obtain a closer match to their wishes. The complaining customer attempts directly to change the firm's policies or behaviour, or to obtain compensation. Voice is more desirable than exit! Complaints are symptoms of dissatisfaction which had not been corrected during the service, and can be regarded as a final attempt by customers to gain a remedy. If that is satisfactory to them, their future custom might be retained, otherwise it is unlikely that they will return to the same company for future services.

Recently the British media and influential tourism bodies including ABTA have focused considerable attention on the way in which travel companies deal

109

with clients' complaints. Editorials and features in the trade press have expressed concern in reporting a growing volume of complaints, but as the value of travel purchases continue to increase, it is not clear whether the absolute complaint rate is significantly higher than previously. Table 8.4 provides a profile of outbound tourism related complaints in the UK.

Table 8.4   British complaints about outbound tourism services

A problems experienced

42% of holidaymakers experienced one or more problems
79% complained about service
77% complained about accommodation
73% complained about the resort, saying it was not as described

B survey of complaints by Ilkeston agency

Complaints to bookings ratio:
Thomson   1 complaint per 85 bookings
Horizon   1 complaint per 87 bookings
ILG   1 complaint per 67 bookings

C formal complaints

In 1988 there were 9 283 complaints against tour operators, and 722 against travel agents

D ABTA conciliations

	Cases	Value of average booking (£)	Value of settlement (£)
1987	15 000	255	112 759
1988	13 500	272	87 058

E Nearly 500 arbitrations, 75% found in favour of consumer

Source: Baxter, 1989

There are two major factors for any company's managers to consider when dealing with a complainant. One is the response to that individual. Companies vary in the hierarchical status, significance and philosophy accorded to their complainant response departments. The responsibility for this varies, from a senior executive to someone with junior status, limited field experience and circumscribed discretion to act in response to the complainant. Some companies have a policy of accepting responsibility when complaints appear reasonable, or reply quickly agreeing to investigate the problem. Table 8.5 indicates the range of responses possible.

The second major factor distinguishing companies is what they do with the data from customer correspondence files. Since it has to be retained until the company is sure that the aggrieved tourist will not bring a legal action against it, management may as well try to benefit from the accumulated experience of its more vocal clients. From a managerial perspective, the problems complainants raise fall into three categories, as indicated in Table 8.6.

Table 8.5   Organizational responses to complainants

Action	Purpose
Apology	To show the customer that the company is aware of the faulty service
Correction	To make the customer aware that the company is trying to correct the fault, and restore normal service
Compensation	A gesture to restore the customer's confidence in the company's goodwill
Follow-up	Tasks carried out on behalf of the customer to solve problems he or she has experienced as a result of the delay

Table 8.6   Solutions to service faults

1 Internal problems which the company can resolve by direct action
2 Problems originating in subcontracted services, which could be tackled by negotiation with other companies
3 Problems reported by some customers which could be turned into marketing advantages. For example, complaints about the quality of in-flight entertainment and the conflicting interests of passengers who wish to watch the screen or the passing scenery, could lead to a solution where each passenger has a miniature screen installed in his seat, giving the advantages of a personal choice of what to watch, and when

The challenge, and the difficulty of acting effectively, increases from 1 to 3, but the rewards are disproportionate as a strong position in the market which other travel firms have not recognized can be identified by analysing clients' serious concerns and responding appropriately.

The costs of service failure

A criticism of marketing literature and practice is that it has focused more on recruiting clients than on retaining them. Increasingly the concern expressed by managers is how to understand the factors which are central in motivating clients to remain loyal to their original tourism company when there are so many alternative suppliers of similar services and so many different services and products to enjoy, with limited funds and time.

An attractive strategy for tourism companies attempting to satisfy their clients is through quality programmes.

> There is no doubt that relative perceived quality and profitability are strongly related. Whether the profit measure is return on sales or return on investment, businesses with a superior product/service offering clearly outperform those with inferior quality. (Buzzell and Gale, 1987)

Gummesson (1988) has suggested that there are two ways to improve profit through quality measures. Improved market performance leads to increased sales and increasing market share (or decreased price elasticity). Increased quality ultimately enables the price to be raised. Secondly, a reduction in defects leads to lower unit costs of production and reduced costs of servicing complainants.

Apart from the consequences for tourists and staff of unsatisfactory services, a managerial perspective highlights both costs and gains to companies implementing quality programmes. The costs include disturbance in the running of departments and a reduction in future sales levels, resulting from dissatisfaction. Further costs are incurred in implementing preventive measures to reduce future dissatisfaction, including the redesign of service delivery systems or training and motivational programmes for staff.

Two related decisions are needed. One concerns the level of service which management sets. If an arbitrary decision is taken, the service provided may not reflect what clients anticipate. The revised standards could exceed expectations, thus increasing the company's costs unnecessarily, or alternatively too low a standard of service would offend clients, and the company would risk the loss of some of its business.

The second problem is how to measure and control the quality system. Lockwood (1989) has explained it in the following way:

> Hotel companies are increasingly aware of the importance of quality and clearly use it in their advertising and promotion to customers and in the standards of performance set for their employees. There is still however some confusion about what quality means. The hotelier should not be concerned with providing the best, but the best for his particular customers. The management of quality is not therefore just a technical problem, but a behavioural one too. The hotelier must consider the customer's attitudes, preferences and perceptions to be able to provide quality.

Research in the airtravel sector has indicated that experienced passengers expect to exercise choice. They claim to base their decision to fly with a particular airline on experience. The following question was posed to British travellers: 'If two or more airlines had equally convenient schedules, how important is previous experience of the airline in your choice?' Half the respondents rated previous experience as an important or very important factor, but 66 per cent of experienced travellers – those spending 50 or more nights a year abroad – stated that they relied on previous experience (Minter, 1989).

Managing tourists' satisfaction

Effective management action for service quality assurance requires an understanding of problems and their causes (and improvement requires a base line for measurement of progress). The point of reference in the consumerist gap method is the level of satisfaction anticipated by a passenger. In the design of their services, managers take decisions about an appropriate level of service to offer each target market segment and have the responsibility for ensuring its delivery. Customers, however, have the prerogative of evaluating their own experiences and of deciding whether (or not) to return to a particular service

Quality of technical responses

	Competent	Incomplete
Competent and caring	**Satisfied** (resale probable)	**Warm** (possible resale)
Competent but distant	**Cool** (possible resale)	**Dissatisfied** (resale unlikely)

Quality of contact staff's service responses

Figure 8.2 Outcomes from responses to a service failure

supplier if they are dissatisfied with the technical or service delivery performance.

Following such an occurrence the subsequent satisfaction of the passenger can be improved by effective responses; or depressed by inappropriate actions or attitudes of the staff. Figure 8.3 suggests how the opportunities for a company to sell future services to a customer may depend on a combination of its technical and service responses.

This model suggests that competent technical responses are judged by the passenger in terms of the perceived attitude of staff. His satisfaction will be boosted more by a caring response than by someone who is merely competent. Grudging service, even when efficient in hard performance measures, may prejudice a future repurchase of that company's services. The significance of the contact staff's attitudes is greater when the technical response to a problem proves inadequate; however, when staff are concerned to help the passenger and work to overcome the particular difficulty he encountered, they can

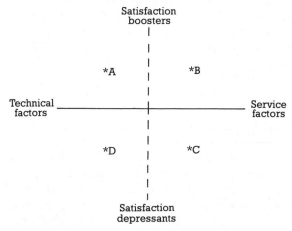

Figure 8.3 Grid analysis of consumerist gap outcomes

minimize his overall dissatisfaction, thus keeping open the possibility of a future sale.

Following the distinction drawn in the consumerist gap model, two dimensions are of interest in service delivery. One is the technological characteristics of the service design, which Chapter 9 reviews for airline services. The second aspect is the quality of service delivery, mainly consisting of the interaction between staff and clients. Technical and service factors form the two poles on the horizontal axis of Figure 8.3. Another foundation of the consumerist gap concept is a recognition that the outcome of service events and interactions vary along a continuum ranging from extreme satisfaction to extreme dissatisfaction. This forms the vertical axis of the consumerist gap outcomes model.

The four quadrants formed by the intersection of these two measures are classified A to D and are discussed in turn.

Most hard measures of service performance are clustered in the technical factors dimension, where it is relatively easy to measure in such terms as on time performance, seat pitch or meal delivery. However, the mere performance of the technically specified criteria are insufficient conditions for the satisfaction of passengers.

Quadrant **A** describes the conditions when a service is operated efficiently at a technical level, for example a flight proves comfortable, arriving on time and offering the passenger satisfying entertainment and meals as well as a pleasing standard of service from the staff.

The quality of entertainment, the control of cabin pressure or temperature and other factors have been shown to be significant factors in the way a passenger experiences a flight. Seats vary in comfort, or are broken or dirty, or situated in areas of the cabin which the passenger finds unappealing for various reasons. The meal (a special request or a normal menu item) may be too cold, or damaged. Thus, quadrant **D** depicts the case when satisfaction may be depressed by technical factors, which otherwise meet a company's performance standards.

Quadrant **B** describes a flight where any technical shortcomings such as delay or the non-delivery of a special meal request have been overcome by the effective responses of staff. It is not sufficient to restore the technical conditions of the service; if it is done in ways which offend or provoke the passenger the result is seen in quadrant **C**, where the acid test has been failed and the passenger is unwilling to return to that company.

Satisfaction management strategies

The involvement model developed in Chapter 5 emphasized the significance of understanding what aspects of a service are important to passengers. It has also been suggested that a company's positioning strategies, and the blueprint and quality controls for its service systems, should reflect the researched needs of its various target markets. Figure 8.4 indicates the connection between varying levels of passenger involvement and the aspects of a service which are important

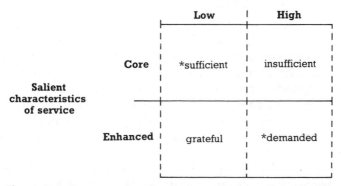

Figure 8.4 Passenger involvement and service characteristics

to them. It draws on the distinction between core and enhanced characteristics of services introduced in Chapter 1.

This model suggests that passengers who regard a service such as airtransport instrumentally, taking little interest in the process and focusing on the personal or business reasons for their journey, are normally satisfied by the efficient performance of the core service. These passengers will be grateful for additional service features offered during their flight and would therefore be likely to repurchase from a company offering such enhancements. (However, there is some contradictory evidence that low involvement passengers may find aspects of enhanced service delivery intrusive and unwelcome.)

In contrast, many passengers take a great deal of pleasure from the various aspects of their flight. They are often experienced travellers, who routinely look for a range of enhancements offered in their class of travel. The basic transport service is unlikely to satisfy them, while they will have the experience to judge the standard of service offered by one company against that of other airlines.

Organizational-wide care for customers

An important factor for managers is that the complexity of tourism services calls for a team-based approach. Consequently, it has been pointed out that 'Team work is the focus of service quality programmes in several firms known for their outstanding customer service' (Garvin, 1986). Table 8.7 draws on several

Table 8.7 Implementing customer orientation

1 The successful Chief Executive Officer develops a compelling vision of the future
2 He or she translates the vision into reality by concentrating on keys to success
3 He is involved in the actions necessary to carry out the vision
4 He motivates employees to embrace the vision
5 He constantly articulates the vision throughout all organizational levels

Sources: Bennis, 1968; Kanter, 1983; Levinson, 1971; Zaleznik, 1977

authorities to show that the characteristics of the chief executive are significant in implementing organizational change.

Many tourism businesses are encountering significant changes in the conditions which define their market. Taken together, the impact of technological, demand, regulatory and competitive changes may precipitate organizational crises, as Herman (1972) recognized: 'A crisis . . . is . . . a situation that threatens the high priority goals of the organization, restricts the amount of time available for response . . . thereby engendering high levels of stress'. Milburn, Schuler and Watman (1983) considered likely responses to such situations: 'An immediate response to organizational crisis is the switch in performance criteria used by the organization.'

A case study in Part Two examines the crisis which BA faced in the early 1980s. It traces the development of the customer care programmes and alludes to the significant role of both the Chairman and the Chief Executive in the change processes. A related case study discusses the importance which British Airways attaches to achieving an awareness of its customers' needs as a foundation of the new organizational culture. The concept of organizational culture has been defined as 'the pattern of shared values and beliefs that help individuals understand organizational functioning and thus provide them with norms for behaviour in the organization. That is, organizational culture is related to the causality that members impute to organizational functioning' (Deshpande and Webster, 1989).

Conclusion

This chapter has contrasted the management of service sector enterprises with the approaches common in the manufacture of goods. It has shown how the quality of services is a factor in clients' future decisions and therefore managers have a critical responsibility for reducing any factors in a service system that cause their clients dissatisfaction, while emphasizing the satisfying aspects of service. But there are two parallel sides to service delivery systems: the technology, which of course varies according to the sector and size of organization, and the human interaction of staff and clients, which has been the major thrust of this section.

Consumers take whatever data they can find, judge it by their own personal standards against their privately held expectations, and decide whether or not they are satisfied. They judge a multitude of facets in the service performance based on their observations of the process and the attitudes experienced.

Service quality is a measure of how well the service delivered matches customer expectations, but: 'Because services are performances rather than objects, precise manufacturing specifications concerning uniform quality can rarely be set . . . Because of intangibility, the firm may find it difficult to understand how consumers perceive their service and evaluate service quality' (Zeithaml *et al*, 1985)

The range of input variables, essentially the customer's unique expectations, make the industrial model of production management of limited value to service organizations concerned with providing a high quality experience. Controlling a service delivery process for uniformity of outcome usually leads to diminishing rather than enhanced customer satisfaction. The service manager's task is to support diversity of response between the customer and the organization, especially between the customer and frontline contact people.

The conclusion is clear: to create a distinctive level of customer service, management must understand and shape the customer's prepurchase expectations, influence the customer's evaluation of postpurchase quality, and ensure that the process of being served is not only painless and easy, but enjoyable.

Questions

1 Identify and discuss the quality control measures implemented by any tourism organization with which you are familiar.

2 Conduct a pilot study on a group of colleagues to gain an understanding of how they evaluate a particular service.

3 Do you agree with the view advanced in this chapter that services require a different quality management approach from manufactured goods?

Recommended reading

Carlzon, J. *Moments of Truth,* Harper and Row, NY, 1987
Garvin, D.A. *Managing Quality, the Strategic and Competitive Edge,* Free Press, NY, 1988
Lovelock, C.H. and Weinberg, C.B. *Marketing for Public and Non Profit Managers,* John Wiley and Sons, NY, 1984
Peters, T. and Austin, N. *A Passion for Excellence,* Collins, Glasgow, 1985

CHAPTER NINE

Transport Operations

Introduction

Tourism has been defined in this book as the industry which moves people from their place of residence to some temporary destination of interest to them, before returning them home. It follows that transport systems are integral to every tourism experience and expectations of travel satisfactions therefore form part of the decision to purchase tourism. Furthermore, any destination depends on the transport system for its supply of tourists, and in turn a transport organization depends on the business strengths of its origin and destination areas. A transport operator's success depends on the appropriateness of the services it supplies to the needs of passengers using a particular route.

Travel decisions

When viewed as part of a tourism system the travel facilities available can be considered as dependent on the overall demand linking destinations and points of origin. The various purposes of travelling between those points including business, family visits, sporting events and vacations then become significant in determining the type, capacity and frequency of transport links. A corollary of this interdependence between transport and destination is that carriers have traditionally invested in other sectors of tourism, particularly hotels, at the destinations they serve. This strategy of integrating the various aspects of tourism gives the lead organization an ability to obtain more leverage over traveller's decisions, and to benefit from all aspects of an expanding trade. Similarly, one of the main advertising themes employed by airlines and railways in points of traveller origin emphasizes the delights of the destinations served.

Tourists seem to regard the travel component of their holiday or business trip in one of two polarized ways. For many, it forms an important aspect in their selection and enjoyment of a journey. They consider the technical processes and style of travelling as pleasurable, interesting or exciting and want to experience particular modes of transport or to travel on particular routes. The trans-Siberian railway, a flight on Concorde, a holiday on a cruise ship, or driving across an Alpine pass are examples of specific transport experiences with strong appeal to certain travellers. Such travellers' decisions are characteristic of high involvement buying behaviour, discussed in the previous chapter.

However, other travellers do not regard the journey as a major part of their experience: people have to travel to get to meetings, holiday-makers and those visiting friends travel to reach their destination. What many of these travellers seek is convenient scheduling and comfort, while keen prices are particularly attractive to private travellers, and this is characteristic of the low involvement buying situations discussed earlier.

Research for market segmentation

It follows that transport operators needs to gain an understanding of what their passengers are seeking from any journey, and accordingly many companies carry out systematic surveys amongst their own passengers in order to build up a profile of their needs and characteristics. In one case the following findings were reported: 'Two market segments were identified: price sensitive vacation travellers; and travellers most sensitive to minimum stay provision of fare plans (mainly business travellers)'.

This finding is typical of the traditional marketing segmentation approach which distinguishes passengers according to straightforward criteria such as purpose of trip. It is helpful for planning purposes, as each segment is affected by identifiable factors resulting in particular rates of growth. Each segment will respond differently to fare changes, foreign exchange fluctuations or many other events. Segmenting the demand for travel into business and leisure is helpful in understanding demand; the base for this approach is conditions in the economy, as incomes rise more travel is likely to be purchased for leisure, and as business activity expands more business travel is stimulated. This understanding is fundamental to decisions on scheduling, pricing and service standards for specific routes, but the focus is on demographic determinants of travel rather than passenger needs.

Scheduled airline development

Transport systems differ in technical ways which are not discussed in this book; here the emphasis is on gaining an understanding of how managerial decisions impact on passengers' experiences. As the majority of international travellers use air services, this section examines the special features of airline operations as they impinge on passengers' experiences. (The exceptions are short sea routes such as those linking Britain with Europe, rail and coach travel, and journeys made by private car, usually on relatively short transborder trips.)

Strategic, technical and marketing considerations underlie the managerial decisions to provide a particular frequency, capacity and style of travel services on a given route, at particular prices. Airlines provide services either on a charter

119

Table 9.1   Service differentiation

---

1 Service strategy, the major decision about service which provides the company with its identity in comparison with the competition
   'In customer care a service strategy should be based on market research and should be aimed at meeting the needs, expectations and motivations of target customers'
2 The system for service delivery, containing visible and invisible components
   'A customer care system should be designed to provide a maximum level of ease of access and convenience to the customer'
3 The people who deliver the service, and form the moments of truth

---

Source: Thomas, 1987

or scheduled basis; the increasingly competitive environment for scheduled airlines has intensified their focus on controllable variables of the marketing mix. However, the problem for all airlines is that what they offer is relatively undifferentiated. Costs, journey times, seat comfort and so on are very comparable both because of the technical constraints of their services, and because of international or bilateral agreements.

It has been shown that three aspects have to be considered for service industry differentiation, as shown in Table 9.1.

Table 9.1 shows that there is more to successful competition than developing a set of technical solutions to clients' needs. It is both difficult and costly for airlines to offer their clients services which are significantly different from other airlines. Regulations dictate many of the conditions which colour a passenger's experience once on board a plane. Within these constraints the opportunities for competition lie in service quality factors including cabin layout; the style of service offered in each class; ground handling and the intangibles which each airline tries to establish. The range of airline improvement options are obviously limited – Table 9.2 sets out the main options. Which to do, and how much to change existing services should be decided on the basis of technical, cost and competitive factors, and with reference to passengers' preferences. This underlines the need for careful market research to understand passengers' views of the services they purchase.

Table 9.2   Airline service improvements

- New equipment (aircraft)
- Increased frequency of service
- Improved schedule timing
- Better seats
- Larger seat pitch and width
- Better or more varied catering
- More effective distribution
- Value added offers
- More focused advertising
- Improved staff ratios
- Improved staff training
- Improved ground handling

Technical aspects of airline services

The major technical constraint on in-flight service is the detailed design of the aircraft and its ancillary equipment for catering, entertainment and comfort. As indicated earlier, research provides a method for understanding the interaction between clients and the physical features of a service, taking this into account at the service design stage.

Mathison (1988) has discussed a note in the annual report of SAS explaining why it had not purchased any planes during 1982/83. This stated: 'What we were really looking for was what we called the Passenger Pleasing Plane, or the three P plane. We needed a 150 seat plane with an innovative passenger compartment including such enhancements as:
- more space to store carry-on luggage
- wider twin aisles for easier mobility
- wider doors
- reduced cabin noise
- no middle seats'.

Mathison reported on the research which led to SAS's decision to purchase the Boeing 767:

> Passengers were asked for ratings of overall seating comfort, seat width and legroom. This information was correlated with data to specify the exact seat and conditions around that passenger.
>
> Passengers seated between two others gave an overall rating of $-.95$; those between a passenger and an aisle $-.38$; those between another passenger and a window $-.25$; and those between and aisle and an empty seat 0. The most preferred seat was that between a window and an empty seat, with a positive rating of .25.
>
> SAS decided to configure its new international fleet without middle seats in business class. The 767 was the only plane which enabled them to do that economically.

The internal company newspaper, *British Airways News,* carried the following message to staff from Sir Colin Marshall in February 1989:

> We are looking ahead. We now have 77 new aircraft on order, worth almost $5000 million . . . and options for another 59 aircraft . . . We must have those aircraft if we are going to remain a successful airline and employer tomorrow . . . That means we need to be sure we can fly them profitably, by identifying our market opportunities . . . Those market opportunities are of course related to our cost levels – because if our competitors can provide a similar standard of service but at a lower cost, they can undercut us on the price they charge the customer.

Airline costs

In the period since the war the operating efficiency of airlines has increased substantially. Technical developments of the airframe, wing and engines, and improved navigation and flight management systems have contributed to a reduction of direct operating costs per passenger mile. Miller & Sawers (1988) have shown that fares fell by about 57 per cent in real terms between 1945 and 1985 while passengers rose by a factor of 75 times on American services.

Airline competition is based on cost efficiency as well as the stimulation of market demand for its services. Even when the same type of aircraft is operated over similar stage lengths, the costs can vary widely. Sawers (1987) has reported that in 1980 it cost SouthWest $1900 to fly a 200 mile stage, while United Airline's costs were $3300, both using Boeing 737s. This range in costs reflects a number of factors including different staffing and remuneration policies and the age of a company's fleet. Typically, as a fleet of aircraft ages it is replaced by new, or newer models. These have the advantage of improved technologies and increased capacity, so the unit costs of operating are likely to fall as capacity increases over time. But although larger planes produce lower seat/mile costs, their total round-trip cost is higher than a smaller plane and, therefore, airlines operating such equipment need to generate increased revenue traffic (both passenger and freight), and they have to adopt an increasingly competitive stance in the market.

Airlines face a wide range of costs, both on the ground and in the air, in relation to routes, aircraft type and the level of service provided to passengers, as shown in Table 9.3. This table distinguishes between the overheads of an airline company, the costs of flying a particular route, and the costs of providing services for each passenger. The latter seem to have fallen as a proportion of total costs, indicating that there is less slack in the range of benefits which airlines can provide to their passengers.

A significant proportion of the costs incurred in servicing passengers are related to the sale of a ticket and check-in procedures, rather than the length of flight undertaken: it is not significantly more expensive to issue a ticket and check a passenger in for a flight from London to Paris (say), than to ticket and board a passenger from London to Sydney. It is clear that passenger costs are a relatively high proportion of total operating costs on shorter routes, although less catering is required than for long haul journeys, and in-flight entertainment costs might be virtually zero. Journeys involving transfers from one aircraft or airline to another at intermediate stages also impose additional expenses on the carrier.

Table 9.3 Airline costs (or revenues)

---

1 **Non-operating costs** (or income)
    Property, interest, foreign exchange, subsidiary companies' government subsidies
2 **Direct operating costs** (or income)
    Flight operations
        crew salaries, etc. fuel airport charges, air traffic control charges
    Ground operations
        staff salaries, etc. crew accommodation, equipment, transport, communications, costs of delays
    Maintenance
        Routine, periodic, components, spares
    Administration
        Promotion, reservations, ticketing
3 **Passenger service costs** (or income)
    Ticketing, baggage handling, check-in, catering

Air fares

In recognition of the varying needs and demands of their clients, many carriers have responded by providing two or more classes of service on their aircraft. This approach entails varying the levels of the service attributes, for example premium fare-paying passengers are given more spacious cabin accommodation, and a better selection of wines is offered to them. They may also enjoy more spacious or relaxed accommodation and faster handling procedures at the terminals. The principal underlying this market segmentation strategy was discussed in Chapter 6. The higher fares charged for these enhanced service standards offer the carrier an improved margin over the costs of providing the service, while standard rate fares signal relatively lower standards of service, but attract more passengers.

A strategy common amongst airlines is to create differential fare plans designed to meet two basic objectives. The first is to stimulate additional traffic to fill any excess capacity, and the second objective is to prevent existing passengers from taking advantage of any fare reductions that may be offered to potential new clients. At any one time, a range of pricing and related service standards may be used in different areas of an airline's route network in order to achieve specific objectives for each route or class of business. The main objectives of these pricing decisions are to match demand to supply, while generating revenue to cover costs and to ensure profit. Other objectives relate to business development of new routes, or for new market segments.

However, this has the disadvantage that passengers connecting say, from an international flight to a domestic sector may encounter noticeably different service specifications, although regulations can produce similar problems for service delivery. An extreme example of this was observed in Australia, where an international carrier was apparently not permitted to serve internal passengers with wine to accompany their meal during a long domestic stage, although passengers continuing on to Japan were able to enjoy this aspect of the airline's service.

A problem for managers is how to stop traffic leaking from the higher fare types, with a consequent reduction in total revenue. Several fences can be erected to stop tariff leaks, including restrictions on the passenger's right to change his dates of travel on discounted tickets, or prebooking conditions which demand unalterable arrangements for the whole itinerary at the time of booking, as Table 9.4 indicates.

Table 9.4   Tariff fences

- Limited, or maximum duration of journey
- Specified time of departure
- Compulsory pre-departure purchase period
- Routing limitations
- No inter-lining
- Inclusive tour package regulations

Source: Sawers, 1987

123

Good, Wilson and McWhirter (1985) have pointed out that the selection of a fare plan may be viewed as an exercise in multi-attribute decision making from the consumer's perspective. Passengers weigh up all the attributes of each fare plan, including such factors as price, departure time, advanced booking requirements, any minimum stay provisions and the level of service associated with it.

> Discounting is a misnomer when used to describe the differential policies practised by airlines. A more appropriate and descriptive term would be fare plans, since price represents only one component or attribute of a fare plan. Fare plans are advertised and sold under the trade names assigned to them by individual carriers. The actual fares, and restrictions governing their use, vary not only from carrier to carrier but from season to season and, in some cases, from day to day. For example, in July 1982, Air Canada listed 28 different fare plans between Calgary and Toronto. Pacific Western Airlines listed 14 and CP Air offered 36. While some duplication existed, each airline offered plans that were unique and restricted to its own system.

Revenues and load factors

Airline operating revenues are earned from the carriage of cargo, mail and passengers. Passenger revenue from a given flight depends on the fare charged to each passenger, and the total numbers carried. However, the complexity of forecasting the total revenue to be earned from any particular operation can be illustrated from two recent reports of the actual price charged for air travel. In the first case, a reporter interviewed passengers during a flight from London to New York and discovered that the fares they had paid ranged between £307 and £2562. The details are shown in Table 9.5. The second case demonstrates the variance in published fares within Europe, calculated by route air miles. An analysis of the lowest scheduled fares available from London found that the charge per mile ranged from 11.4p (on Olympic and BA to Athens) up to a maximum of 31.8p on Transavia flights to Amsterdam (Bray, 1989).

Two main factors determine every transport operator's revenue, the fare and the number of passengers willing to pay it for each stage. While one clear constraint is that a particular aircraft can carry only a specific number of

Table 9.5   Fares paid by selected passengers on one flight (BA 179)
London to New York

Seat	Return fare	Fare type
51B	£307	Standby
38J	£348	Apex (included free return to Rome)
34J	£358	Standby (purchased in New York)
33G	£404	Economy, from Middle East
10B	£890	Economy, upgraded to Business class
8D	£1522	Full Business fare
4C	£2562	Full fare First class

Source: Smart, *The Observer*, June 1988

passengers, the load factor is a measure of the proportion of available seats actually filled. However, not all seats are taken by fare paying, revenue passengers; there are several legitimate reasons why certain people travel without charge. Airlines need to move staff to the point where their next tour of duty will begin, or to return them to base after a tour; its managers have to visit outstations, and travel agents or journalists are offered complimentary travel to familiarize themselves with its standards of operation, or the destinations it serves, as indicated in the case study of Texas' PR campaigns in Britain.

Business travel

Originally most air travel was for business purposes, but as the industry has expanded and fares have fallen in relative terms, business has come to account for a decreased proportion of travellers, perhaps 30 per cent in Europe. While nearly all charter flights are operated exclusively for recreational travel, almost all business travel is on scheduled services, although many passengers are not travelling on business, the mix of business and leisure clients varies according to the route, and between carriers. On some short haul routes, such as between London and Paris, two out of every three passengers are travelling on business.

Business travel decisions differ from those for leisure in several important characteristics. They are paid for by the employer, while leisure travel is a personal expense. Secondly, as business journeys involve meetings and work, people expect high standards of service and accommodation, and thirdly, they often need to change their travel arrangements at short notice according to the demands of business opportunities or crises.

Finally, the business traveller's reservations are often made on his behalf by other people. These vary from specialized implant travel advisers to secretarial staff who make only occasional travel bookings and have limited travel expertise. Of course, the market segment referred to as business travel is itself composed of many subsidiary submarket segments. Senior managers, junior staff and skilled workers travel for business reasons, but expect rather different standards of service. In addition, it seems that an increasing proportion of business travellers are women, and an increasing number of carriers and hotel companies have attempted to develop distinct services to meet their specialized needs.

Scheduled airlines, unlike charter companies, have to operate regular services on the routes for which they hold licences. Within the constraints of such regulations, they might seek to achieve high load factors by limiting the frequency or the capacity of their operation, but in a competitive market that strategy makes it easier for new competitors to service the route. Business routes in particular, that is those linking major cities, need high frequency schedules whereas leisure travellers are more ready to accept restrictions on journey times in order to benefit the lower charges of charter operators.

Charter operations

The basis of most packaged holidays is a charter flight from a local airport to one near the resort. Charter carriers achieve low costs by tailoring their capacity to the market. Most are inclusive tour charters where the whole plane is chartered by one, or several, tour operators; they combine travel with various types and standards of accommodation at the destination. The resultant holiday packages are sold through retail travel agencies, or in some instances, direct to the traveller. Charter-based tours may include various types of accommodation in several resorts on one flight, and may offer car hire, etc. thus drawing together a wider market for a particular route, as indicated in Figure 9.1. This schematic diagram indicates how 12 separate holiday concepts have been created on the basis of a single charter flight.

Sawers (1987) has identified low fares as a key to gaining high usage: 'High load factors can be achieved if an airline specializes in the leisure market, where travellers are less concerned to see frequent services than are business travellers and can therefore be satisfied by low fare and low frequency services run at high load factors. (They can also, of course, be achieved by an airline that has a monopoly, and can make travellers use whatever service it provides.) But in a competitive market, flexible pricing is essential to maintain high load factors'.

Charter airlines do not need the extensive promotional and reservations systems employed by scheduled carriers, as this becomes the tour operators'

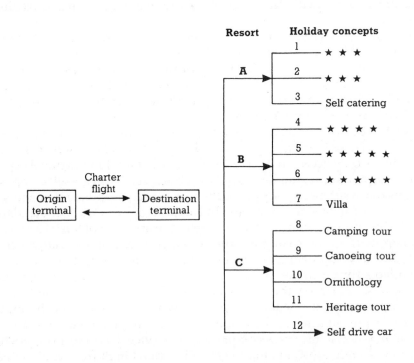

★ Hotel star (quality) rating

Figure 9.1 Charter-based holiday concepts

responsibility. In Europe, around 55 per cent of tonne-miles are charter flights, almost 90 per cent being on international routes. In response, many major scheduled airlines have set up their own subsidiary charter operations; about 55 per cent of charters are operated by scheduled airlines or their subsidiaries.

Responding to delayed travellers

Most transport companies have detailed contingency plans to deal with the operational problems that may occasionally occur as a result of the complex nature of their service. They operate technically advanced equipment, and international schedules are subject to factors beyond the companies' control, such as the weather and political events.

Managerial effort in the face of an operational delay often concentrates on the technical tasks needed to restore normal service. These Type A technical responses focus on repairing the fault, substituting equipment or rearranging an itinerary. Type A responses depend on mobilizing the skills of technical staff, and are backed by the company's inventory and financial resources. But a further type of managerial skill is required to overcome all the effects of an interrupted service. Type B responses are concerned with the management of clients' experiences during the interrupted service. Successful Type B management responses depend on an awareness of customers' needs during a service interruption, and of the problems which customer-contact staff face. These staff act as mediators of company policy. They form the channels of communication for information about the interruption and enable clients to make their needs known to the company. The behaviour and attitudes of staff may improve client satisfaction, but inappropriate responses deepen the consumerist gap, as was indicated in the previous chapter.

Furthermore, an interruption tends to change the role of staff. The need to discuss the situation and explain proposed solutions to each group of clients complicates and delays normal procedures such as check-in. As a result of this delay, tension may rise amongst waiting passengers as rumour spreads. In the face of conflicting demands from waiting passengers for information, or requests for various solutions to meet individual needs, staff may become uncertain of their priorities. An unusually turbulent work environment results, and staff work under less familiar rules. They experience increased role ambiguity and an unpredictable sequence of tasks, in contrast to their normal role which is typically characterized by low discretion and routine sequences. A consequence for staff is an increased probability of role-related stress, and their reactions may further frustrate clients.

One further factor has to be taken into consideration. There is a well-documented strategy for groups of staff to adopt a common occupational self image which results in ritualized, impersonal behaviour towards clients. It is convenient for staff to regard the standard solutions provided by the company as equally satisfactory for all clients involved. A client who claims extra or different attention is regarded as unreasonable, but such attitudes serve to deepen the consumerist gap experienced by an individual.

Management cannot regard an interruption as resolved until the acid test of consumer satisfaction has been passed, and clients are again willing to purchase services from the company in the future. Both Type A and Type B responses have to be implemented effectively before the company can pass the consumerist gap acid test and be sure its clients are satisfied.

Management strategies to gain passenger loyalty

An important way for airlines to improve their profitability is by retaining more of their existing passengers' repeat business. As has been argued earlier in this book, the marketing literature makes a link between client satisfaction and repeat business. In the face of increasing competition, maturing industries or shrinking demand, it becomes increasingly difficult to meet objectives by traditional offensive marketing strategies. The cost of generating a new customer can substantially exceed the cost of retaining a present customer. Defensive marketing is an alternative strategy concerned with reducing customer exit and brand-switching behaviour. Hauser and Shugan (1983) have developed a normative model showing how a firm with an established brand should adjust its marketing expenditure against the launch of a new competitor. One key finding from this study was that varying degrees of customer loyalty can be an effective basis for segmenting many markets.

Two approaches to the management of customer loyalty are to offer bonuses for frequent customers, and to develop services whose characteristics appeal to clients. Loyalty bonuses take several forms, such as frequent passenger awards. This method allows passengers who accumulate a sufficient number of miles with a chosen carrier as a fare paying passenger to obtain a range of benefits. These include complimentary upgrades on the next flight, a free companion ticket with the next purchased, or complimentary flight sectors. A range of such loyalty rewards are shown in Table 9.6. Other entitlements under such schemes are offered by partners such as car rental or hotel groups. Taken together, these benefits can have considerable value for frequent travellers, and represent a rational basis for their choice of one airline. There is some evidence that people actually change their travel plans to take advantage of these schemes and in

Table 9.6   Loyal traveller awards

Award	Internal US	US to Europe
	miles required as a fare paying passenger	
Roundtrip upgrade	10 000	20 000
Companion ticket	25 000	40 000
Complimentary business class ticket	–	65 000
Two roundtrip first class tickets	75 000	140 000

Source: Continental Airlines Onepass Reward Chart

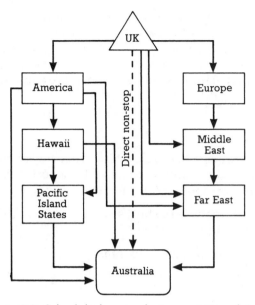

Figure 9.2 Scheduled routes between UK and Australia

particular they may insist on using a particular carrier for their journey, even when its schedules are less convenient.

The fundamental ability of an airline to generate traffic depends on its route network; if it serves many cities it caters to a large marketplace of potential customers. However, the proportion of travellers on a particular route who use one airline rather than others depends on the schedules, fares and service enhancements each offers, and on individuals' subjective judgements and preferences between competing carriers. A perspective on the complexity of decisions facing both carriers and travellers can be gauged from Figure 9.2. This presents schematically the varying route options linking the UK and Australia. At the time this book was completed, a non-stop flight had been made between London and Sydney by Boeing 747-400, although for technical reasons this will not be offered commercially for another few years. Consequently, all flights between the UK and Australia entail a minimum of one stop *en route*, for a change of crew and refuelling. Although many passengers choose to travel through on one plane, many others, particularly those travelling for leisure purposes, prefer to take advantage of one or more stop-overs during the journey. Figure 9.2 indicates the wide range of choices in the Middle and Far East, America and the Pacific. The case study of Hawaii's marketing discusses some of these points (see page 175).

Conclusion

Airlines are the primary means of transport for long-haul and overseas travel and have shaped the modern mass tourism experience. Airline links are crucial to global trade relationships and to the success of tourism destinations. Chapter

10 discusses the significance of airline routeing and fare decisions and the consequent travel behaviour of passengers to those intermediate destinations. The airline industry is constrained by its technology and is regulated by many national and supra-national bodies, so that effective competition between airlines is rather limited. These points are considered further in Chapter 12.

Questions

1 Calculate the approximate seat-mile costs of recent journeys which you or colleagues have taken by various modes of transport. Compare these to the tariffs charged. How do you account for your findings?

2 How might a ferry company on a short sea route, such as the English Channel, segment its services and its markets?

3 What are the limits to the role of passenger preferences in the design of transport services?

Recommended reading

Ansett, R.G. and McManamy, J. *The Customer*, John Kerr Pty, Richmond, Australia, 1989

Miller, J.C. and Sawers. P. *The Technical Development of Modern Aviation*, Routledge and Kegan Paul, London, 1988

Sawers, P. *Competition in the Air*, Institute of Economic Affairs, London, 1987

Shaw, S. *Airline Marketing and Management*, Pitman, London, 1985

Wells, A.T. *Air Transportation, a Management Perspective*, Wadsworth, Belmont, 1984

CHAPTER TEN

Destination Management

Introduction

One of the key components of the tourism system model which was introduced in the first chapter (Figure 1.3) is the tourist destination. This can be understood as the complex subsystem of tourism organizations, activities and attractions which form the foundation for travellers' motivations and on which their satisfaction depends. This chapter examines the structure and functions of areas to which tourists travel, whether their destinations are cities such as Paris, regions such as the Tyrol, or the resorts purpose-built for tourism which typify modern, mass tourism. The common feature of interest in considering any type of destination is that tourists visit and stay temporarily in that area. It follows that any destination has to provide a range of services including accommodation, catering and activities to meet the needs of people who are not resident there.

Each tourist destination has a unique range of features with which it tries to attract visitors, but the marketing challenge they face is that each potential visitor has a very wide choice amongst destinations. The many factors influencing individual choice already discussed include available time, budgetary constraints, and the type of tourism experience being sought. A critical factor explaining why some areas become established as major destinations for tourists is efficient transport links between the destination and its main tourism generating areas. This section of the book focuses attention on the opportunities for destination managers to influence individuals towards selecting their particular resort.

A number of factors contribute to the attractiveness of a tourism region; some are natural features, such as the landscape and climate; some are cultural, such as the traditions or architecture of the region; others are developments introduced specifically for tourism, such as theme parks. An area's success as a destination reflects other factors such as its stage of development, its accessibility and the awareness of it amongst its potential visitors.

Resort development

The location of a resort within a destination country depends on several factors including access, the availability of staffing for 24-hour services, and low value land which offers potential for further development – for example, as second home sites to help in the recovery of capital investment. Many new resorts are therefore built in relatively undeveloped areas, but the risk is that such developments often fail to become integrated into the local community. Such developments may have a limited appeal to visitors seeking cultural contacts. Table 10.1 demonstrates three patterns of resort development.

Table 10.1   Types of resort development

1 The juxtaposition of a tourist development close to but separated from the local population centre
2 A new development away from the highway offering a considerable range of facilities
3 Several isolated resorts away from the road giving a comb effect

Based on Berriane, in Pearce, 1987

Smith (1983) has discussed a measure of the tourist intensity experienced by an area, the argument follows Defert's (1967) TF (tourist function method). He described as hypertouristic those areas where there are more than five times the number of tourist beds available compared to the stock for the resident population. At the other extreme, where there are less than four visitor beds for every hundred residents then there can be virtually no tourist activity. Boyer (1972) has developed six levels of classification, the intermediate stages deal with communities entertaining an increasing proportion of tourist activity. The question underlying Boyer's and similar approaches is what to use as the base for a resident population. In some studies the area of interest is limited specifically to the immediate resort (an area which itself has no clear boundary, but is encompassed within the concept of 'tourist town'). An alternative methodology takes a broader, regional approach to the definition of a tourism-host population. Since tourists generally take day excursions from their accommodation base and as the resort draws employees and other resources from a wide area, this may be a more appropriate basis for the evaluation of local tourism impacts.

Orientation of tourists to destinations

A tourist has been defined as a temporary visitor, and this implies that he has to learn his way around a new resort as he orients himself to it. Initially, his attention is likely to be centred on the places of major interest to him and he is likely to use simple, direct routes between those points and his hotel. During his stay, as he journeys around, an increasing number of local features such as large buildings, prominent signs, restaurants, bars, banks or shops become familiar and his routes become more extensive and complex. If the tourist enjoys his stay and returns to the resort at a later date, his reorientation will be much faster, and a deeper knowledge of a wider area will be gained. It often happens that a returning tourist stays in a different, perhaps more expensive hotel, or opts for a self-catering apartment on subsequent visits, partly as the result of earlier knowledge of alternatives gained from discussion with other tourists in the resort, or social visits to new found friends in their various hotels. By staying in a different part of the resort, he will gain a new perspective and an expanded set of its features will become familiar to him. Table 10.2 shows the steps in this process.

Because there are so many destinations, it follows that a tourist's knowledge of a particular resort can often exceed that of retail travel agency staff, who have to service the needs of clients travelling to a large variety of resorts, and cannot know more than a few in any detail. However, the agent is regarded as an expert, and it can be disconcerting for a client to discover his superior, if localized knowledge. Retail travel agency staff with limited personal knowledge of a specific resort trying to perform their role of recommending the best travel arrangements for a knowledgeable client may experience dissonance in these conditions, as their expert base has been eroded.

Table 10.2   Gaining familiarity with a resort

Stranger stage
1 Arrival
2 Orientation to hotel surroundings
3 Exploration of resort area

Old hand stage
4 Return for a second or further holiday
5 Familiar sites revisited
6 Exploration further afield

The development of tourist destinations

There is an important distinction to be drawn between the arrival in an area of occasional, individual travellers and its later marketing as a destination for regular tourist groups. People visiting friends and relatives may take an active delight in the features of the area, but their requirements for catering, accommodation, and entertainment are easily absorbed by the facilities supporting the local community: in effect they become a temporary part of the community and no specialized businesses depend on visitors for their trade. Others may travel to an area for business or professional purposes, but it could also be argued that the regular arrival of a few specialist travellers is actually a part of the traditional fabric of community life. The many accounts by Victorian travellers indicate that a system of inns could normally be found, even in the most remote areas, although their standards were geared to local tastes.

Table 10.3 sets out a framework within which the evolution of resort areas may be understood. A pre-tourism phase can be identified: a period during which travellers' needs are serviced by existing local community facilities. During the pre-tourism phase travellers would expect to share the local standards of accommodation and catering through which they pass. In this stage of development few areas will receive much attention from casual visitors, and the community will be relatively isolated from outside influences. Visitors may therefore find that they are regarded as objects of interest to the local population. Some areas will be welcoming of occasional visitors, others for cultural reasons may be suspicious and even hostile towards people whose habits seem very strange by local standards, and whose motives for being there are obscure to local people.

Table 10.3   Tourism destination development phases

---

1 **Pre tourism phase**
   Private visits to residents, and business travel
   Effects: *Minimal impact on the community*
2 **Traveller phase**
   Increasing frequency of independent visitors
   Responses: Business opportunities recognized by entrepreneurs, and local people either welcoming or hostile to visitors
3 **Mass tourism phase**
   Regular arrival of tourist groups
   Responses: New businesses established to meet tourists' needs, increasing local employment dependency on tourism, capital investment and consumables imported. The interests of tourists, tourism enterprises and host community may come into increasing conflict
4 **Tourist management phase**
   Tourism recognized as a major industry in the area
   Responses: Destination audit, preferred market segments targeted, infrastructure developed for planned growth, and quality issues including staff development and environmental control addressed

---

It is not suggested that the stages discussed in this model are discrete, rather that they merge into each other, becoming prominent in the particular conditions of each resort as it evolves. Two variants of the pre-tourism phase are worth noting. The first possibility is that travellers will have minimal contact with their destination areas and the people inhabiting them, even to the extent that trekkers carry (or have carried for them) their own supplies, whether or not the areas through which they pass have the facilities to support their needs. Some countries insist that tourists to remote areas have to employ porters to carry their tents, bedding, and sufficient food for the journey as local communities produce sufficient only for their own needs, and the cash economy is too fragile to enable food to be bought locally along the route.

The second variant occurs when a pre-tourism destination has something of great interest to particular visitors: a church, outstanding scenery or an archaeological site might be examples. As word spreads in the origin countries, visitors arrive at such destinations in sufficient numbers and regularly enough to stimulate a response amongst local entrepreneurs. For example, the inn might be expanded and upgraded to provide a few, more comfortably equipped guest rooms, and a rudimentary, but fee-charging guiding service might develop.

Gradually the second variant will blend into the next stage of tourism destination development: the traveller phase. There are two factors contributing to this development. As the attractions of the destination become more widely known, interest in visiting it increases through the reports which early travellers bring back. Through word of mouth and the publication of articles or films, public awareness grows. A concomitant of this process is that potential visitors also learn about access to the destination, and as more visitors arrive, the transport links improve.

Concurrent with an increase in the regularity and volume of visitor arrivals the businesses catering to their needs become more adept at pleasing the tastes and meeting the expectations of their visitors. Competition may develop too, as other locals see opportunities to move away from traditional work, to meet those interesting outsiders and to earn cash from catering to their needs, and as other tourism companies begin to invest in the region's hotels, transport and related sectors.

Under the pressure of these developments, the destination matures, often very rapidly, and it becomes more open to outside influences: the values and expectations of its visitors increasingly drive local entrepreneurs' decisions as previously described, but also the expectations of the wider community begin to encompass aspects of their visitors' behaviour, interests and possessions. Cumulatively, the effect is to induce and support an increasing acceptance of changes in the character and nature of the destination's social, moral and personal relationships. Styles of eating, dress codes, working patterns, social and personal relationships will all change as the buildings, and pattern of the resort changes.

Traditional work and craft skills may persist during this phase, but are likely to lose their central significance in society, at least temporarily. New skills and accompanying attitudes will be sought by employers in the new sector, and this can lead to relatively high remuneration offered by tourism organizations compared to the traditional employment sectors, which will reinforce these changed values (Smaoui, 1979).

Overall, the economy is likely to shift in response to profit opportunities, and a variety of legitimate and some rather questionable ways of extracting profit from the population of temporary visitors will emerge. Local entrepreneurs respond to the profit and new business opportunities during the mass tourism phase, while in the tourist management phase it is quite likely that they will take proactive decisions about the facilities to offer, anticipating the demands and changing tastes of their visitors, and shaping their experiences. Additionally, new residents will be attracted by the work and profit opportunities and the population of the area will increase in size, while its demographic characteristics will change quite rapidly. This will further distort the original relationship between tourists and the community, and perhaps lead to friction with the incomers who are thought to displace local people in the more lucrative and exciting sector of the labour market. This seems more likely to occur when local communities are resistant to the new modes of working. The incomers bring very different values, often taking the more lucrative employment openings as they have a broader range of relevant skills and more experience, or more awareness of visitors' needs, but they are unlikely to share the traditions, tastes and values of the original inhabitants – although visitors will expect these new residents to interpret the more colourful aspects of local culture. Case studies of Tibet and Hawaii present contrasted aspects of tourism development issues.

Tourism service standards in remote destinations

Tourists are often attracted to remote regions, partly by the very different life-styles they expect to encounter there. Dramatic scenery, rare animals or plants, or extreme climates also attract many travellers. Inevitably, they will often meet service standards very different from those they are used to at home. The discussion of package holiday management in Chapter 3 emphasized the benefits of security and certainty offered by the packaged group tour operators in such circumstances. However it can be seen that variances can occur in many aspects of the service experienced during a tour, partly because the need to respond to local conditions requires a flexing of any given organizational style, and also since the distance makes close monitoring cost-ineffective. It is apparent that consistent service delivery throughout one package to remote destinations is an unrealistic objective, not least because the many individual staff from whom a client receives services during the itinerary will be employed by separate companies, operating in varying cultures.

However, it can be argued that variances in service standards are not necessarily a management failure. They can actually form part of the charm of the tourist experience, for example in the tour conditions described in Case Studies D and E. In normal circumstances service variances lead to customer irritation, and even in specialist holidays the attraction of local quirks in service delivery can become tiresome, unless clients are adequately forewarned. One way in which companies can help their clients to understand what conditions to expect is by frank briefing for clients considering such tours. This approach can also give a signal to people who would find the conditions of travel unacceptable.

Another aspect of opening remote areas to tourism which is receiving increasing attention is the high standards of infrastructure which tourists demand, and the effects of this on local residents. An example is tourists' expectations of a plentiful and constant supply of piped water, particularly in their accommodation. A common method of satisfying this demand is to drill deep wells, but often the water table levels fall as a result of this, causing severe hardship to people who traditionally obtain their supplies from shallow village wells. Resentment is often the result, exacerbated by the apparently profligate use of water supplies by the tourists.

Dynamics of resort development

As a destination evolves through the development phases identified in Table 10.3, perceptions of its changing range of facilities attract different groups of visitors. It been shown that some resorts have seen their clientele change completely over a relatively short period of time. For example, the Côte d'Azur started as a winter resort, although now its heaviest traffic is in the summer. From catering almost exclusively to the rich, it now serves tourists representing a cross-section of Western European society, excluding only the poorest sectors (Rudney, 1980).

The majority of visitors to any resort will have experienced other resorts, and this provides a basis for another important development dynamic as it is inevitable that they will make comparisons between the facilities and attractions of destinations with which they are familiar. This comparison process takes two main forms; many tourists will discuss their views of the relative benefits of a resort with their friends and colleagues, thus influencing their opinions. Secondly, they may discuss their opinions with tourism managers and staff, in the resort and after their return home, stressing features of the resort and their experience of service there which they had found pleasing or dissatisfying. In a sense, a dialogue develops between visitors and the resorts' enterprises. This occurs through informal but effective market mechanisms as visitors bring with them expectations about standards of service and the variety and quality of goods they want, which are expressed as economic demands. Their buying preferences and dislikes act as strong economic signals to entrepreneurs. It is so critical for resort managers to understand what their visitors hope for that many resorts conduct formal market research to identify their actual or potential points of advantage from customers' perspectives, to guide their decisions about further development.

Two or more of the development phases may be found in adjacent areas of a destination. While mass tourism is firmly established around a beach area, or centred on the original part of the resort, a more exclusive development may be located on a private beach, or around a sports estate such as a golf course. The most intense examples occur in the self-contained, purpose-built resorts which sometimes incorporate staged entertainment and have many of the organized features of themed entertainment. Its facilities may (or may not) be open to casual visitors, and such developments vary in the degree of interaction which their clients establish with the host community.

McCannel (1976) has commented on this type of development, which he referred to as plantation tourism: 'Tourism may be regarded as a new kind of industry building factories called resorts and amusement parks . . . Some come close to imprisoning tourists within resort compounds'. McCannel pointed out that this type of plantation tourism is exploitive on both sides; the tourist enjoys minimal contact with local people, and locals do not benefit from the money that is generated. He identified plantation tourism as occurring mainly in societies with rigid dualized class systems, and already exploited peasant masses. In extreme cases, employment in the new resorts' shops, catering and accommodation sectors plus estate and facility maintenance is about the limit of contact with locals.

Shopping

A feature of most journeys is the specialized shopping activities which travellers undertake. In addition to personal care items related to conditions encountered in specific destinations, such as sun blockers, travel shopping can be said to fall into three categories, as shown in Table 10.4. An interesting discussion of the factors which underlie tourists' shopping behaviour is summarized in Table 10.5.

Table 10.4   Travel shopping

1 Pre journey	Luggage, appropriate attire, camera and film, travel books and travel insurance
2 During the journey	Local style clothing or artefacts, postcards, luxury items for self or others
3 Souvenirs	Locally produced items, or imports portraying local themes, fruit, models, snow scenes, etc.

Based on Keown, 1989

Table 10.5   Tourists' propensity to shop in destinations

Tourists' propensity to buy goods to bring home depends on:

1 **Types of product available**
  - Domestic
  - Imported
  - Souvenirs and necessities

2 **Level of domestic tax and import duties**
  - Tax free prices
  - Regular prices

3 **Relative value of specific goods**
  - Price
  - Quality comparisons

4 **Retailer strategies**
  - Location
  - Promotion
  - Image

Source: Keown, 1989

The importance of visitors' spending power has been recognized both by retailers who have developed a variety of schemes to attract out-of-town or overseas shoppers, and by governments which tolerate or encourage duty free shopping facilities restricted mainly to overseas visitors, and in some cases to privileged nationals who have access to foreign exchange. Certain destinations, of which Hong Kong is a notable example, have built a significant part of their tourism business through retailing, and careful quality control standards have been introduced for retailers leading to approved status and listings in official publications. This attracts visitors by offering them an additional guarantee and a mechanism to deal with any complaints. Shopping also forms an important part of the service for airports and ferry companies, both of which seek to gain from additional revenue sources. The value and distribution of visitor spending in London's economy was the subject of a study for the London Tourist Board. This report indicated that the impact of their spending varied considerably by class of goods, for example a third of all spending on clothing and footwear was by tourists, compared to 7 per cent of household goods. Table 10.6 provides further details.

Table 10.6   Visitor spending in London

A   Value of London visitors' spending, 1985

	%	£m.
Air travel by UK airlines	19	875
Accommodation	31	1 443
Food and beverage	18	847
Local transport	6	293
Shopping	16	733
Entertainment	7	349
Other	3	129
TOTAL	100%	£4 669m

B   Spending by area

	%
Central London	66
Heathrow (airport) area	22
Other 28 London Boroughs	12

C   Spending by origin

	£m.
Domestic tourists	569
Overseas visitors	3 225

D   Average spending per night

Domestic tourists	31.77
Overseas visitors	50.00

Source: McEwan, 1987

Destination marketing

Given the increasing number of countries and resorts which are accessible to tourists, the challenge for destination managers is to attract a sufficient and regular flow of visitors who will enjoy its particular mix of climate, attractions, activities, costs and quality, its overall style. However, it follows from the discussion of evolving styles of resorts that at any particular point in its development one destination is unlikely to appeal to all potential visitors. It is both possible and desirable to inform potential visitors who would not enjoy the attractions of a particular resort about this. The three major methods which can be used to signal this to potential customers are price, imagery and reputation, spread both through formal trade channels and paid advertizing, or informally in ways already discussed. This strategy minimizes disappointment, reduces irritation amongst those for whom the resort does have major appeals, and is more likely to result in harmonious relations between visitors and residents. The view that service quality is produced in the interaction between a customer and elements in the service organization has been discussed in an earlier chapter. Lehtinen & Lehtinen, (1982) explained this as meaning that quality derives from 'the interaction of personnel with customers as well as that between customers and other customers (cited by Parasuraman *et al*, 1985).

Destinations function as complex systems of businesses and other interests; they depend on a regular flow of visitors. In addition to attracting individuals by the traditional tourism methods of good service leading to word of mouth recommendations, market positioning based on imagery and branding related to the needs of market segments, and tour operator promotions, many destinations also have marketing programmes intended to attract large groups travelling for specific purposes.

These tourism initiatives may be linked with other local drives such as inner city regeneration, or regional development plans. Three major types of large group business can be stimulated, for conferences or conventions of a group of specialists such as medical practitioners, or for annual sporting occasions, such as the Grand Prix at Monaco. The third category is festivals, either traditional ones, such as Mardi Gras, or ones recent in origin such as the Edinburgh Festival. Zhang (1989) has shown, in the case of the People's Republic of China, how cultural festivals were deliberately stimulated as a method of attracting tourists. His article was written sometime before the events of that summer, which had devastating effects on incoming tourism because of the changed political climate and the international outrage which was provoked, as discussed in Case Study A.

Each method of attracting large pre-organized groups requires a specialized marketing approach, as indicated in Table 10.7. Many destinations consider that convention business offers an attractive way of broadening their tourism base and attracting high volume, high spending visitors. Table 10.7 also identifies a number of criteria in selecting venues for preformed groups.

Seasonality

The pattern of tourism activity in an area reflects various features of its geography, culture and development. A major characteristic of the tourism industry is the seasonal nature of demand for particular destinations. In some cases the pull of its tourist resources largely determines the timing or arrivals, and the distribution of tourist activity around the area. The seasonal nature of skiing and the particular location of ski resorts in relation to natural features and purpose-built facilities, is a case in point. In other cases arrival patterns are determined mainly by driving factors in the originating regions – particularly its climate, or socially determined events such as school holiday dates. Travel patterns from cold northern industrial centres of population in America and

Table 10.7   Attracting preformed groups

Attractions

Contests; Food; Music; Displays; Dancing; Theatre; Sports; Children's activities; Parades; Arts; Crafts; Beauty contests; Education

---

Organization

Local authority sponsored; Operated by incorporated company; Voluntary or paid staff; Formal objectives and plan prepared

---

Revenue

Admission charge; Sales; Lottery; Rental of space; Donations; Sponsorship

---

Criteria for success

An attractive destination
A variety of meeting facilities
A range of good accommodation
Good access
Civic commitment to hosting delegates
A coordinated approach to destination marketing and visitor servicing

---

Based on Getz and Frisby 1988, and Friel, 1989

Europe to sun belt destinations such as Florida or the Mediterranean fall into the latter category.

Strong seasonality causes difficulties for destination managers as sufficient facilities to meet peak demand have to be installed, but at other times of the year there are insufficient visitors to sustain their businesses. Uneven flows of business can be influenced by marketing actions to stimulate out-of-season visits, both through pricing tactics and by developing a range of additional activities reflecting the local possibilities for activities at different times of the year. Changing tastes and interests can be harnessed too; mountain areas have been able to capitalize on the growing participation in snow sports to develop strong winter business in addition to their summer visitors who are attracted by alpine scenery and traditions. The discussion of methods of attracting group business earlier in this chapter can be coupled to seasonal flows, so that the strategy usually adopted is to even out fluctuations by stimulating off-season business. The case study of tourism promotion in London is relevant to this topic, and highlights the benefits of a cooperative venture to create an original package of benefits for clients.

Choice of destination

The review of tourists' motivations in Chapter 4 indicated that a wide range of personality and demographic factors underlie their travel behaviour. An important element in tourists' decisions reflects the attractions of destinations: the scenery, the beaches, the historic buildings, the quality and variety of shopping, surroundings providing opportunities to relax or for sporting activities. The initial role of marketing communications is to create a favourable impression, and to attract tourists. But all other destinations are attempting to achieve the same effect, so the stake of tourists' expectations is inexorably raised while the process of product development results in resorts which are increasingly undifferentiated and have less in common with their immediate surroundings other than in superficial ways.

Some studies seem to indicate that there is a correlation between the length of journey to a destination country and the behaviour of tourists within it, for example between the activities and cultural visits of Americans to Holland, or the preference for seaside relaxation by Germans visiting Holland (Lavery, 1989). It seems likely that shopping patterns, small catering establishments such as bars and cafés, and excursion companies' programmes also reflect any local variation in the interests of international tourists.

Understanding what benefits are important to tourists is particularly significant in the promotion or planning of destinations, when success is measured by the number of tourists which it can attract, and the revenue and work opportunities they generate. For it is often the case that tourism offers about the only way to bring employment to many of the destinations which tourists seek out. On the other hand tourism means the arrival of large numbers of people, and to cater for their needs the infrastructure of the receiving area has to be expanded. Often, the style, pace and extent of those developments have disturbing effects for the local population and sometimes for the visitors, as the nature of the destination inevitably changes. The case study of major resort investment in a previously less-developed area of Hawaii illustrates the problems which such proposals cause for residents and planners.

A distinction should be made between the factors influencing the decision of a tourist to visit a destination new to him, and the case where a person decides to revisit an area he already knows, rather than to explore fresh areas. From the tourists' point of view, the satisfaction they experience determines whether they are likely to return to the same area. Fishbein and Ajzen (1957) have shown that the choice of a particular good or service is the result of a comparison of its perceived attributes with the person's set of preferred attributes. For any set of competing destinations, the method involves identifying what characteristics clients consider to be desirable, and measuring the degree to which each destination possesses them. The first step is to compile a list of destination characteristics potentially desired, and a separate list of destinations which the research subjects would choose. Secondly, a sample of people is polled on the relative importance of each characteristic, and thirdly they are asked to indicate the degree to which each destination possesses each characteristic. The average perceived utility of each destination can be assessed by comparing the results. This type of research can be helpful in identifying the appropriate features of a resort to emphasize in its advertising, and can be repeated for each major target group of clients.

Pearce (1987) has discussed a method developed by Mirloup (1974); a Room Comfort Index for a resort which is based on counting the total number of rooms in each star-rated category, and dividing by the number of rooms available there. A related approach was developed by Dewailley (1978), who distinguished ten factors in the comfort of second homes, an increasingly significant mode of tourist accommodation in certain destination areas. A procedural problem which remains unresolved is whether it is possible to provide a consistent weighting scale for such factors. These somewhat general and simplistic methods are helpful in defining the mix of visitor types to whom a particular resort will appeal.

In management terms, the foregoing discussion points to the advantages of adopting a structured approach to the development of new or existing resorts. The method is summarized in Table 10.8.

Table 10.8   A framework for resort marketing decisions

1 Survey current and potential visitors to identify what benefits they are seeking from resorts in general
2 Carry out market research to establish what benefits they consider the specific resort offers
3 Specify the main client groups to which the resort intends to appeal
4 Audit the resort's facilities to identify what it offers
5 Invest in developing appropriate facilities in the resort
6 Devise marketing communications programmes to communicate the facilities which the resort offers to potential visitors
7 Monitor the results

City tourism

In contrast to purpose-built or highly specialized resorts, many destinations are major capital cities, with their own long-established but evolving patterns of habitation, work, leisure and shopping facilities. Within city areas the demand for local transport or road networks results from people's wish to reach various facilities such as shops, entertainment or attractions, and to travel to and from work or school. City transport is provided primarily to satisfy these needs. However, tourists often use existing transport facilities, and in doing so they contribute to the operator's revenue, but affect the rates and patterns of usage, adding to congestion for residents when their travel coincides with local behaviour.

The pattern and timing of travel by residents is dictated by their need to commute regularly, and this imposes a morning and an afternoon peak, for which travel capacity has to be provided. A further, smaller peak can often be detected in the early and late evening as people travel to and from theatres and other entertainment to be found in city centres. However, these facilities will be relatively under-used during the rest of the day, and tourists can be persuaded to travel in out-of-peak periods by advertising, differential pricing, or tickets combining travel and entrance to attractions, but limited to off-peak periods.

This brief discussion of urban transport can be considered in the light of the costs which tourists impose on host communities by using local transport services. Where additional capacity in carriages is required the resultant revenues may not cover the additional costs, but where a new route is required – for example, a city centre connection to an airport – it may be possible to charge to recover the cost, and local people would also benefit from the new service.

Conclusion

It was pointed out earlier that distinct patterns can be observed in the flows of tourist activities, and strong links are established by many destinations with specific points of origin. A key factor is the development of strong, regular transport links, which brings advantages in ways analysed in Chapter 9. Additional reasons why a particular region may attract many people from one point of origin arise as word of mouth recommendation spreads amongst the originating population. As more people with common tastes and habits, including language, arrive in an area, the response of local entrepreneurs is to cater specifically for their interests, and in many cases expatriot businesses will be founded to cater expressly for this market segment – although sometimes in conjunction with local investment or proprietorship to meet local legislation which sets conditions intended to protect local enterprise opportunities.

Thus, the apparent contradiction can be explained that as a destination evolves, perhaps from a remote, agricultural region boasting strong traditions, to become another international-standard resort, it is also likely to see an increase in tourist activity despite any loss of its original character.

Questions

1 Conduct an audit of an area with which you are familiar to assess the potential of local festivals, crafts, etc. as a base for tourism developments, and suggest ways of developing a market for them.

2 What evidence is there to support or challenge the phases of development model of tourism destinations presented in this chapter?

3 What do you consider to be the role of shopping in tourists' decisions and in the functioning of selected resorts?

Recommended reading

Farrell, B.H. *Hawaii, the Legend That Sells*, University of Hawaii Press, Honolulu, 1982
Gunn, C.A. *Tourism Planning*, Crane Rusak, New York, 1979
Pearce, D. *Tourism Today, a Geographical Analysis*, Longman, Harlow, 1987

CHAPTER ELEVEN

The Consequences of Tourism

Introduction

Earlier in this book three groups of people who are affected by the development of tourism were identified; notably tourists themselves, secondly those involved as staff, managers or proprietors of tourism organizations, and thirdly the people who are residents in destination areas. This chapter focuses attention on the beneficial and harmful consequences of tourism for residents, and indicates how economic, social and environmental considerations may be evaluated by tourism planners and managers.

Murphy (1985) has made the significant point that successful destinations need the regular arrival of large numbers of tourists, but increasingly, the ability of a destination to cater for unlimited numbers of visitors is questioned. The capacity constraints of its physical facilities have been one focus of interest (Mitchell, 1979; Hall, 1974). Others have considered the impact of increasing visitor numbers on traditional local values or lifestyles (Krippendorf, 1987; Young, 1973).

Tourists' behaviour and residents' attitudes

Although the benefits of tourism are often very real for local people, bringing employment and expanded leisure opportunities, the arrival of people who are unsympathetic to local values, or appear to be materially better off, may cause them irritation or resentment. Tourists' behaviour is largely unregulated, as it offers a means of relaxation for the individual frustrated by daily routine and the restrictions of society. Often, the tourist leaves many of the social norms which regulate his daily behaviour behind. Relaxed dress code, loose sexual morals, indulgence in illegal drugs, and heavy drinking often characterize tourists' vacation behaviour. One study of the steps in the evolving relationship between tourists and hosts is shown in Table 11.1.

Table 11.1   Index of tourist irritation

1 Euphoric about the arrival of tourists
2 Apathetic, people take increasing arrivals for granted, interest focuses on earnings from tourists
3 Annoyance, facilities must expand to cope with visitors
4 Antagonistic, tourists ripped off and seen as focus of many problems

Source: Doxey, 1975

Assessing the impact of tourism

Modern tourism is characterized by the regular arrival of large numbers of temporary visitors in an area. To attract them and cater for their needs, special facilities have to be provided at the destination in addition to those serving residents. Local residents may benefit from these new facilities, they may object to them, or be excluded in various ways from enjoying them. One approach to measuring the impact of tourism is to compare the extent of specialist tourist facilities, such as hotel beds, to the size of the resident population. A low ratio of residents to each hotel room is evidence of a local economy geared towards tourism (Lundgren, 1966).

The rapid establishment of tourism as the dominant local industry has been characteristic of development in many destination areas during recent decades. With historic and forecast growth rates often exceeding those of other economic sectors, tourism offers attractive investment opportunities to entrepreneurs, but it also poses a variety of challenges for host communities. As any destination matures it becomes more open to outside influences: the values, expectations and lifestyles of its visitors affect those residents with whom they come into contact in the early phases of tourism, but later – although perhaps rapidly – many other people are influenced by their observation of tourists' freedoms and possessions.

Cumulatively, the effect is likely to induce and support an increasing acceptance of changes in the character and nature of all sectors of society in the destination. Styles of eating, dress codes, working patterns, social and personal relationships will all change just as the local style of buildings and the economic structure of the resort changes. The resultant changes will vary on a continuum from benign to damaging, and each situation needs to be considered separately before value judgements can be reached about the beneficial or harmful consequences of change, and the role of tourism in the process. However, it should be emphasized that tourism is only one influence in these change dynamics, and it is likely that such changes would occur even in the absence of a tourism sector.

Tourist activity causes a range of changes for resident populations, but it should be borne in mind that the introduction into any area of alternative new industries will bring change. Chisnall (1985) has given an example, citing Boudon's description of how a sector of French society was totally transformed as the result of a minor change. By switching to hybrid corn from the traditional type, they needed to give more care and space to the new, more productive crop. Increased production required additional land, tractors and fertilizers, and to finance this activity they needed bank loans. Thus, the introduction of a new type of crop had made people more money conscious. Tourism is different in its impact since the essence of the industry is a kind of cultural flux in which people from very different cultures and social backgrounds are brought into direct proximity.

Economic consequences of tourism

Areas vary in the proportion of employment or income which is generated by tourism. The economic gains from tourism tend to be concentrated in major resort or urban areas, even in destination regions where tourism is well-established, such as Hawaii. This point is considered in Case Study B. Accommodation earnings are likely to be much more significant in rural areas rather than towns which offer many other spending opportunities. Pearce (1987) has quoted a study by Britton in 1980 which suggested that rural areas are often rather more dependent for employment on tourism than other areas.

Spending by tourists stimulates an economy by creating work in tourism-related businesses such as accommodation, catering, retailing and transport. That new employment in turn causes an increase in economic activity. This phenomena is known as the multiplier, a concept which was introduced by Kahn. He pointed out that in given circumstances investment stimulates not just the employment directly resulting, but also creates further stages of growth as more employment is stimulated by the extra spending power in the economy. The size of the multiplier depends on the proportion of additional income which people spend to buy goods or services for consumption rather than retain as savings. Spending creates a demand for goods and services which can be satisfied only by production and consequently increased employment is also required. However, this employment may occur outside the locality or country if specialized goods are imported, or if the population prefers to spend its new wealth on overseas holidays. Income spent outside the region under consideration is referred to as leakage.

The effects from a given increase in tourism activity can be calculated from input-output models of the economy, which trace the interaction between its major sectors. The accuracy of the method depends on the number of levels and sectors of the economy through which spending and production effects are traced. The method measures the induced output per unit of spending, and is a valuable aid to planners who need to compare the relative contribution of different industries required to sustain a given increment in tourism activity. Multiplier approaches take the analysis further, by examining the consequences of additional earnings and employment in stimulating yet further demand in an economy. Income multipliers focus on the effect on aggregate income of extra spending, while the employment multiplier is concerned with the additional work created by spending which results from the initial increase in tourism. This can be examined according to sectors and skills levels, as a basis for manpower development and planning. Case Study G deals with methods adopted in London's Capital programme to cope with an anticipated staff shortfall, resulting from increasing tourism demand, and exacerbated by demographic changes.

Beyond the measurable direct and indirect effects of tourism are other economic influences that are harder to estimate. The sector is a major entry point to the workforce for many first time employees. Its seasonal, shift patterns and high client contact work characteristics have significantly expanded employment opportunities for women, and it offers a conducive environment for starting a small business. Tourism has become a key element in the lives of many people and companies, and it builds social and economic linkages between countries and people.

Resort development

The decision to proceed with a specific resort proposal is the prerogative of its entrepreneurial backers, but there is increasing evidence that investment decisions also take into account such loosely linked, long-run considerations as the potential increase in land values of the surrounding area. Developers of major resorts often have a world-wide remit, searching for maximum benefits for their financial backers. Against this, the development of a tourism sector may pose a series of problems for local and state government officials to resolve in the short term. A particular area may have insufficient residents to staff the proposed developments, and they lack the qualifications and experience for managerial job opportunities. Many aspects of the infrastructure may have to be expanded to support the increased visitor and resident populations which will result from even partial implementation of the planned resort developments. The authorities will have to finance such infrastructure improvements ahead of any additional tax revenues which might flow from the developments once they are operating.

Wanhill (1987) has surveyed local councillors' opinions, and found that they expressed fairly strong agreement about the economic benefits of tourism, but a dispersion of views about whether tourists add atmosphere to the area or bring about the provision of better facilities and infrastructure. Crowding, damage to the environment and a burden on local taxes seemed to be the most contentious issues.

As developments take place and the visitor count rises, the character of any area may be expected to change. MacCannell (1976) distinguished between two positions which sectors of the local population might adopt. Planners of marginal economies who look to tourism as a new source of profit or development tend to favour tourism, while urban dwellers are more likely to question the value of tourism for local people. In most areas, the interests of the various groups are less polarized. One example is the small, local construction firms which could profit from increased building activity. However the scale and pace of resort development may be beyond their technical and staff resources, or may attract bidding from large scale specialist contractors for one-off work. Conversely, small firms may be reluctant to bid themselves if the project requires their investment in new equipment when the prospects of further large-scale work in the area is uncertain.

In these conflicting interests, the role for government planners is to assess the impact of proposed expansion in resort areas and intermediate the varying interests. This point is developed in the next chapter, while the case study of plans for development in West Hawaii, the Kohala and Kona areas of the Big Island, examines the planning approach adopted in Hawaii. In contrast, where planning has been undertaken in tourism resorts, it has often been remedial, attempting to intervene after much development had already taken place, on an *ad hoc* basis dealing with individual projects rather than viewing the destination systematically.

Development expertise

Many of the poorer nations hoping to derive developmental benefits from tourism lack the entrepreneurial and business strengths to exploit their own natural tourism resources in ways which are acceptable to internationally mobile, experienced travellers and to their own citizens. There is seldom a strong nationally-owned private sector, a vigorous entrepreneurial class, or an adequate range and depth of public sector management skills. To bridge these gaps, they tend to place considerable reliance on foreign skills and finance. A common strategy is to retain specialists as consultants. Bodlender (1985) has explained the advantages to be gained from consulting experts. His points are summarized in Table 11.2.

Table 11.2   Advantages of retaining tourism consultants

---

1 Consultancy firms can provide specific specialized expertise on a project basis which is not needed regularly
2 The specific skills required may not be available within the country or region and the most appropriate or quickest way to progress the assignment or project is to buy in these skills
3 An independent professional opinion by experts not directly involved in the assignment or project and not benefiting from it financially is required

---

Based on Bodlender, 1985

Another strategy is to base development on the skills and resources of multinational companies. The key assets of multinational enterprises are access to international finance, their established marketing power, highly developed communications systems and organizational skills. Typically, most tourist destinations, even in developed countries, rely heavily on foreign operators to package and market vacation opportunities in origin countries. At another level, a local venture can collaborate with overseas interests to gain expertise and technical skills. Hotels and airlines being established in developing countries often contract with large companies for start-up support, and many continue the relationship once the scheme has been established. Other facilities in the destination, including handicrafts, excursions and catering have less need for foreign partners, although they too may benefit from foreign expertise and organizational abilities at the start. In many destinations, an expatriot community takes root, attracted by the natural attributes of the region, and the opportunity to establish small enterprises. This often takes the form of joint ownership with a local citizen, to meet legislative requirements designed to promote entrepreneurial opportunities for their own citizens.

Social impacts

> The most noticeable impact of tourism on traditional values is that certain social and human relations are brought into the economic sphere: they become part of making a living . . . goods or services that used to be part of people's social lives have now been commercialized and are offered as commodities. (Kadt, 1979)

In developing countries, tourism is often regarded as a potent 'modernizing' influence on values and morals. Some Government and religious leaders see these effects as beneficial, and take policy decisions to encourage the process, while in other cultural contexts they are regarded as a cause for concern, and ways are sought to limit the transfer of new values from tourists to the local community. Demonstration effects can result from merely observing tourists' behaviour, and is most often seen in the changing patterns of local consumption. The new facilities built to accommodate and cater for tourists also influences local expectations and values.

Chisnall (1985) has argued that the more cohesive a community, the more likely its members are to share very similar attitudes, and he quoted Banton:

> Backward societies look to the past. Each generation learns its roles from its fathers and continues to regard them as teachers and exemplars. People strive to be as worthy as their fathers, not to surpass them . . . Industrial societies look to the future. They see history as the story of progress up to the present elevation . . . the cultural characteristic of industrial societies is their need to believe in the future.

Residents' attitudes towards tourism

Several factors influence the ways in which local people regard tourism. Sheldon and Var (1984) considered that distance of residence from the tourist zone would have an effect, but pointed out also that their length of residency in a tourist locality was a factor in inhabitants' perceptions of tourism. Um and Crompton (1987) have suggested a methodology to evaluate 'attachment' which appears to indicate that residents with a strong cultural tradition are less enthusiastic about visitors than newcomers to their community. Research is inconclusive, but the topic is a critical one given the goals stated for many tourism developments of enhancing residents' lifestyles, and the earlier discussion of tourists as a potential source of irritation to local residents.

The potential damage to the tourism sector is sufficiently serious that a number of destinations have instituted programmes designed to educate members of the host community to have a more receptive attitude towards their visitors. In part, this strategy is designed to counteract the negative aspects of tourism, such as congestion, but it is also intended to counter existing or potential concern that people's traditions are becoming objects in a spectacle. In many tourism destinations traditional, and perhaps private ceremonial or celebrations are portrayed as part of the image underpinning marketing communications designed to attract visitors to the area. Visitors therefore expect to see and enjoy these spectacles, and local performances are arranged on a commercial basis for their entertainment, thus debasing the integrity of cultural traditions.

Examples include Hawaii, where the Hula became a dance staged regularly on a commercial basis, entirely for the enjoyment of tourists. Often, the performers were newcomers to the Islands, and the style of this ancient dance rapidly diverged from its culturally pure form. More recently, Hawaiian native culture has experienced a renaissance of local interest and the traditional forms of expression are being revived. Several community dance groups, organized on a voluntary basis, now perform traditional Hula for their own interest, their members are keen to explain the meaning to interested visitors. The distinctions between pure forms of folk tradition and commercially driven variants is seldom easy to draw. In Europe, mock or simulated mediaeval jousting tournaments are sometimes staged in genuine historic castles, or on the site of important battles. Some are performed by expert groups who are interested in the historical or technical aspects, while others are organized as spectacles to attract clients. Several tourist regions have well-established performing groups which are sometimes taken to international tourism fairs, such as World Travel Market, where they function as an effective promotional tool.

Performances of traditional culture, pure or interpreted, please tourists who are able to see something of an ancient tradition, and provide opportunities for many local people to benefit from a cash income for the display. The arrival of visitors with an interest in their culture also creates a market for the sale of associated craft work. Local people may also feel glad that outsiders are taking an interest in their old way of life; in Tibet, the brief gateway that opened for visitors in the mid 1980s brought important cash sources to the temples and gave the Chinese administrators a reason for permitting, or encouraging, their restoration after the damage inflicted in the Chinese occupation of Tibet. This is discussed further in Case Study D.

Island tourism

Many destinations are small islands. Their economies are confronted with a host of problems arising from their isolation, small populations and limited resources. Typically they experience high unemployment, slow economic development, including low capital investment, and foreign debt. However, their climate and relaxed lifestyle make them very attractive destinations for tourists seeking benefits such as relaxation and water sports. When tourism is introduced to exploit the attractive natural attributes of climate, scenery and sea, and to generate employment, a set of new problems result for residents, as discussed in Case Study B. Many islands which develop a significant tourism sector, such as the Balearics or Hawaii, may receive more visitors than the entire population, sometimes by a factor of five or more. Residents in resort areas want to preserve traditional features of life and they tend to oppose developments, while developers see new facilities as the key to business opportunities from increased numbers of visitors. Thus, tourism development implies change, and conflicting interests characterize such situations.

Tourist attractions and tourist impacts

The major evidence of tourism in a region is the regular arrival of large numbers of visitors and this inevitably has consequences for the destination. The rapid increase in built environments in attractive areas, coupled with invasive architectural styles or imported materials for the new buildings, can be offensive to residents and has often proved unattractive to holiday-makers, particularly when the skyline or beach front is obscured. As an area is developed for tourism its characteristics inevitably undergo change. The existing ecological balance is altered and the survival of particular animal, bird, reptile or floral species has sometimes been put in jeopardy by tourism, although it is evident that investment in alternative activities such as mineral extraction or manufacturing can have even more damaging impacts.

There are many examples of hillsides or parklands where thin topsoil cover has been worn down under the pressure of visitor numbers, causing long-term damage from the resultant erosion channels. Individual visitors indulging their natural curiosity and picking rare flowers, or uprooting plants to take home, cause more environmental damage. Isolated and relatively unresearched archaeological sites may also suffer from casual souvenir collecting: some of the greatest museum collections in the Western world were formed in this way, but the dangers are better understood now. However, more people are in a position to visit exotic sites, and often succumb to the temptation to return home with a momento which seems to have a more immediate personal value if it was selected from its site by the individual. A related trait is the habit of writing or carving names on monuments; many Roman and Greek archaeological sites have the signatures of notable visitors carved over the centuries in prominent positions. Two factors should be considered, but their overall impact is uncertain; the dangers to scientific understanding and to national heritages of haphazard collection or spurious damage are well understood now, but against that many sites are still derelict. The evident interest of visitors gives local authorities a strong rationale for the investment of resources in their repair and preservation. One example is the Ming tomb site outside Beijing, where a few of the most prestigious buildings have been renovated, and guided tours are readily available. Within an hour's walk, unsignposted tomb buildings of striking beauty are gradually falling into disrepair. These, rather than the formally interpreted tombs, are the preferred picnic sites of local people, and expatriots working in Beijing. With some investment, these sites could be protected and their delights made available to visitors for a fee. Revenue from tourism could thus be used to offset the expenses of preserving an important aspect of China's heritage.

Tourism also provides an economic justification for setting aside vast areas of land for national parks and wilderness areas. The revenue and interest which tourism brings to such areas contributes to their preservation and provides governments with the rationale for the preservation of parkland and historical sites. Bleak, open countryside is attractive to many tourists seeking solitude or traditional lifestyles, but it is also a recreational facility for local people. The nature of such areas implies a limit to the number of visitors who can be supported without altering or damaging the environment. A joint programme between the Countryside Commission and English Tourist Board was announced in 1989 to ensure that the National Parks are not damaged by insensitive or excessive tourism. The parks had been established to protect unspoiled areas and to enable people to enjoy these important areas. They are natural magnets to many tourists. Table 11.3 shows the main principles of tourism development which were proposed.

Table 11.3   National park tourism management proposals

1 Support for practical conservation and wildlife measures
2 Make the most of opportunities for quiet, open-air recreation and improving access
3 Support the rural economy
4 Ensure new tourism developments respect the landscape and environment
5 Ensure that the design of new developments is in keeping with the landscape
6 Use marketing opportunities to deepen people's enjoyment, appreciation, understanding and concern for the parks

Source: *Countryside Commission News*, No. 40, Nov/Dec 1989

In remote areas where there are sites of major historical interest, such as Hadrian's Wall in Northumberland, a typical response on the part of local government seeking to stimulate the economy is to provide additional tourist amenities. Toilets and car parks are necessary when visitor numbers reach a certain threshold. Paths are liable to erosion and they may be paved, or edged to stop the erosion spreading, a necessary but potentially intrusive protective measure for the environment. Lighting may be installed, and catering facilities built as visitors are attracted in increasing numbers, but more people bring pollution, noise and a reduction in the original quality of solitude which had been a significant attribute of the area for many visitors, and is often an essential feature for wildlife.

One reaction to the congestion which many tourist sites experience is to adopt localized 'negative promotion'. Increasingly, selected beauty spots in Britain's National Parks are deliberately omitted from tourism promotions in an effort to prevent them being overwhelmed. The Council for National Parks (a watchdog body supported by 40 conservation organizations) proposed another solution based on the designation of areas which could only be reached by buses from specially built car parks, located away from the main points of interest. The number of car parks in park areas was reduced. Such steps reflect the inevitable conflict between tourism and conservation interests and shows how they may be minimized.

Shopping for authentic souvenirs

In many areas of interest to tourists, a variety of goods are produced primarily to meet local needs. These strongly reflect local culture and traditions and traditionally were made of locally produced materials. Examples of such goods include carpets, cooking and storage vessels, baskets, hunting tools and ceremonial clothing. Such artifacts are often regarded as attractive souvenirs, as was indicated in an earlier discussion of the importance to tourists of shopping opportunities (see Table 10.4).

However, modern production technology and materials, and changing tastes influenced by exposure to the media and the arrival of tourists, is contributing to a change in the way such goods are produced, the materials used in their construction, their design and decorative style, and even the way they are used. Although the goods displayed in resort shops and airport departure lounges may seem authentic, following local patterns, often they are produced elsewhere by modern methods, or using modern materials. Kadt (1979) has argued that to be authentic, arts and crafts must be rooted both in historical tradition and in present day life; true authenticity cannot be achieved by conservation alone, since that leads to stultification. Against this, tourism may revitalize certain crafts under the impetus of new cash demand. Kadt discussed Schadler's study of Africa, which found that objects such as carvings had been created for use in cults, and commented 'with the demise of traditional religious beliefs and their associated rituals, the objects to which craftsmen devote themselves become meaningless fragmentary husks of a cult or religion'.

Responsible tourism

In many spheres of economic, social and political activity the 1980s saw an increasingly widespread sensitivity and concern for the general quality of life. Consumerism, and the apparent end of the cold war, together with a spreading vision and understanding of the world's ecological systems, tended to accelerate public, business and governmental concern with these issues. In tourism, an understanding of the impact on other people of individual and organized leisure and travel behaviour became a focus of concern.

Earlier in this book it was pointed out that tourism can be viewed as that part of leisure time spent in travelling. Krippendorf (1987) has pointed out that 'the recreation cycle begins with man and the spheres of everyday life: work, home and free time'. Tourism serves as a break from every-day life and is itself characterized by particular influences, motives and expectations. The tourist destination represents counter-routine to its clients, who expect not to have to observe the restraints and conventions of every-day life and routine which they have paid to leave behind. The consequences are interactions between tourists and locals which can be exploitive, and are potentially harmful to both sides. Krippendorf commented:

> The goal must be to develop and promote new forms of tourism which will bring the greatest possible benefit to all the participants – the travellers, the host population and the tourist business, without causing intolerable ecological and social damage.

D'Amore (1987) has distinguished between three generations of tourism thinking in Canada: small scale, followed by the development of large scale national and multinational corporations, and thirdly a stage characterized by collaboration between public and private sectors. He argued that the new priority must have as its focal point people, and has developed a set of guidelines, shown in Table 11.4. These seek to balance community aspirations with the type and pace of tourism development.

Table 11.4   Guidelines to aspiring destinations

---

1   Make residents aware of the advantages of tourism, demonstrating economic benefits and encouraging them to share tourists' resources and amenities
2   Base tourism planning on goals identified by local residents so that they can maintain their lifestyle, keep developments within local carrying capacity, and match the pace of change with local desires
3   The images used in the promotion of local attractions should be endorsed by residents
4   Co-ordinate public and private efforts to maintain local opportunities for recreation
5   Retain respect for traditions and lifestyles through local involvement in tourism development
6   Local capital, enterprise and labour should be invested in local tourism developments
7   Broad based community participation in tourism events should be encouraged, as it is local residents' homes which are being put on display
8   Destinations should adopt themes which reflect history and local lifestyles and enhance local pride in the community
9   Mitigate local growth problems before increasing tourism activity as tourism is an agent of change

---

Based on Murphy's account of D'Amore, 1983

Conclusion

The effects of tourism on a destination area are complex and varied; in some respects they may harm some local interests, while other consequences are beneficial to the same, or different groups in the community. It is not just a case of the overall number of tourists arriving in a destination area; the concentration of tourism in specific localities is also significant. As the intensity of tourism activity increases the consequences become more visible, and more people are affected

155

The early enthusiasm of locals for tourists, and the spontaneity and warmth of personal encounters in the early stages of tourism development, can quickly wane under the pressure of increasing arrivals, resulting in increased impersonalism, resentment and commercialism at later stages of development. Table 11.5 provides an overview of the benefits and disadvantages of tourism-led development.

Table 11.5   Beneficial and harmful effects of tourism

Aspect	Positive	Negative
Economic	Job creation Multiplier Infrastructure developments Foreign exchange	Pressure on labour supply New demand patterns Increased population
Social	New attitudes Culture preserved New business skills	New attitudes Culture debased
Political	International recognition	Restrictions on international travel
Conservation	Enhanced protection	Irresponsible behaviour

But for many areas, tourism represents one of the few activities which can be developed there, and as the volume of tourism increases more destinations will inevitably be brought into the tourism system. It is therefore necessary for business and government leaders to develop their understanding of tourism, and to manage its effects in the context of local conditions.

Questions

1 With reference to any area which is developing a tourism sector, analyse the probable consequences for local people, distinguishing between problems and benefits in the short and long term.

2 What advice would you offer to a community which wishes to gain economic benefits from its traditional costume, dance or crafts as an attraction to tourists?

3 What role does national and local government play in the development of two tourism destinations with which you are familiar, and how do you account for any differences?

Recommended reading

de Kadt, E. (ed.) *Tourism, Passport to Development*, Oxford University Press, London, 1976

Mathieson, A. and Wall, G. *Tourism – Economic Physical and Social Impacts*, Longman, Harlow, 1982

Murphy, P.E. *Tourism, a Community Approach*, Methuen, New York, 1985

Smith, V.L. *Hosts and Guests*, Blackwell, Oxford, 1978

Young, G. *Tourism, Blessing or Blight?* Pelican, Harmondsworth, 1973

CHAPTER TWELVE

Regulation and Competition in Tourism

Introduction

The concluding chapter of Part One of this book extends the discussion of tourism management to a consideration of the environments within which the tourism system exists, and which constrain the operation of tourism enterprises. So far in this book, the view taken of the tourism industry has been that it is a system composed of many specialist organizations interacting to supply tourism services, but an important characteristic of the systems concept is the attention it focuses on the variety of forces external to the main elements which affect the actions of the entire system. Many of these have already been identified; this chapter focuses more closely on selected aspects of the tourism environment, and considers how they affect the quality of tourists' experiences. Further perspectives are provided in the case studies which conclude this book.

Government roles in tourism planning

The fundamental task for planning authorities is to establish a clear framework to determine what factors should enter into their decision making. The main impact of any development falls on those who live in the communities which become tourism destination areas as a result of developers' visions and investment. Equitable and effective management of their varied interests depends on formulating priorities which take into account all such concerns and needs, and then applying appropriate executive instruments to defend the rights of all groups while creating conditions within which the development can flourish.

Two further areas of concern to local or central government agencies are how to fund the large infrastructure developments required to support increased tourism activity and populations (of visitors and supporting residents); and secondly the validity of the demand forecasts on which resort or hotel expansion plans have been predicted. In some areas, several independent developments may be planned or under construction, suggesting that a massive increase in overall demand for tourism to that area is expected. If the planned demand does not materialize, the tourism sector will suffer from oversupply, with detrimental consequences for the profitability of new and existing resorts as prices drop, reduced levels of employment and lower flows of tax revenue for local or central government. Consequently, planners have a role to play in deciding the general level of resort development, or they may have an influence on specific proposals and, as discussed below, many national tourism authorities play a significant role in promoting their destinations in international tourist generating markets.

In addition to attracting overseas visitors, governments have another role in tourism through their planning mechanisms, as indicated in the previous chapter. They frequently become involved in major capital projects, typically by granting, blocking or altering development proposals, or in granting investment incentives. Bodlender and Ward (1989) have identified three purposes, which are summarized here. Firstly, a project which is considered desirable can be accelerated by giving it higher priority for investors through offering quicker returns; obstacles to private sector profit objectives such as the repatriation of profits can be eased and, thirdly, positive discrimination can stimulate certain types of development in less favoured areas. The methods available include grant aid, government loans or guaranteed commercial loans, tax incentives or technical aid such as training programmes.

To coordinate tourism promotional and planning activities, and to form a framework for the private sector's operational decisions, many countries develop a tourism sector plan, usually as part of a broader strategy of economic and social development. The tourism plan normally has two focuses; marketing and development. Typical objectives of national tourism marketing plans are to increase the number of foreign visitors, extend their length of stay and their spending, extend the tourist season, or encourage a fuller regional spread of activities. The purposes behind this may include the generation of foreign currency flows, or a reduction in overseas holiday-taking by the country's inhabitants, and the creation of new work and investment or enterprise opportunities, particularly in regions which have little alternative prospects. Table 12.1 indicates the developmental issues identified by the English Tourist Board (ETB).

Table 12.1   Key development issues for the ETB

1 To satisfy changing tastes, exploit areas of growth and counter competition from abroad
2 To raise standards aiming for quality of product, design and management with improved training programmes
3 To channel more investment, both public and private, into tourism and leisure
4 To gain commitment from local authorities to Tourism Development Action Programmes and Local Tourism Strategies

Based on *A Vision for England*, ETB, 1987

Tourism as a strategic tool for national development

Any country wishing to stimulate its tourism trade faces considerable demands for investment in infrastructure specific to the tourism sector, such as airports, or of more general benefit such as expanded and improved transport, water and power systems. In addition, training for tourism staff as well as promotional campaigns to attract investors and later tourists, will also be required.

Many destinations are developing countries, and the decision to invest scarce resources to bring infrastructure for the specific benefit of tourists up to internationally acceptable standards can be politically difficult in the face of other local priorities. It is a basic tenet of economic theory that all resources are limited in supply, and diverting funds or skills towards the tourism sector means fewer resources in the short term for residents. However, tourism offers an alternative to primary exports as a generator of both foreign exchange and waged employment. A number of disadvantages of primary exports have been suggested by Bond and Ledman (1977, quoted in Smith, 1983). Commodity prices depend on world market conditions, and export markets in raw products are unstable, so that foreign currency earnings are uncertain. In contrast, the tourism host country has more opportunity to control prices; tourism diversifies the export base while it generally requires relatively little import to generate a unit of earnings.

Government roles in tourism promotion

The economic significance of tourism points to reasons why many governments take an active part in its promotion. These include the flow of tax receipts it generates, its contribution to the national Balance of Payments, and its potential to generate employment. A fourth factor is that the many small enterprises which form a major part of the tourism industry have no prospect of influencing the flow of tourists to a destination area, although they may compete effectively on a local scale to attract the attention and business of people who are already visitors to the region.

Despite the foregoing discussion, there are political points of view which argue against the participation of some governments in tourism promotion. For example, America's share of world tourism had fallen from 13 per cent in 1976 to 10 per cent in 1986. The three reasons identified were high dollar exchange rates, making the US a more costly destination, global economic and political circumstances, and the reluctance at that time of its government to fund tourism promotional activities. The US spent three and a half cents per head of population on tourism, and ranked 83rd in the world in per capita spending by national government tourism organizations. The average spent was $3.64 and the highest was the Bahamas, $118.64. Commenting on this, Ronkainen and Farano (1987) wrote:

President Reagan has repeatedly called for the elimination of the USTTA [United States Travel and Tourism Administration]. He recommended that Congress phase out the USTTA by only providing it with $4m in close out funding. Administration officials believe that the private sector can better safeguard America's share of the world tourism market than can a bureaucratic agency. In fact they do not deem tourism promotion as an appropriate federal activity. Further, they do not want the general public to pay for programmes which benefit specific segments of society. Finally, the President contends that tourism promotion has little impact in inducing increased receipts from foreigners. At the heart of their position, the Administration officials do not believe that it is possible or beneficial for the USTTA to attempt to unify the diverse range of travel and tourism firms into a single industry.

Devising effective promotional strategies for a destination country depends on an understanding of its particular tourism supply strengths, and detailed knowledge of the various markets it serves, particularly differing population's preferences for various tourism benefits, and their media habits. The typical pattern is for destination countries to establish a network of National Tourist Offices (NTOs) in their major generating countries, although some prefer to rely on the services and expertise of a local marketing consultancy. These offices have a dual function: educating the trade channels about their destination, and promoting the various tourism opportunities to the public, or responding to their enquiries. NTOs seldom offer a reservations service to travellers as their remit is to represent the generic destination and all tourism operations within it, although many perform a facilitating function bringing together the various companies which together create tourism concepts.

Regional tourism promotion

Many tourists, particularly on long haul journeys, visit more than one destination during a single trip and national boundaries in tourism areas such as the Himalayas, South East Asia or Europe are an irrelevant obstacle to travel behaviour. Although each destination is in competition with the others in the region there is also a sense in which cooperation between them can bring advantages to each, including an increase in the value of tourism activity within the region, rather than to more distant countries. Several areas have adopted this approach for tourism marketing, often drawing on already established regional political supra national groupings.

With the formation in 1992 of a single market within Europe, members of the European Economic Community will trade with each other on equal terms, and Europe will in effect have no internal frontiers. As part of the preparation for this, the Commission designated 1990 the Year of Tourism. The objectives identified for this project were to prepare for 1992, to turn the integrating role of tourism to account in the creation of a people's Europe, and to stress the economic and social importance of tourism in regional development and job creation. Each country developed its own response; in the case of Britain this consisted of three strands. Product standards and the visitor's reception was one target for improvement; the presentation of tourism products was to be developed, particularly stressing regional and seasonal tourism spreads, and thirdly tourism was to be included in the curriculum of schools and colleges.

The Commission provided some 5 million ECUs (approximately £3 million) for the operation of the Tourism Year, about half of which was intended for assistance with projects connected to the Year's specific themes. These are shown in Table 12.2. The criteria for eligibility are shown in Table 12.3. Each country was expected to set up an Examining Committee to assess projects from that particular country and recommend those worthy of support to an EEC steering committee in Brussels. Those accepted would receive 40 per cent of the total cost of the project, within the budget allocated to each country. In the case of Britain, this was set at £150 000, and therefore sponsorship was sought to boost the funds available. In addition some £300 000 was set aside by the Commission to promote pan-European projects – that is those covering three or more member countries.

Table 12.2   Themes of the EEC Tourism Year

- To promote greater knowledge among the citizens of the member states, particularly young people, of the cultures and life-styles of the other member states
- To encourage the staggering of holiday dates
- To encourage the development of new holiday destinations
- To encourage the development of new forms of tourism and of alternatives to mass tourism
- To promote intra-community tourism, particularly by facilitating the movement of travellers
- To promote tourism from third countries to Europe

Source: *European Tourism Year 1990*, Tourism Society, October 1989

Table 12.3   Criteria for Tourism Year project funding

- Promotion of off-season tourism
- Promotion of cultural, rural, social and other forms of tourism alternative to mass tourism during the high season
- Promotion of travel by persons up to the age of 26 aimed at greater knowledge of cultures and life-styles of other member states of the Community
- Projects facilitating intra-community travel
- Projects contributing to the horizontal cooperation between professions of several countries
- Projects contributing to the development of new destinations
- Projects that can serve as a pilot to similar projects in other countries or regions
- Projects that are environment friendly in character, meaning that they embellish, or at least do not damage the natural or man-made environment

Source: *European Tourism Year 1990*, Tourism Society, October 1989

Monitoring tourism activity

An important basis for Government's decisions in any sphere of influence is accurate and timely tracking of the social, economic, demographic and technological trends throughout society. Tourism is regarded as a rather difficult sector for researchers, due to its diversity, lack of central co-ordination, its huge scope, and disagreement over definitions of its key aspects. Other factors identified by Allard (1989) were the recency of the tourism sector, compounded by the relatively low esteem accorded to service sector activity by many governments.

Methods of collecting statistics about tourism activity vary. The usual practice is for countries to record the country of a visitor's origin. The length of stay is important, but it may not be recorded even though bed nights give a clearer picture of the tourism intensity for a destination than arrivals figures. The two main points for data capture are a country's ports of entry, and the registers of accommodation operators. In addition, many governments and destinations carry out surveys for special purposes. None of these methods provide a consistent or full picture of tourism activity. In 1976 the United Nations statistical commission suggested a harmonization of statistics as indicated in Table 12.4. Whatever methods are used to collect and process data on the tourism industry,

---

Table 12.4 Recommendations for tourism statistics

1 Data desirable on individual demand:

- Number of visitors during period
- Duration of visit
- Place of origin
- Destination
- Arrival period
- Transport
- Accommodation
- Socio-demographic details
- Purpose of visit
- Reasons for taking trip
- How trip was organized
- Spending by type
- Image of destination
- Satisfaction after trip
- Opinions on prices, infrastructure, quality . . .

---

2 Data on tourism production unit services

- Capacity
- Occupancy
- Economic performance
- Employment
- Prices
- Potential growth

Based on Allard, 1989

some of the information may be inaccurate, for reasons indicated in Table 12.5, but in the absence of reliable statistical data, it is difficult to take appropriate decisions on the many aspects of tourism destination development with which local and national governments become involved, and nor can entrepreneurs accurately assess the likely demand for their projects.

Table 12.5   Reasons for inaccurate hotel returns

1 A tour leader makes a single return for a group – the nationalities may not be recorded accurately
2 Certain types of tourist accommodation may not have to make returns and privately owned second homes may not be counted at all
3 The data will (probably) be collated according to traditional administrative criteria, e.g. districts, but the pattern of tourist activities may have a different basis
4 Fraud

Predicting the demand for tourism services

Earlier in this book, it was pointed out that individual tourism organizations need to understand the characteristics, motivations and expectations of their clients as a basis for effective marketing and service delivery. It is equally important for countries to monitor the trends in international travel behaviour, although a number of difficulties and inconsistencies in data collection have just been noted.

In addition, several experts have cast doubt on the accuracy of forecasting methods and models in current use. The evidence for this, and its effect, can be seen in the inadequacy of Britain's major transport systems, and particularly their failure to keep pace with the expanding demand for both private and public modes of travel. Despite these problems, several methods of forecasting are available, mostly based on statistical projections of currently recorded activity levels and trends, so that their accuracy can be no greater than that of the data which they employ. A second major approach to forecasting method harnesses the experience of managers through scenario writing or delphic oracle methods. These bring several experts together to speculate in a structured way about the foreseeable future. Interesting discussions of these and related techniques are contained in an article by Calantone et al (1987). Witt and Martin (1987) have examined the implications of forecasting methods of tourism demand in the context of assessments of the effect of marketing programmes.

Regulatory impacts on passenger experiences

In common with all commercial activities, tourism has become a target for regulations intended to protect those people who might be affected by its operations, including staff, residents and customers. These restrictions are imposed by trade bodies, governments and international bodies. The effect on service standards is now examined in the special case of scheduled air transport.

The civil aviation industry is subject to a range of regulations, both national and international. Governments have always felt a need to control access to their airports and airspaces (flightpaths) and to protect the markets for their developing national airlines; in 1919 the International Airconvention of Paris established the basis of control for commercial operations.

Historically, most major airlines were either state-owned, or depended heavily on government subsidies. A further factor was the connection between civil and military transport in the mind of governments. Recent evidence of this has been the use of hastily converted cruise ships for troop transport in the conflict between Britain and Argentina over the Falkland (Malvinas) Islands, and the sale by BA of part of its tristar fleet to the RAF for conversion into fuel tankers. Common specifications for components between military and civil versions of transport fleets is quite common, both for economic and strategic reasons.

Public concern over safety, noise and pollution requires that high standards be set for control over aircraft servicing, staffing and operation. Passenger safety is also widely considered to be safeguarded by licensing and supervision. The majority of technical and safety regulations are general, and apply to all passenger carriers. (In Britain they are contained in the Air Navigation Order.) Variations between countries are very slight, and based on a series of International Standard and Recommended Practices provided by ICAO (International Civil Aviation Organisation) within the Convention on International Civil Aviation.

Traditionally, air tariffs have been set by IATA, and must be approved by the Governments concerned. Economic regulation of the international civil aviation industry is arranged under the Chicago Convention. Taken together, airlines face a series of economic and other regulations, and the regulation of air-routes and congestion at airports imposes further restrictions on all operators. The cumulative effect of all regulations is indicated in Table 12.6 while Table 12.7 deals with their liberty to operate routes.

Table 12.6   Regulations on airlines

A **Non economic**
1 The airworthiness of aircraft
2 The timing, nature and supervision of airframe, engine and other maintenance
3 The numbers and qualifications of both flight and cabin crew; their training, licensing and schedules of work
4 The ways in which aircraft are operated
5 Standards dealing with civil aviation infrastructure

B **Economic regulations**
1 The exchange of airtraffic rights (freedoms of the air)
2 The control of fares (and freight tariffs)
3 The control of frequencies and capacities

Based on Doganis 1985, and Sawers 1987

Table 12.7   Freedoms of the air

Freedom	Airline rights
First	To overfly one country to reach another
Second	To land in another country for technical reasons such as to refuel
Third	To drop traffic from its own country in another
Fourth	To carry traffic back to its own country from another
Fifth	To fly from its own country to pick up traffic from another country en-route, and deliver them to a third, or vice versa
Sixth	To carry traffic to a gateway in its own country and then abroad, when the traffic originates elsewhere
Seventh	To operate entirely between two other countries
Eighth	To carry traffic between two points in another foreign country

Based on Gee, Choy and Makens, 1984

The result has been to constrain the ability of international airlines to take business decisions in two ways. Airlines are not free to enter a market (route) at will and, secondly, their revenue and growth is limited by capacity controls, frequency rules or the imposed need to share a route with other airlines. The following discussion illustrates the range of problems reported by one operator, Air Mauritius.

> Compared to traffic statistics of about two decades ago the growth has been phenomenal. This growth has been mainly due to the introduction of jet aircraft in the early sixties and the wide-bodied jumbos in the seventies. They have developed in their wake an equally phenomenal growth in world tourism. Air transportation it can be said has been the single greatest motivating force in the development of world-wide tourism and in particular in the opening up of new far away tourist destinations.
>
> Air Mauritius has built up significant volumes . . . in the twelve month period 1984-85 Mauritius-Paris traffic grew from 26 000 to 44 000 . . . On the European routes the number of aircraft seats each way rose from 156 in 1982 to 858 in 1986 . . .
>
> The concept of a national flag airline as a chosen instrument whereby a country utilizes a national airline to display its flag in other parts of the world is a well-established tradition for both large industrialized countries and small developing ones . . . It has been demonstrated in our case to what extent air transportation has a key role to play for stimulating economic development and growth.
>
> The decision on the part of the government to set up an international airline requires that constant attention be given to new air routes and new political relationships with other countries.
>
> Since independence the government has entered into some 20 Bilateral Air Services Agreements with other countries. Of these the carriers of only eight countries exercise the rights exchanged and operate to Mauritius . . . Australia . . . has a substantial tourist market for Mauritius, but has for the past ten years consistently refused air access. Qantas does not want to operate to Mauritius nor does it want Air Mauritius to fly to Australia. The official reason is that there is not enough origin and destination traffic. The real reason is protectionism. (Tirvengadum, 1986)

Changing market conditions for airlines

For more than three decades the regulatory framework which constrained airline managers' economic and other decisions placed severe limitations on their decisions, and had remained largely unchanged:

> The cumulative effect of all the constraints has been that scheduled airline managers have been constrained in their ability to compete with other carriers, especially if their own airlines were IATA members. (Doganis, 1985)

The justification for the regulatory framework outlined above was based on the quasi public-goods nature of transport, and the belief that regulation would limit wasteful competition. However, the emergence of charter carriers to service the special needs of holiday-takers may be seen as a denial of the second point of view as it demonstrated vividly that demand for travel by air is responsive to price.

After the 1973-4 fuel crisis the regulatory frameworks outlined above were increasingly challenged. The change began in the US, and was linked with President Carter's arrival at the White House in 1977. Together with the effects of the oil crisis, the three factors shown in Table 12.8 are said to have contributed to deregulatory pressures.

Table 12.8   Pressures for deregulation in America

---

1   Consumerism had been a key element in Carter's election campaign: he sought the reduction of fares, and new direct international links from more US cities
2   His belief in the benefits of competition: domestic deregulation was expected to reduce internal airfares and increase airline profitability. The protected positions of Pan Am, TWA and other international carriers could not then be justified
3   His desire to increase the US share of international traffic

---

Based on Doganis, 1985

In 1977 a bill was introduced to Congress to permit greater (domestic) competition. The Airline Deregulation Act was passed in 1978. By 1979 entry to routes was virtually uncontrolled, and airlines were empowered to vary their fares by 80 per cent. In Europe airline regulations were also changed, somewhat later, and on a smaller scale.

Competitive market theory

Baumol (1982) has identified the crucial feature of any market place open to unrestrained competition (a contestable market place) as 'its vulnerability to hit and run entry'. Traditionally, economists have considered that incumbent firms gain advantages from insurmountably high fixed costs barring entry to a market. It has been shown above that capital costs in the airline industry are very high. The alternative to utilizing retained profits for fleet purchasing-raising loans or equity stakes, is still a formidable barrier. Baumol and Willig (1981) defined entry barriers as 'anything that requires an expenditure by a new entrant into an industry, but requires no equivalent cost upon an incumbent'. Another feature of contestable markets is that exit costs are minimal as other businesses, incumbents or new entrants will be willing to buy the equipment.

On the other hand, a technical barrier to entry for airlines is the need to obtain the necessary operating permits. The actual cost of such permits will be variable, dependent on the scale and scope of planned operations. It is also affected by the responses of incumbents who can challenge new applicants' applications, or raise the stakes by petitioning for increases in deposits and guarantees. Such costs are normally regarded as sunk once incurred, in contrast to the investment in capital equipment which may be recovered, at least in part, on the resale market.

However, a competitor may be persuaded to defray incurred expenses during a takeover, and Sawers (1987) pointed to evidence that route licences or landing and similar rights can be treated analytically as a commodity, with utility to be traded. Richard Branson (Virgin Airlines) is reported to have said that his airline and others like it should be able to pick up those routes that Britain's Monopoly Commission had said BA would have to give up if it bought BCal.

Barrett and Purdy (1987) have argued that the airline industry was so heavily regulated at that time that it cannot be considered contestable: 'The traditional system of aviation regulation in Europe does not allow customers the choice between the established airlines and allegedly inferior alternatives'.

However, regulatory controls over airline companies seem likely to be relaxed:

> In an industry whose firms use only capital on wheels or wings, some or all of the capital must be fixed, but it is not sunk. This means that in the absence of other barriers to entry, natural or artificial, an incumbent dare not offer profit-making opportunities to potential entrants because even if he can threaten retaliation after entry, an entering firm can hit and run, gathering in the available profits and departing when the going gets rough. (Baumol and Willig, 1981)

Two further points are significant in this brief review of contestable market theory as it applies to scheduled air transport. The market structure which may emerge from a contestable airline industry depends upon the economies of scale to its participants. To the extent that average costs will decline as output increases the evolving market structure will favour increasingly large firms, and will tend towards oligopoly or monopoly. But the authors previously cited also foresaw a limit to this trend: 'For the monopoly that operates in a contestable market the analysis shows also that potential entry can control undesirable behaviour' (Baumol and Willig, 1981).

In a discussion of American experience since deregulation James (1986) also disputed the tendency towards monopoly in deregulated markets:

> Many critics of deregulation predicted that regulatory reforms would eventually encourage the airlines to form natural monopolies. This is unlikely to happen . . . Competition will continue to challenge the marketing creativity of large carriers who have recently learned to take advantage of their size . . . Surviving smaller carriers will be tested to find special marketing niches beyond low prices.

This policy does, of course, have its dangers. Average yields (revenue per passenger mile flown) are always difficult to control in a competitive environment where market share is heavily influenced by price. Even nearly eight years after deregulation, it is not certain that the industry has developed complete mastery of pricing. This is one aspect of deregulation which offers a number of lessons for non-US carriers. Price instability is of course a major reason why non-US carriers remain very apprehensive about the relevance of the North American experience for their own environment. Another spin-off from deregulation, and most useful to the large airlines, has been the frequent flyer programme, pioneered by American, and quickly emulated by the other carriers.

In 1978 as deregulation began, there were 36 certified scheduled carriers (Section 401). If all those who have received certificates since 1978 were still in business, there would be over 225 Section 401 carriers. However, due to mergers, bankruptcies or just closing down of operations, this figure is down to 100 (in 1986). From 1978 to 1985, 32 carriers went into bankruptcy, 13 of which were declared in 1984. Of the 17 moving into bankruptcy since 1983, three were National carriers (between \$75m and \$1b in annual sales) and 14 were Regional carriers (below \$75m). None was a Major (sales above \$1b). (James, 1986)

The existing members of an oligopoly may combine together against potential entrants. One way of doing this is by raising entry costs through marketing strategies. For example, Koutsoyiannis (1987, drawing on Williamson, 1963) has shown that an industry's advertising spend may be increased without additional revenue benefits to the incumbent firms, it it rises beyond its profit-maximizing level.

Competition through service quality

An alternative strategy, which has been a major theme throughout this book, is to build customer loyalty or to offer a range of (perceived) benefits to selected market segments. An example discussed in Chapter 9 was the free mileage promotions which several airlines offered during the 1980s, awarding free flights or upgrades to higher service cabins, and merchandise to clients who had passed a mileage threshold to trigger the awards. As these were desirable to many passengers, but increased with the mileage paid for, the philosophy of this method was that people would try to arrange their flights with one carrier, rather than choosing an airline on the basis of schedule convenience and so on, in order to boost their mileage in pursuit of the most valuable awards. The concept was extended in several ways. Extra notional miles were awarded for enrolling in the programme, or for recruiting a colleague. Higher mileage awards were given for travel in premium classes, or at certain times of the year. In contrast, awards could not be taken at peak travel periods, when sufficient fare-paying passengers wanted to travel, filling available capacity.

Another strategy discussed in this book is to gain an improved understanding of customers' perceptions of the service and to manage the service towards their greater satisfaction. This will have two effects. In the first place it will induce customer loyalty, as a previously satisfying experience is likely to be repeat-purchased. Secondly, the judicious use of advertising messages will position the firm in the target public's awareness, as Chatburn (1985) has indicated, quoting from British Airways marketing director at that time:

> Through a perhaps more imaginative research approach than previously adopted the airline (BA) identified a number of salient features of service for its major passenger segments . . . This research . . . pointed to a need to promote the facets of courtesy and sympathy, the elements of the . . . Putting People First campaign . . . The airline's need to become more single-minded about what it actually was, was underlined when Landor Associates, trying to design a new corporate design and slogan for BA asked it what sort of company it saw itself as being. The lack of any coherent response showed BA's executives how much they needed to develop a single personality for the airline . . . Manhattan (the advertising campaign which had featured the New York island apparently on final approach for a landing) was designed to raise the perception of BA, to give it prestige, to rebuild its image. 'We had come out of a fairly bad track record both in terms of profitability and things like overmanning. And we had moved from being a technology led company to being market led.'

The management turnaround at British Airways is examined in Case Study K, and Case Study L provides an analysis of the airline's approach to understanding its customers, and meeting their expectations.

Conclusion

The emphasis throughout this book has been on analysing the way in which tourists experience the services they buy. Aspects have been identified which tend to provide satisfaction, while other approaches to service provision are considered to be more likely to lead to disappointment, with consequent ill-effects for all concerned. Often, these service failures can be traced to inappropriate management decisions. These may be about the promotion of service benefits which cannot be delivered, the setting of inappropriate quality standards, or the adoption of poor monitoring systems. But another set of weaknesses can arise from environmental influences on the service system, particularly regulation by government or other bodies. Of course, such interventions can be justified on various grounds, including the protection of consumers, employees or other interest groups. Furthermore, government participation in the tourism system can have beneficial effects through co-ordinated development and more effective promotional campaigns, as a coherent policy framework is set out.

The nature of companies' market place relationships with other organizations and clients is characterized by varying degrees of competition, and it has been suggested that this often gives the impetus for service enhancements based on an understanding of customers' evolving expectations. But as the Director of the German National Tourist Office in London has pointed out in the Preface to this book, stable economic social and political conditions, and personal freedoms are prerequisites for the devleopment of a consistent tourism sector. Many destinations experience problems in one or more of these respects, with consequent disruptions to their tourism sector.

The next section of this book provides a dozen case studies illustrating the complex and changing realities with which managers from various tourism sectors have to deal.

Questions

1 Identify the restrictions under which managers of any tourism sector with which you are familiar have to operate and analyse the effects on service standards.

2 Distinguish between the appropriate level of local or central government control over established tourism destinations in contrast to a new development in an area which has not previously had a tourism sector of any significance.

3 Discuss the factors which foster or inhibit the overall development of the tourism industry. To the extent that you consider its growth is limited, is this a matter of concern?

Recommended reading

Brent Ritchie, J.R. and Goeldner, C.R. *Travel, Tourism and Hospitality Research,* John Wiley and Sons, New York, 1987

Doganis, R. *Flying Off Course, the Economics of International Airlines,* George Allen and Unwin, London, 1985

Richter, L.K. *Politics of Tourism in Asia,* University of Hawaii Press, Honolulu, 1989

Witt, S.F. and Moutinho, L. *Tourism Marketing and Management Handbook,* Prentice Hall, Hemel Hempstead, 1989

PART TWO

Service Management Case Studies

Marketing Tourism to the State of Hawaii

Introduction

In 1987 the State of Hawaii had a resident population of 1062000, but received 5.8 million visitors; its tourist arrival count had increased for the seventh year running. Tourism has become increasingly important in the economy of the State, accounting for 9 per cent of the State gross product in 1963; 18 per cent in 1973; and 24 per cent in 1983. By 1987, over a third of employment and of personal income in Hawaii depended on the tourism industry (*State of Hawaii Data Book*, 1987).

Development of tourism to Hawaii

High volume tourism really began with the introduction of jet aircraft on routes to the Pacific island State in February 1960. Before that, the flight from the West coast of America, by unpressurized DC4, had taken about 14 hours, and many tourists at that time travelled by ocean liner. However, in February 1960, United Airlines began to operate DC8 jets between New York and Honolulu, and from Chicago. The Pacific sector now took less than six hours. Qantas and Pan Am also initiated jet services linking America with Australia and Japan through Hawaii, and the airlines began major promotional efforts to fill their greatly increased capacity to carry passengers to and from the islands. From a quarter of a million arrivals in 1959, tourism increased within seven years by a factor of four, and rose again from 1 million in 1967 to 2 million in 1972. By the end of the 1980s about 6 million tourists visited Hawaii annually. Table A1 shows the increasing rate of development of tourism in Hawaii.

Improved air transport has made Hawaii accessible from all continents. Hawaii's central Pacific location, its scenery, climate and complex history of settlement from many nations, combine to make the islands an attractive holiday destination for both American and Asian travellers, and it is an important business centre for the Pacific region's thriving economies.

Table A1   Development of Hawaii's
visitor industry

Year	Visitors	Spending $m.
1927	17451	8.2
1937	21987	9.5
1947	25000	12.1
1957	168829	77.6
1967*	1124818	380
1977	3433667	1845
1987	5799830	6600

*Base of series changed; all expenditure
figures in current dollars.

Westbound Visitor Survey, 1987

For statistical purposes the Hawaii Visitor Bureau (HVB) categorizes its tourists into Westbound (that is, arriving from America), and Eastbound. The main sources of tourism business for Hawaii are the American mainland and Japan. Japanese tourists accounted for about 12 per cent of visitors in 1987, while the 117000 Europeans who visited the Islands represented a 70 per cent increase over the previous year. Europeans were still only 3 per cent of total visitors to Hawaii; 66000 were British, while the 63000 German visitors had more than doubled over 1986. A report in the *Travel Trade Gazette* identified nine airlines providing services between the UK and Hawaii in 1989. The same article listed some 30 tour operators offering packages to, or including Hawaii from Britain. Most were small operations, carrying between 600 and 2000 clients, the largest had 3500. Seventy per cent of tourists from the UK were said to visit Hawaii as an add-on to a visit to the West Coast of America.

California, Washington, New York, Illinois and Texas together produced 52 per cent of Hawaii's US visitors. Table A2 summarizes the findings of a study of tourists arriving in Hawaii from America and provides a contrast spanning the decade between 1977 and 1987. The methodology for this survey was based on a combination of monthly reports, supplied by carriers, and questionnaire forms distributed for the HVB on trans-Pacific flights. In 1987 about 62 per cent of

Table A2   Profile of visitors to Hawaii,
(west bound) 1977 compared with 1987

Age	1977	1987
Under 19	13%	14%
20–29	22	23
30–39	22	20
40–49	18	18
50–59	14	13
Over 60	11	12

continued

Table A2 continued

	1977	1987
Travel arrangements		
Organized tour group	42%	15%
Individual	57	79
Incentive	–	6
Government and military	0.5	0.5
Male	44	45
Female	55	55
Length of stay (intended)		
2 to 6 days	8	9
7 to 12	62	68
13 to 18	24	18
19 to 24	3	3
More than 24 days	2	2
Purpose of visit		
Pleasure	78	82
Business	2	2
Business and pleasure	9	10
Government and military	0.5	0.5
Visiting relatives	4	3
Convention	5	2
Accommodation		
Hotel	92	80
Condominium	1	10
Hotel and condo	–	3
Friend or relative's home	6	5
Occupation (head of party)		
Professional and technical	33	38
Business, managerial	25	25
Clerical	11	9
Retired	13	14
Students	4	4
Number of visits to Hawaii		
1st trip	59	50
2nd	17	19
3rd	7	9
4th or more	16	21
(percentages rounded up)		

passengers disembarking in Hawaii from America completed the HVB information form and a 10 per cent sample was taken for analysis. The results were then adjusted for passengers who had not completed the form, based on carriers' figures.

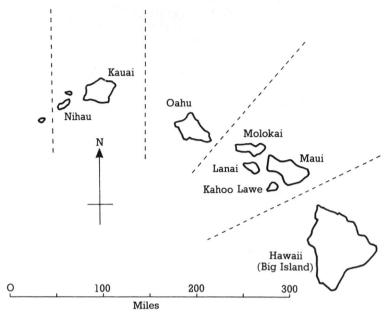

Figure A1 Hawaiian islands

Roles of the Hawaii Visitor Bureau

Tourism activity is centred on Waikiki in the County of Honolulu (see Figure A1). Of the 69 000 tourist accommodation units in the State registered by the Hawaii Visitor Bureau in 1987, 37 800 were on Oahu. Each of the six main islands in the Hawaiian archipelago has its own attractions, and the promotion of tourism to Hawaii has both competitive and collaborative strands. The primary role of the HVB is to promote tourist visits to the state. In addition to this generic marketing each of the destination areas, as well as the main Hotel groups, car rental companies and inter-island airlines, promote their own services. Tourism is becoming increasingly important for the outer islands of Kauai, Maui and Hawaii, 'the Big Island'; developments on the Big Island are considered in two other case studies, B and C.

Marketing planning

At the time this case study was prepared, the State's dominant status as a Pacific destination seemed less secure. Alternatives such as northern Queensland were gaining awareness in the main tourist generating regions amongst both trade and consumers. New aircraft technology could erode Honolulu's significance as a refuelling point for trans-Pacific traffic. Against that, the opportunity of the 1990s promises to be regional direct long-haul flights at relatively low unit cost, making Hawaii accessible from an increased number of origin points. A report in

Travel Trade Gazette at the end of 1989 indicated that non-stop charter flights from London by MD11 aircraft were under consideration.

The Strategic Marketing Plan for the State of Hawaii called for a diversification in the State's visitor marketing mix, the enhancement of its current markets, and new initiatives. Fifteen per cent ($1.2m) of the HVB 1987-8 budget was earmarked for 'the development of new world-wide markets and specific Hawaii island destinations'. For the future, the HVB was charged to 'select and target markets based on constantly updated research'. Thirty-seven per cent of its 1988-9 budget was to be devoted to new market development initiatives. The following quotations are drawn from the State's strategic marketing plan (1988).

> The tourism focus is changing from maintaining market share in established markets to developing new markets and new market segments. The new approach takes into account the quality and value of the visitor segment desired. This means we are attempting to place more emphasis on higher spending visitors, new visitors who are likely to be repeat customers, visitors who will come in off-peak seasons, a diversified geographic visitor base and visitors who will come to Hawaii during adverse economic times. It appears the best interests of the state lie with low, steady rates of growth which are consistent through all seasons and protect the economy against large fluctuations in revenues and employment . . .
>
> Marketing segments must be broken down in more detail than previously. Instead of looking for generic upscale visitors, it is necessary to pinpoint the expectations and vacation desires of specific groups. (Hawaii State Department of Business and Economic Development Strategic Marketing Plan 'Tourism' 1988)

State funding for the work of the HVB was increased in response to the developments on the islands and in the face of new competitor destinations, and the opportunities to develop new markets for tourism to Hawaii. This is shown in Table A3.

Table A3   Growth in HVB funding by the State of Hawaii

1987-8	$12.3m
1988-9	16
1989-90	21

Influences on visitors to Hawaii

A number of factors influenced Hawaii's visitor arrivals. The 1987 year for American tourists started slowly as a result of the drop in stock market prices and competition from other destinations. The main increase was Eastbound traffic, particularly from Japan. It was reported that 69 250 passengers arrived in Honolulu on Japan Airlines' 237 flights during August 1989, an increase of 18 per cent over the previous year for the carrier. It seemed that this was due in part to the negative effects on tourism to China of the events in Tiananmen Square that June, with the result that many Japanese tourists sought alternative destinations. At the same time, relaxation of the American visa regulations meant that Japanese citizens could take an instant decision to visit the USA. Hawaii was the top destination for Japanese tourists, but as only 7 per cent of the population have travelled overseas there is still a large potential (*Honolulu Star Bulletin*, 30 August 1989).

Distribution of visitor activity in Hawaii

The amount and patterns of spending differed between west bound visitors staying on Oahu, and those visiting neighbour islands in 1978, as indicated in Table A4.

Table A4   Visitor spending on the islands of Hawaii

Expenditure purpose	Oahu	Other islands
Accommodation	$37.62	$54.37
Restaurants	$15.41	$18.53
Dinner shows	2.87	1.01
Night clubs	1.88	1.60
Groceries	2.15	2.67
All food and beverage	$22.31	$23.81
Attractions	6.10	5.66
Entertainment	0.86	1.96
All entertainment	$6.96	$7.62
Bus, etc. fares	0.85	0.67
Self drive cars	2.37	5.42
Inter-island travel	1.92	18.87
Sightseeing tours	3.06	3.92
All transport	$8.20	$28.88
Clothing	8.95	6.43
Gifts and souvenirs	8.70	7.15
Other spending	6.13	6.32
Total		
Average spending per visitor per day	**$99.05**	**$125.58**

Source: HVB Visitor Expenditure Survey, 1987

Perceptions of Hawaii

The increased advertising budget, and a creative cooperative campaign with key airlines and tour operators carried the message of Hawaii's attractions to a widening audience. A new slogan, COME TO LIFE IN HAWAII, was adopted.

Extracts from the media plan which was prepared in the form of a calendar are given in Table A5.

However, the marketing power of major resort developers also heightened awareness of Hawaii as a vacation destination. Hyatt operated five resorts in the Islands, and was reported to be expecting $500m. sales by 1991. To create awareness on this scale, the organization invested $12m. in its promotion for its

Table A5   Come to life in Hawaii, Hawaii Visitors Bureau Marketing and Advertising Calendar

	August 1989	*September 1989*
US Travel Trade and Consumer Shows	Spotlight on Hawaii, Woodland Hills San Diego Bridal Bazaar Huddle West, Reno	Hawaiian Airlines/Big Island
US Meetings and Conventions Trade Shows	American Society of Association Executives Boston	Boston Quest Trade Show, Atlanta JCP Golf and Tennis Classis, Oahu Incentive Travel and Meeting Executive Show, Chicago
International Trade Shows	Australia Sales Caravan Agent Canada, Vancouver	Canada Premium Incentive Travel Show, Toronto Korea World Travel Fair Travel Agents Association of New Zealand
Research Reports	Monthly Research Report, Monthly US Mainland Visitor Origin Study Top 20, Quarterly Metro Production Report	Monthly Research Report Monthly US Mainland Visitor Origin Report
HVB Publications	*Hawaiian Beat*	*Hawaiian Beat*
US Consumer Advertising	(JULY) **New market newspapers** Sunday, 9 July *Boston Globe* *Buffalo News* *Chicago Sun Times* *Cleveland Plain Dealer* (partial list)	*Pacific Travelogue* *Travel and leisure* **Base market newspapers** Sunday, 10 September *Denver Post* *LA Daily News* *Los Angeles Times* *Long Beach Press Telegram* (partial list)
International Advertising	*Travel Week Australia*	*Canada Travel Press*

Source: HVB Marketing Calendar, 1989-90

181

Hawaiian properties, and has an international sales and representation network to service trade or consumer enquiries. Such resorts, and their marketing communications, are targeted at new and affluent visitors, with two potentially difficult consequences for the HVB. There is a fear that Hawaii will increasingly be perceived as an expensive destination, or alternatively that its image will no longer match that of many of its existing visitors. Secondly, a high proportion of the new entrants working in the travel industry, particularly at retail agency level, are unfamiliar with Hawaii, and therefore are not able to provide accurate information to influence their clients' decisions.

In 1989 a newly appointed Director of Market Research explained the need for the HVB to understand their tourists' reasons for visiting Hawaii:

> Visitor counts and expenditure surveys are historical snapshots. The new focus is on traveller motivations, awareness, attitudes and behaviour . . . to forecast trends and find market niches. (*Honolulu Star Bulletin,* 23 July 1989)

Questions

1 Which destinations can be regarded as competitors to Hawaii?

2 Prepare an outline SWOT analysis for Hawaii's visitor industry and discuss the benefits of a strategic planning approach to its marketing.

3 Based on the information provided in this case study, and an examination of current tour brochures, what market segmentation possibilities can you identify?

Relevant chapters

2, 4, 5 and 6.

Planning Responses to Tourism Investment Proposals for the Big Island of Hawaii

Introduction

This case study examines the way in which the authorities in a major tourist destination responded to the conflicting interests of developers, tourists and residents, within the culture of enterprise and consultation which is characteristic of American society.

Tourism development in the Big Island of Hawaii

A context to the probable impact of proposals for a six-fold or greater increase in visitor accommodation in an attractive and relatively undeveloped rural area of the Big Island can be gained from earlier experiences in Waikiki:

> Tourism's development was dramatic. It grew from an enthusiastic roar by the 1950s to a resounding crescendo in the 1960s when concrete monoliths were constructed in every available space. Still, from a room count of 10 700 in 1967 the number grew to 25 000 in a little more than a decade. The rate of increase was unbelievably fast until 1971 when growth flattened out after most areas, zoned appropriately, had been taken up. By this time two new regulations were enforced; apparently foreknowledge of these encouraged the earlier frantic activity. (Farrel, 1982)

Concerns resulting from tourism proposals

The scale of expansion of tourist activity proposed for the West Hawaii area caused a variety of concerns for local and State officials, summarized in Table B1.

Table B1   Government concerns

1 Projected visitor forecasts suggest that demand will not support the expanded tourism stock at the prices intended by the developers
2 The region has insufficient residents to staff the proposed developments and in general they lack the qualifications and experience for managerial job opportunities
3 All aspects of the infrastructure will have to be expanded to support the increased visitor and resident populations which will result from even partial implementation of the planned resort developments
4 The State and County will have to finance the infrastructure improvements ahead of any additional tax revenues which might flow from the developments

Source: derived by the author from Hawaii state documents

Residents have expressed many reservations about the impact on their lifestyle of the proposed resort development, and the inevitable increase in tourists which the new resorts would attract to a quiet area. Formal planning consultative meetings were convened by the State to provide a forum to debate these issues, and many people wrote to express their concerns through the correspondence columns of local newspapers, as indicated in Table B2.

Table B2   Residents' concerns

1 Increasing visitor numbers will result in congestion and related problems on the Island's roads, or an expensive expansion of the existing network
2 The costs of house purchase or rental and taxes (which are based on property market value) will rise beyond the reach of the present residents under the pressure of 'immigrant' workers' demands
3 Developments are sited around the most attractive beaches and past experience of resort hotels suggests that access for local people will become more controlled than at present. The best beach areas tend to be 'reserved' for hotel guests, despite legislation intended to preserve the beaches as public areas

Sources: Public debate during State of Hawaii Planning Consultative meeting at Waimea, August 1988, and content analysis of all letters published in correspondence columns of *West Hawaii Today* during August 1988

Planning in Hawaii

In his introduction to the State Tourism Functional Plan, Governor George Airyoshi wrote,

> The Hawaii State Plan is a document second in importance only to our State constitution ... it is the only legislatively adopted state plan in the nation. It is the blueprint for Hawaii's future. It sets forth broad goals, objectives and policies to guide the long range growth and development of our State, and establishes a system for co-ordinating activities of state and county agencies towards the achievement of these common ends. This system has included the formulation of 12 State Functional plans ... (which) can be the basis for cooperation between the public and private sectors. (Hawaii State Tourism Functional Plan, 1984)

The State Plan for Hawaii builds on the General Plans of each County, and the technical State Functional Plans for the twelve major areas of activity in Hawaii specifically: agriculture; conservation lands; historic preservations; education; energy; health; higher education; housing; recreation; transportation; water resource development; and tourism.

The priorities of the State Functional Plans and the State Plan are reviewed biannually. Every four years a more comprehensive review is carried out to revise the long range goals, objectives and policies of the State. Corresponding adjustments are applied to the State budgetary decisions.

The Tourism Functional Plan

The Tourism Functional Plan recommends policies and actions for all regions of the state and proposes specific action for certain areas. Its priority guidelines recognize the pervasive nature of the visitor industry in Hawaii. In the face of the cumulative impacts generated by the rapid growth of tourism the State's aim is to protect the 'quality of life', and its concern is that private development may outpace infrastructure investment. The main objective for the State Tourism Functional Plan is to facilitate '. . . a visitor industry that constitutes a major component of steady growth for Hawaii's economy'. Action programmes are recommended for the lead agencies responsible for each of its four major concerns: tourism promotion; physical development; employment and career development; and community relations.

Each State Functional Plan identifies both links and potential conflicts with other planning domains. For example, the housing needs of future employees in the tourism sector will impose quantifiable demands on the Housing Functional Plan, while the training needs of the industry are linked through the State Higher Education Functional plan to developments recommended for the University of Hawaii School of Travel Industry Management; and expansion and curriculum changes in the Community Colleges. In contrast, changes in land usage resulting from resort developments place tourism in potential competition with agriculture and recreation planning.

The West Hawaii Regional Plan

At the local level, the West Hawaii Regional Plan is expressed in terms of a vision for the region. The direction and commitments towards which the State will work are grouped into four main objectives, shown in Table B3.

Table B3   Objectives of the regional plan

1 To co-ordinate state activities in the region to gain the most effective response to emerging needs and critical problems
2 To address areas of state concern
3 To co-ordinate the Capital Improvements Program within a regional planning framework
4 To provide guidance in State land use decision-making processes

Source: West Hawaii Regional Plan

Demand and revenue projections

Most proposals for the area are for expansive and upmarket resorts such as the 1200 room Hyatt Waikaloa which opened in September 1988. Statewide hotel occupancy for 1987 was reported as 81 per cent; Waikiki, which has most of the rooms, runs at about 87 per cent. But the more expensive resorts are believed to experience much lower occupancy, thus there is grave concern at Government level about their long-term viability as major local employers and their ability to generate forecast tax revenue. An additional concern identified in Case Study A is that the advertising budgets of individual resorts can exceed State capabilities, and the fear is that the resultant perception of Hawaii as an expensive destination will reduce all traffic. (Sources: Hawaii Visitor Bureau Annual Research Report, 1987, various tables, and discussions with State officials, and resort managers.)

Demographic, employment and income effects

In Hawaii, developers are required to submit environmental impact statements to the Government as part of the planning process. Projections based on computerized modelling of the impacts of selected developments in the region suggest that 46 000 jobs would be created if all resort plans were fulfilled.

The 1986 resident population of the whole of the Big Island was 111 800, having virtually doubled since 1970. In that period the resident population of West Hawaii had increased threefold, to 33 per cent of the Island population. The surplus above present unemployment of job vacancies resulting from further resort development would create a significant demand for housing from people moving into the area attracted by employment opportunities. It is believed that perhaps as many as 32 000 extra homes will be needed, and projections suggest that West Hawaii will become home to 45 per cent of the Big Island population by the year 2005.

In July 1987 there were 43 000 'housing units' on the Island, with an average vacancy rate of 6 per cent. But in Kona, the main conurbation in West Hawaii, only 1 per cent were vacant. The two employment growth sectors for the area are services and retailing. Both sectors are categorized in the West Hawaii Plan as 'dominated by lower wage jobs'. The cost of housing in the area is high and with low wages in the tourism sector the regional plan forecast that 75 per cent of all households might qualify for government housing assistance by the end of this century.

A further implication of the developments is an increase in demand for specialized skills training provision, and a change in general education curricula towards service sector (and certain other) skills.

Alternative development strategies

The West Hawaii Plan calls attention to opportunities for diversifying the region's economic base. It suggests that the area's natural energy resources (geothermal, wind, solar and ocean thermal) could underpin initiatives in aquaculture, high technology research and diversified agriculture, thus partially counteracting the effects on per capita income of a significant increase in the region's low wage sectors. The Big Island's traditional agricultural market for sugar has collapsed and new markets are being sought for high margin products including tropical flowers, macadamia nuts, coffee and papayas. This development depends mainly on enhanced airport and air transport facilities currently being planned to provide fast, regular and direct access to Mainland markets.

Access by air

The 6500 foot runway at Kona is likely to be increased to 11 500 in the hope that mainland and international carriers will operate into the Big Island. At present only one airline provides a direct service from the West Coast of America, and there are no customs facilities at the airport. Virtually all passengers and most freight traffic is routed via the State's international airport at Honolulu, where passengers transfer to one of the two main inter-island carriers.

This interruption to the journey increases passengers' uncertainty after a long trans-Pacific flight, and passage across several time zones, and causes extra delay and expense. An improved and expanded airport facility at Kona is regarded as a key to the fuller development of the West Hawaii region's tourism and exporting industries.

Infrastructure

Ahead of the anticipated expansion of resident and visitor populations, a wide range of projects are needed to maintain the present quality of community lifestyles and values, and to ensure that the area remains a quality visitor destination. Achieving those aims is thought likely to result in continuing growth for the region which will put more pressure on the environment. State lands might be released for public infrastructure development, but against the scale of investment required for the projects indicated in Table B4, present budgeting is inadequate.

Between 1983 and 1987 infrastructure investment for the area had totalled $24m. but the scale of resort development under discussion, together with the consequent expansion in resident populations would require an investment of $622m. The regional plan commented, 'The general consensus among State agencies is that the State will have difficulty in providing all necessary services and infrastructure'.

The timing of private sector developments is a matter of entrepreneurial judgement, but the resultant uncertainty poses a problem for State planning and decisions. The State will have to fund much of the infrastructure development needed if new resorts are to succeed, and might expect to recover the investment from the increasing flow of tax revenues. However, if developers were to decide to postpone (or withdraw) their proposals, the region would not be able to support the investment costs from existing taxes.

Table B4   Infrastructure estimates

	$m.
Airport expansion	156
Major road improvement	106
Harbours	36
Hospitals	12
Library	14
Police and emergency services	28
Schools	72
Water supply	47
Sewage	25
Drainage	55
Solid waste	5
Recreation and parks	65
Total public infrastructure estimate:	**$622m**

Source: West Hawaii Plan, Appendix C

About 80 per cent of planned units are in rural areas lacking support populations and resources. Thus the inflow of people seeking employment will further strain the local infrastructure. 'This situation has led to a co-ordinated State effort . . . to balance rapid economic growth with the need to have quality services, programs, and resources in place' (West Hawaii Plan).

The nodal solution

Individual resort plans exploit the many attractive sites along the coast. Figure B1 illustrates the resultant sprawl of development. This conflicts with the State's overriding objectives; including the provision of open spaces and recreation areas, and the protection of heritage sites, many of which are located along the coastal areas of West Hawaii. The West Hawaii Plan proposes a solution based on clustering new resorts around existing developments, which would also minimize infrastructure costs. The nodal solution is illustrated in Figure B2. These nodes would become employment centres and to succeed will require mass transport, day care and employment training facilities.

A further problem for the State authorities is to determine the probable and desirable levels of development. The three steps which were taken are shown in Table B5.

The nodal concept proposed by the West Hawaii Plan would accommodate about 22 000 resort units. That is about 10 000 less than the total currently planned by individual developers, but this still represents a threefold increase to existing tourism stock. The Plan considers three alternative scenarios for resort development and recommends the nodal approach as it will best enable the quality of visitors' and residents' experiences to be maximized. This concept was put to developers and residents in the form of a draft regional plan for discussion during late 1988.

Figure B1 The West Hawaii region showing actual and planned developments

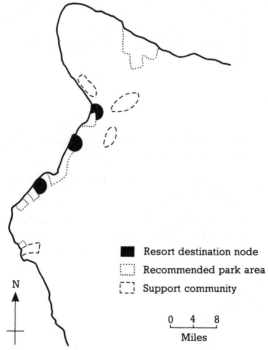

Figure B2 The nodal planning solution for West Hawaii development

Table B5   Determining development levels

1 To identify all planned resort developments
2 To identify those falling in the recommended resort nodes
3 To estimate the resort developments within those nodes likely to be completed by 2005. This is based on:
  a) forecast market conditions
  b) availability of finance

Source: West Hawaii Plan

Planning issues

Two main issues emerge from the six-fold increase in tourism activity in West Hawaii proposed by individual developers. One is the vast infrastructure improvements which would be required. Necessary work includes roads, water, energy, sewage, housing and social support systems such as schools, clinics and police. As the existing local population cannot fill the job opportunities to be created, the expanded infrastructure will also have to support a significantly increased resident population.

The second issue concerns the vision of the future towards which the State is striving, including the preservation of the area's many natural and cultural attractions for both its resident and visitor populations.

In summing up, the draft West Hawaii Plan calls for a more moderate and balanced development to meet the State vision. The solution proposed is based on the location of all future tourism developments around a number of nodes which will become the focus of major infrastructure investment. This solution implies a limit to the increase in visitor accommodation, and consultations with all interested groups are being carried out.

Questions

1 Identify the stakeholders in the development proposals outlined in this case study, and discuss how their interests might be identified and protected.

2 Who, in your opinion, should finance the infrastructure required for this type of development to succeed?

3 How do you account for the 'upmarket' nature of all the developments for this area? Do you consider this to be a cause for concern?

Relevant chapters

1, 10, 11 and 12.

Marketing Tourism to the Big Island

Introduction

The island of Hawaii is the largest in the American State of the same name and identifies itself to tourists as The Big Island. It is 4038 square miles in area and had a population in 1986 of 111 800.

Tourism is regarded on the Big Island of Hawaii as the major antidote to the declining agricultural sector. Facilities are concentrated on the Kona and Kohala coasts of West Hawaii which is considered one of the most attractive tourist areas in the State, both for developers and visitors. Three-quarters of the Island's total visitor accommodation is located in West Hawaii which had 5800 units in 1988. 3874 are classified as hotel units, and 1916 as resort residential units.

Tourist attractions on the Big Island

In addition to the delights typical of tropical islands Hawaii, the Big Island, has desert areas, alpine pastures and the largest privately owned ranch in the USA, which is now developing a range of visitor facilities. Visitors to the Big Island can enjoy a surprising variety of attractions including active volcanoes and private art collections. Several industries, including coffee mills, orchid nurseries and macadamia nut processing facilities have visitor centres offering formal interpretation, selected viewing of the processes, and products for sale.

Recently a 48 passenger submersible craft began ferrying tourists and locals to depths of 200 feet where ex-oil industry divers explain the colourful sights of the reef. The geothermal energy plant offers visitors an interpretation programme and, among the observatories in the University of Hawaii campus on the 13 000 foot summit of Mauna Kea, is a small optical telescope where amateur astronomers can join guided visits for night-time star gazing. At the 9000 feet level a visitor centre has been dedicated to a Hawaiian astronaut who died in the Challenger space shuttle disaster.

The effects of the development of major resorts in the Kona region can be seen in Table C1, which shows room rates and occupancy for the State and for Kona in July of 1988 (while the Royal Waikoloa resort was still under construction) and in July 1989, after its opening.

Table C1   Room rates and occupancy, July, Hawaii and Kona Coast

	Average rates		Average occupancy	
	1988	1989	1988	1989
State	$81	$90	81%	81%
Kona	$85	$124	56%	64%

Source: Summary of Pannell Kerr Foster report published in the
Honolulu Advertiser, 29 August 1989

Marketing the island of Hawaii

Until the mid 1980s the Big Island had been promoted by as many as seven organizations representing various tourism sectors or regions. There had also been some confusion about the name of the island, which some organizations promoted as the Orchid Island while others referred to it as the Volcano Island.

During 1984, a simple survey was conducted to establish the strength of the Big Island's image. Some 300 visitors to tourism promotional shows around America who approached the Hawaiian stands were asked if they had visited the Big Island, and what they had enjoyed most about it. The majority named attractions such as the *Arizona,* a warship sunk in the notorious Japanese air raid on Pearl Harbour, now a memorial, which is actually on another island, Oahu, near Waikiki.

Most marketing funds had been spent from Honolulu, in the generic promotion of tourism for all of the State of Hawaii. In 1985, when a Big Island Chapter (branch) of the Hawaii Visitors' Bureau was formed to promote the island, it was allocated $10 000 for promotion and further funds for its operations from central State budgets.

The organizational challenge was to integrate all marketing efforts for the Big Island, and this was achieved by arranging for all interests to be represented on the Chapter Marketing Committee. The key issue to be addressed was to redefine the identity of the Big Island as part of, but different from, the State of Hawaii.

Promotion by the Big Island and other counties of Hawaii were now encouraged within overall state tourism objectives. The funding voted by the State senate for promotion increased rapidly under the pressure of County lobbying for the surplus from hotel room taxes, as shown in Table C2. The $512 000 allocated in 1989 compared with $700 000 for Maui and $450 000 for Kauai.

Table C2 Growth of State funding for Big Island marketing	
1986	$50,000
1987	$175,000
1988	$200,000
1989	$512,000

The Chapter's role is to promote the generic concept of Big Island tourism; other organizations continue to promote specific aspects such as resorts, hotels and excursions. The Chapter operates by getting private sector support for specific activities, typically seeking one or more partners to match its advertising spending. In such cases the promotion has to be seen to be beneficial to the island as a whole.

An example of the leveraged spending that can be developed was the budget for certain tourism shows at which the Big Island is represented. The Chapter's initial $50000 was doubled by a contribution from the Kohala coast resorts, and that total itself was matched by a contribution of $100000 from United Airlines, giving a working budget of $200000. These shows enable Chapter staff and delegates from the contributing organizations to meet 10000 travel agents in a year.

Other activities of the Chapter have included commissioning a logo for the Big Island, which led to the granting of a concession for T-shirts, and the production of a range of tourism publications for visitors and the trade.

Big Island Information Guide

The Information Guide is a key resource for travel agents, providing information on all the tourism activities on the Island. Details of up to five Chapter members providing each type of activity are given, but for minority interests which are not served by Chapter members, one non-member is listed. The guide also presents a general introduction to the geography, history and climate of the Big Island. It lists a wide range of accommodation including hotels, condos, B&B, cabins, home rental, and retreats. Restaurants are classified under the subheadings of American, coffee shops, continental, fastfood, oriental, and so on.

The transport operators include car rental, taxi, airtour, cycle, and limousine. Greeting, ground handling and four-wheel drive tour operators are listed. Activities include art/craft, attractions, beach sports, bird watching, boating, camping, diving, fishing, golf, hiking, hunting, horse riding, luaus, museums, parasailing, snowskiing, submarine rides, surf sports, tennis, whale watching and windsurfing.

Hawaiian products are featured, especially coffee and macadamia nuts. These products are a reason to visit the Island and are popular promotional give-aways at trade fairs. Banking services, medical facilities and so on are also listed. An annual calendar of events is included in the Information Guide. Some two thousand enquiries are generated by the Big Island's print advertising each month – the Guide is the fulfilment piece mailed in response to enquiries.

Parker Ranch diversification

One of the interesting tourism attractions on the Big Island is tours to the house and estate of the Parker Ranch. The ranch was founded in 1847 by John Palmer Parker who had been befriended by King Kamehameha and married his granddaughter in 1816. Parker showed the King how to domesticate the wild cattle and horses which had been brought to the Island and in return he was granted land rights.

Now, the ranch occupies 225 000 acres, stretching from the Pacific to the high pastures of the volcano. The present owner is Richard Smart, once a Broadway star, and a direct descendant of John Palmer Parker. The estate regards itself as a part of the Hawaiian heritage and has donated land for an airport, the observatory headquarters, civic centres, and other community developments. Many estate staff are fourth generation and a plan (Parker Ranch 2020), has been developed 'to ensure that what occurs on these lands is consistent with the goals of the community'.

The ranch has 50 000 head of cattle, and accounts for a third of the State's beef production and a tenth of its consumption, but the management has decided to diversify from the fluctuating red meat market. The first step was to lease part of the estate beachfront to Rockerfeller for a luxury resort development in order to create work for the region; the Mauna Kea Hotel opened in 1965.

The original estate home, an impressive log-built house, has been transplanted to a site adjacent to the modern family home, and restored. Now it is a family showcase of original documents and photos. The new house has a good collection of impressionist paintings, and both were opened to the public in 1987.

Tours of the estate have been established to enable visitors to see the unique ranch. The tourism staff are drawn mainly from the ranch, and give visitors a graphic insight into a day in the life of modern cowboys. This is achieved through a visitor centre in the town and a short tour through the corrals to a converted stable; the main work of the ranch takes place in remote locations which at present are inaccessible to tourists. The ranch is centred on a small town and does not suffer from the general shortage of labour in the State. Instead, the ranch managers have to maintain a balance between creating new work, and drawing cowboys away from the main tasks of the ranch.

Further developments are planned, including wagon rides, and mini rodeos for incentive groups, and the small hotel in the town is being expanded. A unique opportunity will occur in 1991. A full solar eclipse will be visible from the upper ranch. Plans are being prepared to entertain 20 000 visitors, who will benefit from technical presentations by the astronomers working in the summit observatories. The optical fibre lines from the observatories will be tapped to feed large screen video of the eclipse, which will also be transmitted live by two major television networks, ABC and CNN. The resultant free nationwide publicity is important to the ranch.

Interest in the eclipse is such that all hotel and tour bus capacity was reserved two years ahead. This provided the cue for the ranch to establish a special package. Accommodation together with catering and the facilities necessary for 20 000 visitors staying for two or three days will be provided in a specially built, temporary tented village high on the mountain pastures. In order to avoid pressure on the regular tour operators, and as the eclipse happens to fall in the school holiday period the ranch has contracted 150 school buses for a week. The event is expected to be both educational and fun.

Questions

1 What advantages can you suggest for any area to market its tourism differently from the region of which it is part, and what limits do you see to this strategy?

2 How do you account for the data shown in Table C1, and A4, and what implications has this for the Big Island's marketing strategies?

3 Drawing on the information presented in Cases A, B and C, propose a marketing plan for the Big Island some years in the future.

Relevant chapters

1, 2, 6, 10, 11 and 12.

CASE STUDY D

Issues in Developing Tourism to Tibet

(Part of this case study was presented in Vancouver, October 1988 at the conference 'Tourism, A Vital Force For Peace'.)

Introduction

The attractions of Tibet include magnificent temples set in soaring mountains, vivid under compelling sky scapes, and high altitude pastureland contrasting with colourful gardens and spectacular ceremonies. In 1980 Tibet first became accessible to tourists joining organized groups, shortly after the Peoples Republic of China itself began to accept tourists. The first tourist groups to visit Tibet were carefully supervized and, although individual travellers were later allowed entry, the need to obtain a permit from the authorities in addition to a Chinese visa effectively limited their numbers. Statistics published by China's tourism administration show that arrivals built up gradually; 1500 tourists visited Tibet in 1986. In part, this early rationing of the Tibetan tourism experience seems to have been a policy response to the limited resources considered suitable for Western visitors, particularly transport, accommodation and guides.

Early in 1987 tourism to Tibet seemed to enter a new phase when Lhasa was declared open to anyone with a Chinese visa. 35 000 tourists arrived in that year and plans called for 80 000 visitors annually by 1990. However, the political climate within China changed radically after the events in Tiananmen Square in 1989, and taken together with civil unrest in Tibet those targets seem unlikely to be achieved.

Importance of the tourism industry in Tibet

Tourism had been introduced as both an economic and a social tool in the developments which are reshaping the way of life in Tibet. The Chinese authorities in Tibet regarded tourism as part of their strategies to attain the four modernizations of industry, agriculture, defence and technology. Tourism could contribute to the development of Tibet in two main ways: tourists would bring foreign exchange, and their presence would speed the move towards decentralization which was one of the planks of Chinese policy in Tibet at the time.

Tourists expect familiar standards of comfort and service: meeting their demands stimulated investment in the infrastructure and required training for local recruits to the industry in both technical skills and awareness of visitors' different expectations. Tourists' spending power encouraged the establishment of small enterprises. Their interest in Tibet's cultural traditions gave administrators an important rationale for the preservation of Tibet's remaining religious centres, and for investment in schemes to develop remote areas of the vast, beautiful country.

To support this new business significant investment in tourism infrastructure was planned. The few airports, roads and hotels which had been constructed during the previous two decades were upgraded. New roads and hotels were being built or planned. The primary objective of certain investments was to improve tourists' experiences, but they also conferred benefits on local people. Other infrastructure improvements such as air transport, electricity supplies and plumbing were part of the community development programme, but also had the effect of improving conditions for tourists. A variety of financing and management schemes were offered by the Chinese government and Tibetan business interests, some in collaboration with foreign investors. In common with moves throughout China, training programmes for guides, drivers and hotel staff were initiated.

Travel to Tibet

Difficult access is one of the major problems any travel destination seeking to attract tourists must overcome. Tibet is one of the most difficult countries to reach, as it spreads northwards from the Himalaya Mountains into the great deserts of central Asia. Its capital, Lhasa, lies in a fertile valley at nearly 12 000 feet, and is one of the lowest points in the country. There is also a political aspect to Tibet's isolation which is rooted in its ancient religious and social systems; until the Chinese occupation its traditional patterns of life had remained virtually unaltered for centuries. This remoteness, and Tibet's colourful, ancient culture is attractive to many tourists.

There are two major routes into Lhasa and both cause significant problems to travellers. Tibet's land border with Nepal was opened in March 1985; the grandeur of the scenery and the exhilaration of a challenging three or four day journey across passes reaching 17 000 feet in altitude attracted many adventurous travellers. However, tourists planning itineraries to Tibet had to expect delays, alterations and even the cancellation of their journey. The Nepal–Tibet border road was washed out for weeks during May 1987 and again in July: tour companies warned intending travellers of the necessity for long arduous walking at high altitude with their luggage.

The problems for the majority of travellers who arrived by plane via Chengdu were different. Even with reservations, it was difficult to get seats on the daily Boeing 707 flight. From Gongaar airport the hotel or airline bus takes about two hours on good roads to make the journey into Lhasa through interesting rather than breathtaking scenery. But passengers were not permitted to claim their luggage at the airport, and CAAC, the only carrier operating into Lhasa seemed unable to arrange delivery of luggage to the hotels until the day after arrival. Altitude affects people to different extents, and several days may be needed to acclimatize to the 12 000 feet altitude for those arriving from sea level. (The manager of the Lhasa Hotel pointed out that complimentary piped oxygen was available and is often used in guest rooms.)

The Lhasa Hotel – improving service standards

The Lhasa Hotel provides an interesting case study which encapsulates many of the challenges and opportunities facing tourism in Tibet. (This section is based on interviews with the Hotels' managers in 1987.) The Lhasa Hotel had been built as one of five projects to mark the twentieth anniversary of the founding of the Tibet Autonomous Region. The prefabricated building was started in April 1984 and opened in September 1985. It has 486 twin rooms offering two standards of comfort at two rack rates, plus two self-contained suites equipped to the standards expected by such visiting dignitaries as the past President of the US, Jimmy Carter. There are work shops, gardens and residential accommodation for nearly 700 staff in the hotel compound which backs onto the Norbilunka park, the Dalai Lama's traditional summer home. Despite its incongruous design, its prefabricated concrete construction and the fact that it has no direct line of view to any of the major sites in Lhasa, the hotel was awarded a national architectural award.

The Managers discussed the special challenges of bringing the flagship of Tibetan hotels up to the standards of the Holiday Inn group which had taken on the management contract. The first priority had been 'to minimize shouting by the guests', as their company had been brought in when service standards were poor. The Chinese 'iron rice bowl' policy had made it very hard to sack staff: 98 per cent of the people working in the Lhasa Hotel at that time had to be retained by the new management. The turn-around in service standards was based on training and motivational programmes.

Training concentrated on language skills, especially English, and service skills – a totally new concept to Tibetans. Training was about basics: teaching local girls the appropriate dress for restaurant service, and emphasizing personal cleanliness. 'It was not customary for young Tibetan ladies to clean their finger nails, and in the winter they objected to covering their newly acquired jeans with the uniforms we issued, so we had to compromise by getting them to roll the legs up.'

Jobs in the hotel were considered to be prestigious because of the opportunities to meet Westerners. Pay was good by local standards and supplemented by incentive schemes and employee service recognition programmes. The dormitory was said to be the only one in Lhasa to provide central heating in the winter and staff got three meals a day plus free medical care. Staff from other hotels were also attracted to work in the Lhasa Hotel by the greater work discipline and the training opportunities offered. In July 1987 the compliment was 650 staff recruited locally, with 15 managers from Hong Kong, 28 from Beijing and five from overseas.

Tourism managers spoke of a 'golden season' in Tibet, lasting from April to September,

> At first tourists thought that winter was too hostile to come to Tibet. Now we are building the winter business with special inclusive packages which can be linked with other Holiday Inn properties throughout China. Actually it is a beautiful time of year, but it can certainly be very cold, and the roads can be cut by bad weather – but that happens at any time of the year.

The market for tourism to Tibet

Convenience and economy encouraged many visitors to join inclusive tours. Another advantage was that the tour escort had to bear the uncertainties of travelling in China. The most serious problem confronting tour managers was the loss of control over itineraries and accommodation, typical of conditions elsewhere in China, to the frustration and annoyance of their clients. The high cost of package tour itineraries which included Tibet was exacerbated by two factors common to group tourists' experiences in any area of China. Language difficulties and the often bleak modern urban landscapes intimidated many clients who, unable to sample life at a local level, remained insulated in the expensive coffee shop environments of tourist hotels. Secondly, service in those hotels (with a few notable exceptions) did not match the standards in other destinations and was often unacceptable to tourists who had travelled in other Asian countries at lower rates.

A third problem for tourists in Tibet was the pressure on limited schedules when there is so much of interest. The formidable difficulties for travellers of obtaining current information or of reaching the many fabulous minor attractions was a further argument in favour of joining a group. However, it seemed from observation that most tourists, whether independent or group participants were experienced travellers, keenly interested in the culture and the country around them and frustrated by the inevitable delays.

Although many group members were experienced travellers they were very dependent on the local group leaders for their excursion and visit schedules. However, tourists participating in group arrangements complained about the limited excursion opportunities afforded them and expressed dissatisfaction with the quality of Chinese tourist guides.

Most tourists expected to spend most of their available time visiting temples and palaces, and to take excursions into the mountainous countryside accompanied by guides who would explain the sights for them. The tourists encountered in Tibet fell into two main categories. One group comprised younger, adventurous backpackers seeking the maximum contact with local people and traditional lifestyles, and having minimum concern with comfort in accommodation or transport. These tourists were able to reach Lhasa through a window relaxing entry restrictions during much of 1987, but were the first targets for exclusion after the civil turmoil which broke out again in October 1987.

The second major category of tourists were those who required standards of comfort and certainty in their travel arrangements which more closely echoed conditions they were familiar with at home. Typically, they stayed in the Lhasa Hotel, paying American rates for standards which approximated those normal in international hotels. Few of them patronized the roadside canteens catering for local people, nor the cheap restaurants targeted at the backpackers. They tended to be strongly motivated by a keenness to visit the temples, palaces and sites during their stay and many were knowledgeable about them. These tourists included some independent travellers (who again were excluded after the October troubles), but the majority came in organized groups. Groups rather than independent travellers were welcomed back to Tibet after the riots died down, partly because of the limited accommodation and transport available, and partly it seems, because groups are more readily supervised during their stay.

It seemed that most tourists came expecting to see a special way of life consisting of colourful religious observations, spectacular scenery, unique architecture and a traditional agricultural way of life. A minority of travellers encountered in Lhasa were there because, they claimed, it was a desirable place to say they had visited.

Tibetan responses to tourism

Tibetans responded quickly to the opportunities for small enterprise offered by tourist spending pull. Shortages of milk, fruit and vegetables in the main hotels were tackled by local producers. The authorities encouraged this diversification from the traditional staple diet as a means of improving local health, and they hoped for a surplus to export to other parts of China.

In the absence of a network of town buses, transport was provided by amused farmers to tourists who happily rode in their unsprung tractor-trailer combinations to outlying temples, or around the town. The revenue from fares was said to exceed earnings from agricultural efforts, and the scale of diverted resources cast some doubt on the feasibility of meeting local agricultural production targets.

English-speaking Tibetans interviewed in Lhasa stated that they considered that tourism was a significant factor in the Chinese policy decision to protect the remaining heritage of buildings and culture. Pilgrims had traditionally donated money or jewellery to the temples, or added yak butter to the ever-burning lamps, and it seemed that tourists' contributions had quickly become a significant element in the finances of major temples. Their donations boosted centrally-funded restoration work and sustained the monks whose traditional sources of support have been eradicated. The monks were very keen to receive photos of the exiled Dalai Lama, although possession of these pictures was deemed illegal by the Chinese authorities, and were happy to pose for photos and to show foreign visitors around the temples. Many local people crowded into the temples and seemed pleased that tourists were taking an interest in their traditional pilgrimages and ceremonies.

Tibetan tourism managers and staff were keen to help tourists understand the culture, traditions and lifestyle of local people. The approach of larger Tibetan-managed enterprises was focused on enhancing visitors' experiences through knowledgeable, enthusiastic and trained staff. They were enthusiastically developing itineraries personalized to meet the interests of their clients, and welcome-packs were devised to help individuals' orientation. These were to include a white silk scarf, a traditional gift in Tibet, a schematic map of the main sites around Lhasa, and a pamphlet introducing the highlights of a stay and outlining the main features of Tibetan culture. In contrast, tourists expressed discontent with Chinese-managed tours, complaining in particular that their guides lacked empathy with Tibet's culture and knew little of traditional ways of life, such as local farming methods, or the country's religious beliefs and practices.

Increasingly, the authentic nature of travellers' encounters with Tibetan culture is changing. There were plans to simplify the traditional dances and stage them regularly at tourist hotels. Electric lighting was replacing the guttering butter-lamps in the Potala and certain of the temples and poorly prepared, hand-written signs appeared against major religious idols. It has also been suggested that the monks who are such a central feature of any visit to Tibetan temples are now often appointed by the political authorities.

Civil unrest in Tibet

In common with several other tourist destinations, Tibet is embroiled in a conflict between factions. The development of a tourism sector in Tibet cannot be considered in isolation from the conflict between Chinese and Tibetans; it seems significant to consider two aspects of Tibet's history. The first is that Tibet has long experience as a buffer between the major political (and military) players in the Asian arena, including Russia, Britain and China.

Other countries see Tibet as an attractive conquest, as is indicated by its Chinese name Xizang, which means 'Western Storehouse'. The second signficant lesson of Tibetan history is that religion has been an integral aspect of life for all Tibetans with an intensity matched in few other nations.

Tibet has experienced the full range of trauma; political, ideological, military, racial and religious, but until 1951 Tibetans had remained essentially independent. In May that year the Governor of Chamdo province signed a 17 point agreement for the liberation of Tibet with the Chinese who had invaded the region. Under the agreement, the Chinese were to provide military support and conduct Tibet's foreign affairs, introducing schools, hospitals and other infrastructure and guaranteeing religious freedoms and the Tibetan language. The present Dalai Lama, the fourteenth, was then about 15 years old. Within a few years Tibetan resistance to the substance of Chinese reforms in Tibet grew serious in frequency and intensity. The Chinese retaliated and in 1959 the Dalai Lama left Tibet, renouncing the 17 point agreement from his exile in India.

In 1965 China established the Tibet Autonomous Region and the dismantling of its unique way of life began in earnest, accelerated by the Cultural revolution which, it should be acknowledged, did so much harm to many sections of China's own society and culture. Gradually a new liberalism spread through China, but resistance to the Chinese occupation of Tibet continued sporadically.

As has happened in other countries, tourists became pawns in the struggle, their presence in Lhasa increased the stake of international attention. Photographs and video of riots have been shown on the Western media, where previously little had been known of events in this remote country. The authorities typically refuse entry to Tibet to all tourists for some weeks after any rising, later allowing their return only as members of organized groups. In 1989, further trouble in Tibet closed it again to tourists, but later in the year small groups organized by State, Provincial or Municipal agencies were again permitted entry.

Questions

1 Compare the benefits and problems of a developing tourism sector for Tibetans to the results of tourism development described in the Big Island Case Study (B) and account for any differences.

2 What role has tourism to play in the planned change of traditional societies?

3 Read the chapters in this book dealing with tourists' motivations and tourism marketing and suggest how the market for Tibet might be segmented.

Relevant chapters

1, 10 and 11.

See also:
Bhutani, V.C. *Tibetan Aspirations; China Report*, pp. 311–17, July–September 1987
Harrer, H. *Return To Tibet*, Penguin Books, London, 1985
Snellgrove, D. and Richardson, H. *A Cultural History of Tibet*, Weidenfeld and Nicholson, London, 1968
Tucchi, G. (Translated by J.E. Stapleton Driver) *Tibet, Land of Snows*, Paul Elek Ltd, London, 1967
Year Book of China Tourism Statistics (English Language Edition) National Tourist Administration of the PR China, Beijing 1986
Zhang Guangrui, *Tourism Education in PR China; Tourism Management*, pp. 262–6, September, 1987

CASE STUDY E

Briefing Tourists Travelling to Remote Destinations

Introduction

Premier Holidays is a diversified tour operator which had been established in the 1930s as a coaching company. It is organized into the following divisions, America, Far Away, Channel Islands and Golf. The coaching operation is now a separate company. The Premier Travel Group's Far Away division includes Study China Travel Ltd (SCT-China). This company had been appointed an accredited agent of Luxingshe (China International Travel Service, Beijing) in 1972.

The philosophy behind Premier's China operation is to run profitable inclusive tours to areas of outstanding natural beauty or to parts of China which are of particular cultural or specialist interest, and particularly to pioneer travel to new areas of China. SCT-China arranges itineraries on an *ad hoc* basis for individuals or private groups such as University expeditions which approach it for its logistical expertise. But most of its business is in the form of pre-packaged tours marketed through the retail agency network in a separately branded brochure. Many of its tours are physically demanding, due to the extensive travel itineraries, high altitudes and the lack of facilities on tour to which most Westerners are accustomed. As one of the earliest companies to operate tours into the Peoples Republic of China, Premier felt that intending travellers should be offered frank and factual information about the difficulties which they could potentially encounter, so that their decision to join a group would be based on an understanding of the conditions on the journey as well as the attractions of the destinations portrayed in the company's brochure.

Briefing conferences

One of the methods adopted by Premier had been instituted by its director earlier in his career at Thomas Cook. Pre-tour briefings were arranged for people interested in joining any of the company's tours. Here, they could meet company staff and tour guides, and could discuss recent travel experiences with members of previous tours or obtain detailed information on the areas to be visited from experts.

These briefings proved popular and eventually developed into day-long workshops held at prestigious centres such as the Queen Elizabeth II Conference Centre in London. The January 1987 briefing was attended by some 300 people, a nominal fee was charged to recover the expenses incurred in staging the event. In the morning, an introductory lecture provided an overview of the workshop, the Director of SCT-China gave an illustrated introduction to travel in China and an experienced independent traveller shared his recent experiences of China. After a break for lunch, the workshop desks were opened. These operated on an 'appointment' basis, and people signed up for a ten minute discussion on any of the tours offered by SCT-China, including the Trans-Siberian train, Kashgar and Eastern China, Tibet and Buddhism, China Highlights, and Chinese art tours. Another facility was a display of oriental books and guides to China, for which orders could be placed. After tea, a film was shown and the workshop concluded with a practical and participative introduction to the Chinese language.

People attending the briefing also received an A4 spiral-bound booklet which included hints on 'how to select a China tour' and introductory notes and travel tips together with guidance on topics such as photography, health care, climate and what luggage to take. The highlights of each of the main towns or areas which SCT-China visited were described, and suggestions were offered on reading or other sources of information about travel to China. In addition to its function as an exercise in education about travel to China, the briefing resulted in some 20 bookings, a conversion rate which is better than SCT-China's brochure produced.

Tour briefing documents

The second approach was to send tour members a detailed briefing document shortly before departure. This was presented in the form of a 30 page (approximately) spiral bound A4 booklet containing both general travel information, and specific details for the tour booked. In addition, it carried limited advertising for travel clothing, and for other Premier Far Away tours of special interest such as whale watching in Baja. Table E1 provides excerpts which indicate the approach adopted in the briefing booklet.

Table E1   Excerpts from the briefing booklet – Tibet

China is – – – – –	a great travel experience tiring, constant travelling, sometimes frustrating beautiful and fascinating an absence of our Western standards of time and punctuality full of friendly hospitable people
China needs –	patience and flexibility; it is best to flow with a tour
Remember –	China is still developing as a tourist destination, but has to do this under great pressure of travellers who all want to visit a country that hardly ever fails to come up to expectation
Luggage	Everything that is not personally carried must have a lock . . . The Chinese will not transport anything that is not locked
Itinerary	Arrival and departure times are sometimes later than we would wish. If you are travelling in the early evening, it is a good idea to carry an overnight bag with you as luggage can be delayed (luggage is transported separately from the group)
Hotels	Standards vary a great deal, from basic to recently built, but even new hotels suffer from various plumbing difficulties . . . For those travelling to remote areas, hotels can be extremely basic and facilities can be below standards that are normally encountered in Far Eastern countries. Travellers should prepare themselves for hotels of varying standards
High season	Journey costs are higher in Spring and Autumn. This is a charge made by the Chinese, not SCT-China
Local tours	Some tours start early and you may find you are away from your hotel all day and arrive back with very little time to change for dinner
Weather delays	If due to weather or for other reasons your onward travel is delayed, it is highly probable that your itinerary will be disrupted in some way . . Our escorts and CITS (China International Travel Service) will do everything possible to minimize the problem but please consider that the transport/hotel infrastructure within China has no overlap and it may be impossible to take the next scheduled form of transport . . . Timetables tend to be misleading and scheduling is only possible through CITS and its liaison with the various transport departments
Overnight trains	Timings are unknown in advance of the group's arrival in the city of departure, or at the earliest on arrival in Peking. Sometimes the train will depart in the morning and travel all day and night and arrive early the following morning Time spent on trains is considered a part of the China experience and has been included at popular request from past travellers
Yangtse boat	We use normal Chinese boats which have limited Western accommodation. First class boats just for tourists are available but

continued

Table E1   continued

	at an increased cost and SCT-China does not contract for this form of travel. The Chinese boats are traditional and offer an experience of China that is different from the tourist class boats. Accommodation is in four berth cabins but in some circumstances beyond SCT-China's control, this can change to larger cabins. Our escorts are aware of this and keep an eye on the situation, but demand for space is high and overbooking can occur
Priority groups	In most cases groups from the USA, Germany and Japan pay higher costs to CITS and by doing so obtain space and food priorities
Conduct at altitude	Most people initially feel very fit on arrival at Lhasa airport (12 000ft). The air is crisp and fresh, usually with sunshine. However, even the fittest person should treat the first day as a rest day, even taking to bed in the afternoon! Never try to walk quickly and if others walk faster than you, let them go on. Breathlessness is normal, but panting is not. Walk accordingly
Remember –	Go slowly at altitude. Your visit to Tibet depends on your well-being and it is therefore important to rest on arrival.

Source: STC-China briefing booklet, 1988

Objectives of briefing methods

Three main purposes can be identified in this communications strategy. In the first place the briefings formed an integral part of the selling process and many people were converted into clients at these sessions. Having made personal contact with Premier staff it was easier for them to make a booking for these specialist tours through their local travel agency. Secondly, people who had been uncertain about the rigour of the conditions they were likely to encounter could talk with others and decide whether they would enjoy making a journey which could include digging buses out of sand, or enduring long delays, or extreme cold. By making this clear through talks, films and slide shows, potential disappointment or distress for individuals, or difficulties for an entire travel group were minimized, as intending travellers could learn about the reality of tours. At the same time, the briefing made an interesting day, as people saw recent film taken in areas of real interest to them. However, by the end of the 1980s it was felt that travel to China was sufficiently understood for these briefing conferences to be no longer necessary.

Thirdly, the pretour booklet, which is revised each year, makes it clear that tour operators to China do not have the degree of control over arrangements which is normal in most other destinations, and it provides travellers with a realistic assessment of the unpredictable conditions which they might encounter. The booklet also provides much useful detail on health care, Chinese culture, customs, cuisine and language and tips on shopping and activities as well as a comprehensive reading list, so that travellers are able to make effective preparations for their tour.

Questions

1 What are the advantages to a tour operator and to potential clients of explaining the hardships which might be encountered before a tour to remote areas?

2 What is the significance of models of pre- and post-purchase search behaviour to the briefings described in this case study?

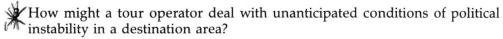 How might a tour operator deal with unanticipated conditions of political instability in a destination area?

Relevant chapters

2, 5 and 8.

Coping with the Slack Season

Introduction

London Entertains is a subsidiary of Mecca Leisure Group PLC. The division acts as the sole source of reservations for restaurants in the Group. One aspect of the operation is theme meals, notably Cockney and Medieval banquets with live entertainment at an inclusive price.

Sources of business

Nearly all of London Entertain's business comes in the form of group bookings, either from incentive organizers or on a regular basis from tour operators. The latter book in one of several ways. Some overseas groups (notably those from Israel) have very limited budgets due to their government's restrictions on the export of hard currencies. Typically the leader of these groups sells all excursions for the itinerary at the first stop, which is normally Rome. This gives the tourists a basis for budgeting their shopping and other personal expenses during the trip, while ensuring that they will be able to participate in a full schedule of optional excursions and activities of their choice. The leader then communicates the group's needs to a London agent who places the reservation with London Entertains and is responsible for collecting and forwarding payment. The Israeli groups have special dietary requirements and a special group rate reflects both the ceiling on their spending, and the special arrangements made for them.

Other groups are recruited in London, either during the coach transfer from the arrival airport, or at an orientation meeting in the hotel, typically the morning after arrival. A variety of methods of payment and different levels of pricing are available to suit the differing needs of the group leaders and the interests of the groups.

Reservations

In each case the numbers, dates and so on are sent to the booking office, which employs a manual reservations system that can cope flexibly with the different levels of price, methods of payment, special requests and the various restaurant seating capacities in the system. Each restaurant contributes to the overhead for the reservations service which is available seven days a week. Another reason for retaining a manual system is that part-time staff can use the traditional method with ease and confidence, while training would be required for a computerized system.

The office also has a panic board which is used to monitor the reservations in each restaurant for the next few days. A ceiling on capacity is set by the physical configuration of each restaurant; this is lower than the 'safe numbers' permitted by fire regulations. Inevitably, some group reservations are altered at the last minute, either as people drop out of the tour, or when more than the organizer anticipated decide to join the event. Experience allows the office to anticipate the likely pattern of uptake from each regular organizer, and to build a degree of flexibility into the bookings accepted. A more difficult judgement concerns the occasional situation when small numbers book into a restaurant. The operation is staff-intensive, as the concept is dining with themed entertainment and this calls for a high degree of interaction between servers and guests. It is difficult to achieve the optimum level of participation when guest numbers are low, and sometimes a decision is taken to consolidate two restaurants to gain a bigger audience.

Coping with reduced demand

One recurrent feature of demand in this industry sector is the slack season following the New Year. In 1988 the company had faced a particularly slow January following American raids on Libya which had reduced the numbers of Americans visiting London. The company had identified other organizations such as hotels and coach operators which experienced similarly reduced demand. The challenge was to develop a way to package what they each offered, and to attract new sources of business.

The Daily Mirror South Pacific weekend

The solution which London Entertains created centred on discovering that a mass circulation newspaper was interested in meeting a large group of its readers. It had never previously had the opportunity to talk at length with a cross-section of readers, but felt that it would understand their interests better were it to do so. London Entertains had the knowledge and resources to prepare a packaged weekend which would appeal to the readers, while the newspaper promoted the package which London Entertains had prepared, and branded the weekend under its title.

209

The main features of the package were preview seats for the musical *South Pacific*, ahead of its public opening; two nights at a four star hotel; and excursions to two London Entertains restaurants: one Cockney lunch, and one gala dinner with the theme of *South Pacific*. An additional feature of the concept was the link to a charity which attracted support from many of the paper's readers. An inclusive price was set which was significantly below the perceived value of all the components and featured a donation of £5 for each guest booked to the Great Ormond Street Hospital for Children.

The newspaper carried three features advertising the weekend during December 1987, providing coupons inviting readers to book through London Entertains. Five hundred and forty people booked for the weekend. The Sales and Marketing manager for London Entertains summarized the benefits in the following way,

> The weekend allowed London Entertains to fill certain venues for lunches and gala dinners, whilst strengthening our relationship with an important national newspaper group – bringing us free advertising to ten million readers and creating a useful mailing list. It enabled us to raise £2660 for a worthy charity.

Briefing staff

A special briefing was held for London Entertain's staff, emphasizing two key aspects of the arrangements. The first was that all clients are VIPs, and should be looked after with the utmost courtesy and understanding. Complimentary letters from participants to the *Daily Mirror* were expected to stimulate further business for London Entertains.

Secondly, it was stressed that when dealing with large numbers of people, good cooperation between colleagues would be essential. Each of the staff was assigned a principle responsibility, but all were expected to be aware of the arrangements for the weekend as a whole, so that they could be interchangeable, as needed. Table F1 shows the responsibilities allocated before the tour. During the weekend, staff were assigned specific duties at the hotel, in relation to coach transfers, and at the theatre and the lunch or dinner.

Table F1 Responsibilities

- Updating the hotel on rooming lists and numbers
- Supplying updated rooming list to all staff
- Checking coaches and guides
- Setting up the hospitality desk
- Training all staff in its operation
- Preparation of information packs and theatre tickets
- Liaison with *Daily Mirror*

Development of the concept

The event was regarded as successful by the company and the other organizations involved, and the participants were very pleased. It was decided to develop the concept into a regular product. It was offered in the form of two night's accommodation at a four star London hotel, seats for a musical, an evening at one of the theme restaurants and a Thames cruise on an all-weather boat. This package was offered to coach operators around the country, for them to sell either through local newspapers or in other ways. With a minimum of 25 paying passengers, free accommodation and breakfast was provided for the coach driver.

Questions

1 The Great Ormond Street Hospital For Sick Children, and the *South Pacific* musical featured strongly in the publicity for this weekend. It was entitled *'Daily Mirror South Pacific* Weekend' yet it was conceived and coordinated by London Entertains. What were the advantages to each of these organizations of this arrangement?

2 How do you account for seasonal fluctuations in tourism demand, and what are the implications for companies supplying tourism services?

3 Prepare and cost (at full prices) an inclusive two day 'event' for your local newspaper, giving a rationale for the components, and identifying the target audience.

Relevant chapters

1, 3, 6, 7 and 8.

'Capital' – The London Tourist Board Training Initiative

Introduction

In 1986 the London Tourist Board (LTB) established a Forum to develop a tourism strategy for London in recognition of the importance of tourism in the capital. Over 23 million visitors stayed in London each year and the 210 000 jobs then dependent on tourism were increasing at the rate of about 1000 per month.

The London Tourism Forum, whose members were drawn from public and private sectors, considered ways to harmonize the interests of visitors and residents, enhance tourists' experiences and improve the environment in London, improve usage of existing facilities, stimulate selected sectors of the market, and to create a better understanding of tourism employment.

Tourism employment and training

The increasing demand for tourism services would evidently create more employment in the sector, but the demographic forecasts for London predicted a shortage in the supply of traditional tourism workers. The 16- to 24-year-old age group on which the industry had mainly relied was forecast to drop by over 20 per cent and to remain low until the end of the twentieth century. Employers in all sectors of the economy were becoming increasingly aware of the developing problem and were beginning to turn their attention to the older age groups as additional sources of labour. A specialist group was established to consider the issue of employment and training for the tourism industry. Training was identified as a key component of the tourism strategy both for those in work and for those seeking employment, and it was also regarded as a key business growth tool. The recruitment and retention of staff was seen as critical to the industry's future; unless tourism manpower was planned and managed effectively, three problems were foreseen, indicated in Table G1.

Table G1   Potential problems for tourism in London

1   An uncontrolled wages explosion leading to higher prices
2   Falling standards of service through manning shortages
3   A deterioration in London's international image and its market position

The Capital Training Project

The diversity of tourism in London, together with the wide range of training in the capital, was regarded as a major problem. The difficulty was that small tourism companies did not find it easy to make contact with the many training experts in the London area, and employers had little experience of judging the competency of trainers or the relevance of the training they offered.

The LTB believed that a co-ordinated training strategy was needed to develop the variety of skills required for the varied tourism businesses in London to compete effectively. The objectives of the Capital tourism training initiative were to increase the number of tourism, leisure, accommodation and catering companies using training, and to stimulate further training in those already having a programme. The first year was spent researching the needs of all tourism sectors in London, mainly by case research methods. Various gaps in the training provision for each sector were identified through over a hundred in-depth interviews. Customer care awareness emerged from the research as a key priority for all tourism staff, in all sectors of the industry.

The Board commissioned trainers and educationalists to work with trade and professional bodies to produce a range of training materials. The initiative was organized under the Local Collaborative Project scheme (LCP), and funded by two Government departments, the Department of Education and Science, and the Department of Employment's Training Agency, together with commercial companies. The project was given the title of Capital – Get into Training for Tourism (with the banner 'Capital – Training for Tourism') and launched in November 1989. It was managed by the Hotel and Catering Industry Training Board.

A £100 000 grant was obtained from the Training Agency to develop a Pilot Innovatory Programme of Training (PIT) which would be easily accessible to the many small tourism operators who could not afford expensive off-the-job training for their staff. The innovatory feature which Capital developed was a video-based package which offered staff from every tourism sector an accessible, common language approach to understanding and meeting their customers' needs. The funding enabled Capital to commission professional production of the video but still to offer it within the LCP guideline price of £99.00.

213

The Capital programme produced a set of training packages which businesses in the tourism industry in London could purchase. The packages could be supported by additional information and consultancy if required. The challenge for Capital at this stage was to market the training material; its strategy was based on seminars and a series of leaflets distributed through the LTB. Table G2 provides excerpts from its promotional brochure for tourism organizations which illustrate the persuasive approach of the Capital tourism training project.

Table G2   The Capital training approach

London is where 40 million day visitors and 21 million staying visitors choose to spend time each year; where business exhibitions and conferences attract more than 250 000 high spending overseas delegates annually; and where more than 200 000 people are employed in tourism-related jobs – 7 per cent of the working population.

You're in direct competition with other companies for a share of that business.

And London itself is also competing for that spending power – with other business and leisure destinations around the world.

We have to work together. If you can increase your business in tourism, you'll do better. London will attract more word-of-mouth and repeat business, and you'll do better still . . .

Guide to educational qualifications

The initial period of research had uncovered a widespread lack of understanding amongst managers of the many new qualifications which had been introduced into Britain's educational system during recent years. Their difficulties were exacerbated by the accompanying use of educational jargon related to a hierarchy of assessment targets and attainment levels. The consequence was particularly severe at the recruitment stage of employment, when managers were uncertain of the comparative values of qualifications, subjects, examining boards, and grades which candidates offered. Capital's response was to produce a leaflet available free of charge to tourism employers which explained these details in a jargon-free way.

The benefits of training

The Capital promotional leaflets identified a series of benefits which training would provide for tourism organizations. These benefits are summarized in Table G3.

To further convince employers that training would be beneficial to them, Capital spelt out ways in which the benefits could be evaluated by comparing selected performance criteria before and after training. These are summarized in Table G4.

**Table G3   Benefits of training for
tourism employers**

How training will help
- Your business becomes more efficient
- You offer a better product or service
- You gain more new business
- You gain more repeat business
- You recruit more effectively
- You reduce staff turnover
- You improve morale
- You manage your staff better . . .

Table G4   Measuring the benefits of tourism training

Staff
- Turnover
- Under three months – induction
- Over three months – retention
- Cost of staff turnover
- Absenteeism
- Time keeping
- Productivity
- Commitment

Operational yardsticks
- Staff costs
- Total
- % margin on sales

Operating costs
- Total
- % margin on sales

Sales
- Absolute sales
- Repeat business
- Average spending
- Guest comments/complaints
- Customer reaction/perception

Wider issues
- Management time (including recruitment)
- General business reputation
- Staff reaction to training, number of requests to be trained and staff attitudes to training
- Number of job applicants
- Recruitment costs
- Career development
- Effect on pricing policy
- Productivity/service issues

Capital's training portfolio

Capital has produced a portfolio of 13 training packages targetted to the needs of specific tourism sectors such as visitor attractions, travel and tourism, and tourism training. Its list of titles includes 'Courier Training', the 'Promotion of Visitor Attractions', and 'More Training, Better Training'. In addition there is a key programme common to all sectors, 'Better Customer Care'.

The courier training package identifies the basic competencies for trainee couriers and provides support for managers responsible for the induction of new couriers. During the 20 hours of the course, basic customer skills are illustrated, meet and greet techniques for groups are discussed, the varying roles of couriers are explained and further training opportunities are outlined. The course consists of texts, audio cassettes, self assessment tests, and an element of field work, to introduce students to specific aspects of the work.

Training for Visitor Attractions is a series of packages which deal with merchandising, marketing and promotional techniques, legal aspects and information services. These are designed to reflect the wide range of operating conditions encountered in small or large visitor attractions.

Part of Capital's strategy for action focuses on developing training skills for experienced tourism managers. 'More Training, Better Training' is adapted from Hotel and Catering Industry Training Board course material which had proved very successful for the Hotel sector's managers and supervisors and has now been transferred to other tourism sectors. The programme consists of three elements: Trainer Training, Supervisor Training and Health and Safety Training. Two schemes were developed for trainers, both leading to special qualifications. The Craft Trainer Award is a three day course intended for those who carry out on the job training on a one-to-one basis. For managers who organize short off-the-job training sessions, a five-day course which includes group training techniques, the organization of training sessions, and assessment leads to a Training Certificate. Another practical three-day course has been designed to improve the work-based skills essential for supervisors, including communications, problem-solving, leadership and motivation. The third element of the training programmes focuses on Health and Safety. This one-day course is intended to alert both staff and employers to their responsibilities under the Health and Safety at Work Act to ensure a safe working environment.

'Better Customer Care', a package of two videos and support training material, is intended to achieve improved customer satisfaction, with accompanying benefits in staff recruitment and turnover from enhanced company morale, and improved profitability for the company. Its approach reflects the customer care investment of larger companies, but tailored to the needs of smaller businesses. One video, 'The People Factor', focuses on four key areas, attitudes and behaviour of staff, communications with fellow employees and customers, taking personal responsibility for customer service, and teamwork. The philosophy underlying this programme is to establish a common language and approach from which all staff can contribute to increased customer satisfaction. The second video, 'The Quality Factor', follows the efforts of the new owner of a fictitious hotel to transform it into the best in the area. His attempt raises critical questions about the meaning of quality in services, and the video focuses on staff motivation, the importance of team work, and the flexibility of working practices in seeking answers.

Standards for trainers

The early phases of Capital's work had suggested minimum standards which trainers should offer their clients and students. However, Capital's role and resources did not extend to a policing function of the many organizations, private and public, which offered training in the London area to the tourism sector. It was felt that employers and also staff would benefit from an understanding of how to choose appropriate trainers, and so checklists were produced providing advice on what questions each should ask in assessing courses, or deciding which organization to use as a trainer. These were provided free to students, and employers, as appropriate. A companion guide offered advice to training providers outlining the standards which they would be expected to attain for recognition and recommendation by the LTB and other relevant bodies.

A computerized register of all training courses considered relevant was established to provide easy access to training solutions to employers' problems. Though the Training Access Programme (TAP) had previously been developed across industries on a geographical basis, the Capital version was for a single industry, specific to London, and thereby an innovation in itself.

Recruiting trainers

Colleges and commercial trainers were attracted to participate through the benefits which the scheme offered them. Five key benefits were identified in a consultative document, and are shown in Table G5.

Table G5   Benefits to trainers

1 Training providers would gain new contacts and clients, thereby increasing their market penetration
2 Industry wide marketing in London would increase the exposure for training, and be cost effective for providers
3 They would have access to comparative information on their own position in the market, and on the industry's needs. This would aid in course development, and costing
4 Training providers would gain prestige through association with a quality group
5 They would gain through inclusion in a comprehensive listing of training provision for tourism enterprises in London

Demonstrating the benefits of training

To reinforce the message that training confers substantial and measurable benefits to tourism employers, a series of case studies showed how training has enhanced the performance of a range of businesses. One of the case studies discussed the benefits which the Belgravia Sheraton had gained from implementing a training programme. Detailed material had been developed for three main groups of employees; those in rooms-related work, food and beverages, and support service. These programmes were based on the Sheraton Guest Satisfaction System which is aimed to attune employees to the needs of customers and are supplemented by a planned system of courses for employees at all levels including senior executives. The Sheraton's training material had been produced centrally, but adapted to local conditions. Table G6 draws on this case study to indicate the results of this training investment.

Table G6   Benefits of training for the Belgravia Sheraton

- Better occupancy rates than comparable hotels in London
- Reduction in food and beverage costs
- Improved departmental profits
- Better staff turnover rates than comparable hotels

Questions

1 What changes in the market for tourism staff can you predict in your area over the next few years, and what steps should be taken in response?

2 In the absence of a centralized, industry-wide training initiative such as that described in this case study, what steps might tourism organizations of varying sizes and complexity take to improve selected aspects of their service?

3 What, if any, additional developments do you consider necessary to raise the quality of services provided to London's visitors?

Relevant chapters

1, 3, 7 and 12.

The Hilton International Acquisition

Introduction

Hilton International had been formed in 1949 as a separate subsidiary of the US based Hilton Hotels Corporation. In 1964 it was spun off as an independent public company quoted on the New York Stock Exchange and given the exclusive right to use the Hilton name outside the USA. In 1967 Hilton International was acquired by TWA; however the airline group was reorganized in 1979 and again in 1986 prior to the sale of Hilton International to Allegis (United Air Lines) in April 1987. In June of that year, Allegis decided to sell all its non-airline subsidiaries. This turbulent and directionless period in Hilton International's history ended when it was acquired by the British company, Ladbroke Group PLC, in October 1987 for $1.07b (£645m).

The strengths of Hilton International

Certain names stand as landmarks in their industry: they are recognized around the world for the standards of performance or service they offer. Just as Rolls-Royce or Ferrari evoke impressions of particular albeit differing high quality approaches to the engineering of private passenger transport, so certain brands in tourism are widely recognized for their special styles and quality. Two worldwide surveys carried out by National Opinion Polls and Landor Associates in 1988/89 established that Hilton is the most powerful brand name in the hotel industry.

An indication of the quality for which Hilton International is renowned is given by the number of medals won by the company at international catering competitions. At the Salon Culinaire Mondial held in Switzerland in November 1987, Hilton International chefs had won 11 gold, 21 silver and 3 bronze medals. The International Culinary Olympics is held every four years and is regarded as one of the leading events in the industry: from 1400 participants Hilton

International's 24 entrants won 43 medals at the 1988 Frankfurt event. In both competitions, Hilton International's performance surpassed all other hotel groups.

Ladbroke Group PLC

Ladbroke's original business had been founded in the Warwickshire village of Ladbroke, in 1887. It was formed as a credit betting partnership and developed gradually until the Betting and Gaming Act legalized off-track betting in licensed betting offices in 1963. From 1971, when it operated 660 licensed betting shops, the group began to diversify into the property and hotel industries in order to balance its cash flow businesses with valuable property assets. This was the start of the group's development into its present four core businesses: hotels, racing, property and Do-It-Yourself (DIY) retailing through the Texas Homecare chain.

Prior to the acquisition of Hilton International, one of Ladbroke's core businesses was a mid-market chain of hotels, mainly located in Britain but with some properties in Europe. It had acquired small chains such as Myddleton and Comfort (the latter purchased in 1985 for £70m). Its policy was to upgrade the three star properties situated in city centres to four star standards, and by 1986 Ladbroke had established itself as the second largest UK hotel operator. An analysis by Shearson Lehman Securities ascribed this success to several factors in addition to those outlined above:

- concentration on particular types of business, particularly conference and business travel, and the establishment of strong leisure weekend sales to gain high occupancy rates
- maximizing the revenue from food and beverage sales
- tight control of labour productivity.

The 1986 Ladbroke Annual Report stated,

> In the UK, Ladbroke Hotels made good progress in the year, increasing profits by 14 per cent, the division's commitment to providing good quality accommodation at competitive tariffs, to the business community in particular, enabling it to gain market share. The extensive programme of expansion, rebuilding and upgrading which is continuing at an even faster rate is providing the base for profitable growth.

The acquisition of Hilton International

Prior to its acquisition by Ladbroke Group PLC, Hilton International operated 91 hotels with a total of more than 35 000 rooms in 44 countries: 27 in Europe; 26 in the American continent, and 38 in other parts of the world. It owned and operated 44 hotels and partially owned and operated a further 14. In addition, Hilton International operated 33 hotels under management contracts for which it received a percentage of revenues and operating profits.

The Chairman's statement to shareholders in the Ladbroke Group PLC Annual Report and Accounts, 1987, put the acquisition in the context of the group's strategic objectives of growth for the four major businesses.

In my report to the shareholders on 1986, the centenary year of the company, I referred to the progress made by the group through having clearly defined strategic objectives and by focusing on the growth of our four major businesses. At that time, however, an important part of our strategic plan had yet to be accomplished: the promotion of our hotel business from the ranks of a leading national operator to the level of a world leader in the industry.

The possibility of purchasing Hilton International Co. at a reasonable price was seen by your directors as a 'once in a life-time' corporate opportunity to achieve our strategic goal. To have succeeded was a great coup for Ladbroke, particularly since the brand name of Hilton is, more than any other, synonymous with first class international hotels.

Funding for the acquisition was raised by a 1 for 5 rights issue of approximately £254 million net of expenses, with the balance funded by term bank facilities provided by Barclays Bank PLC and National Westminster Bank PLC. A press release was issued by Charterhouse, Ladbroke Group's merchant bank, in September 1987 to explain the thinking behind the acquisition. Some excerpts are presented here: 'The revenues and capital values of Ladbroke's hotels will be enhanced by the association with the Hilton name . . . and the joint ownership of one of the best real-time reservations systems in the world. In addition, the removal of uncertainty which has long surrounded the ownership of Hilton will result in the stability and direction necessary for its consistent growth. Furthermore, significant benefits will accrue to the combined operation through economies of scale.

The scale of the acquisition may be gauged from the increased significance to Ladbroke of its hotels division in the company's profit performance. In 1987 Hotels had contributed 29.5 per cent and Racing 38.7 per cent to company profits before tax. After the Hilton International group was acquired Hotels contributed 45 per cent and Racing 29 per cent. Table H1 provides more detail.

Table H1   Ladbroke Group PLC pre-tax profit by activity

	1986	(£m.) 1987	1988
Hotels*	21.8	47.2	118.9
Property (after interest)	21.4	22.3	32.2
Racing	49.5	62.0	77.5
Retail	13.8	26.0	34.5
Media	0.6	–	–
Discontinued businesses	12.9	11.8	–
TOTAL	120.0	169.3	263.1
Interest	(18.7)	(9.1)	(10.8)
TOTAL	101.3	160.2	252.3

Source: Ladbroke Annual Accounts

(*It must be noted that the hotels division profits reflect two different portfolios. 1987 includes the first 13 weeks of Hilton's operation as part of Ladbroke Group PLC)

The post acquisition policy

The following discussion of the hotels division policy after the merger is extracted from the Chairman's statements in the 1987 annual report.

> Our current strategy is to increase profitability through investment and organic growth ... We now estimate that it will take some five years of substantial annual profit growth before the group generates the full potential profit from the existing Hilton International business.
>
> We intend to maintain Hilton's reputation for excellence, while introducing the strong financial disciplines and entrepreneurial skills which are applied to all the group's activities. The division is now destined to become the largest individual contributor to the annual profits of the group.

Ladbroke considered that Hilton International's marketing had lacked focus, and that it relied too heavily on the ex-US market and individual business travellers. The intention, following the acquisition, was to concentrate on about 12 main markets, in some of which, such as conferences, Ladbroke already had considerable experience.

The new Hilton International Board also identified opportunities for considerable savings in the operation and administration of the business; it relocated sales and marketing functions from Manhattan to Watford with the corporate HQ remaining in New York. The number of regional offices was reduced and the cost of marketing reviewed. Cost efficiencies resulting from streamlining and improving central and regional offices and marketing, together with economies of scale and the start of benefits from improved purchasing combined to give a 70 per cent profit improvement for Hilton International within a year of the acquisition.

Rationalization after the acquisition

After the acquisition Ladbroke continued to build its core businesses, both by divesting itself of peripheral businesses and by purchasing additional businesses which complemented its core interests. Ladbroke sold its 17 UK holiday centres and a catering business to Mecca Leisure in December 1987 for £55.1m. The Chairman commented in a press release:

> The sale is in keeping with our policy of disposing of businesses which are peripheral to our core activities of hotels, property, racing and DIY retailing, all of which continue to show excellent potential for further substantial growth.

The challenge in Britain was to manage the existing range of hotels alongside the newly acquired Hiltons. A trade publication, *The Caterer and Hotelkeeper*, commented on this in September 1987:

> The key to the long term success of the acquisition will be Ladbroke's ability to rationalize its existing hotels and those of Hilton into the two brands of Hilton National and Hilton International.

Of the 63 hotels which Ladbroke operated in Britain and Europe before the acquisition, 26 were retained to be operated as Hiltons, and a multi-million pound refurbishment programme commenced. In April 1988 these hotels, together with the three established Hilton Internationals in the UK, were relaunched. The revised portfolio comprised 10 Hilton International hotels and 19 Hilton National properties. The latter were positioned as first class hotels in regional hubs offering quality leisure and conference facilities aimed at the domestic, rather than the international, market.

Thirty-four of the original 63 hotels were disposed of by Ladbroke Group over the period October 1987 to December 1989. As at January 1990, three hotels (two in the UK and one in France) remained under Ladbroke ownership and operated as associate hotels. Table H2 provides a profile of the Hilton Hotel portfolio as at February 1990.

Table H2 Profile of Hilton Hotels, February 1990	
Hilton International	117
Hilton National	20
Associate	5
	142

Announcing the group's half year figures for 1988, the Chairman gave his view of Hilton's progress since becoming part of the Ladbroke Group in October 1987:

> With considerable organic growth achievable in the short and medium term, the Hilton acquisition is proving to be one of the best value purchases ever made by a British company . . . Nine new hotels (3 628 bedrooms) have been opened since October 1987 when Hilton International was acquired by the group, and ten more are planned to open before the end of 1989. Management contracts, which require minimal capital investment, are being negotiated at a fast rate . . . The group's UK hotels, now trading under the Hilton brand name, also produced record first half figures. Here, too, capacity is being expanded, with new Hilton National hotels under development in addition to Hilton International's 415 bedroom luxury Langham Hotel which (will be) . . . the group's sixth major London hotel. The division now operates a total of 138 hotels with more than 45 000 bedrooms worldwide.

Management style of Ladbroke Group PLC

During the 1980s, Ladbroke had evolved from a long-established British based betting company into a $5 billion international hotel, real estate, racing and retail business. This had been achieved by applying an entrepreneurial management style calling for the close involvement of senior managers in every aspect of the group's business. The Chairman, Mr Stein, discussed Ladbroke's management style in an interview for *Leaders Magazine,* (April, May, June, 1988). The following remarks are extracted from that article.

Hands-on management means being both visible and involved. In the case of the Hilton purchase, we made certain that, in the days immediately after the completion of the deal, every single hotel manager heard about and understood our philosophy and culture. They were initially brought together in three groups geographically and subsequently seen individually at every Hilton and Vista International hotel,* not just one to announce our arrival, but as part of a continual programme of regular visits . . .

We bring a degree of management involvement which, in Hilton's case, certainly did not exist before as part of a decentralized corporation . . . Even within the network, individual hotels had operated independently of each other, acting virtually as if separate companies. And while decentralization may well be a fashionable business theory, we believe it results in losing control, particularly when it comes to maximizing revenue and controlling costs.

In our experience, you cannot operate hotels or any other consumer service in a totally decentralized way. Their success, both in the service they provide customers and in financial performance, depends on attention to detail . . .

An important part of our culture is that the hands-on policy of a centralized management has to work two ways. We find that maintaining control over the operations of the group encourages, rather than stifles, enterprise . . .

When I go into one of our Texas Homecare superstores in Britain, I look to see how well the major product lines are being displayed. I look at the way staff are reacting to customers' requirements. I see how long it takes to answer the telephone and how long the lines are at the check-outs. You can relate all those aspects of service and performance to hotels in exactly the same way.

We operate 2000 individual units in Britain and another 1200 abroad, and yet we have no problem in maintaining a hands-on policy because our senior management recognize how important it is to be out where the business is and not isolated at headquarters by corporate bureaucracy.

Mr Stein put forward the idea that one must decide whether one is in the numbers game of how many hotels or shops are operated, or whether he is in a profits game, where one keeps in mind the need for every asset to produce an acceptable level of return. He continued:

While I don't attach much importance to luck in business, because it can cut both ways, if there has been an element of luck it has been in our being in the right businesses at the right time. If, in a few years, we were to decide that we were ready to put commercial resources into another business, it would still need to meet the criteria of being substantial, capable of operating internationally, and able to benefit from our existing skills in consumer services. But the success of our strategy in the '80s means that its scope for profitability would have to be considerably more than the £20m. (core business) target we set for ourselves early in the decade.

The 1988 Ladbroke Group Report commented:

A common theme throughout all our businesses is the importance we attach to staff development and training, not only to provide a high calibre of central and divisional management but also to encourage, among the 69 000 people employed in our businesses worldwide, the highest standards of customer service . . . senior and middle managers from 46 countries attended courses in 1988 designed and operated by (the group's Human Resources Development Centre) to imbue in them the entrepreneurial

*It should be explained that Hilton International operates under the Vista International banner in the US.

management style and 'culture' which are the hallmarks of Ladbroke's success ... All our businesses are encouraged to develop more flexible organizational structures and to question traditional thinking; the result is constantly improving two-way communication ... incentives for local management are now based on the performance for each hotel, rather than the global performance of the chain as a whole. This encourages entrepreneurial flair and ensures that each management team makes the most of local opportunities ... Sales strategies are in place to ensure that innovations which succeed in one country are exploited in others. An example of this is the successful short-breaks and special interest programmes which were initially developed for the European market and are now being introduced throughout the world.

A new look for Hilton International

In October 1989 the Chairman of Hilton International announced the group's strategy for the 1990s. Following worldwide research to assess the strength of the Hilton International brand, the company introduced a new corporate identity in print, guest amenities and signage. National Opinion Polls had been asked to identify the profile of the consumer who uses Hilton International and other first class hotels, estimate the size of the market and Hilton's share of it, and assess the awareness of and attitudes to Hilton versus its key competition. 12 000 face-to-face interviews were conducted throughout the world. Results showed that Hilton ranks as one of the world's most powerful brand names alongside Coca Cola, Disney and IBM. Hilton is the best known first class hotel brand, gaining 82 per cent spontaneous awareness and is perceived as the most prestigious, business oriented, efficient and reliable hotel chain in the category. Hilton is the first choice for a business trip, especially a trip abroad, and is preferred by 50 per cent more people than its nearest competitor. It was ranked twelfth in terms of esteem and twenty-first in terms of a combination of awareness and esteem compared to Hyatt, the next hotel company, which ranked fifty-fourth.

A worldwide branding and image enhancement programme was launched to achieve consistency in corporate identity through design, advertising and public relations to create greater awareness in the minds of frequent business travellers. The objective was to attract and retain the world's top 300 000 travellers. One aspect of the programme was to place the geographical location of the hotel before the hotel name, in recognition of the importance of location in business travellers' selection of hotels. The names of unique landmark hotels were to be retained, identifying them as being operated by Hilton International. A new logo was developed to encapsulate the new corporate positioning and the new graphic approach was applied consistently to support the corporate identity.

The advertising strategy was to position Hilton International as the natural choice of discerning travellers the world over. The theme was 'The Hilton. *The* Hotel.' Most hotel advertising campaigns tended to show stereotyped pictures of bedrooms, lobbies, restaurants and so on. The Hilton approach, developed by Saatchi and Saatchi, was to concentrate on the traveller's expectations of what Hilton International will provide. Mr Richard Humphreys, Chief Executive

Officer, Saatchi & Saatchi Advertising International, explained the philosophy in Hilton International's launch booklet, 'The New Look',

> In the campaign, we invite the businessman to identify with more unusual travellers in exotic situations, to rediscover the romance of travel, to share the savoir-faire of making the same choice as the most seasoned of travellers.

A global advertising campaign with the headline 'Take me to the Hilton' commenced in November 1989 to launch the new identity and enhance business travellers' awareness of the brand. Another aspect of the strategy for the 1990s involves the sale of part of the equity in wholly owned hotels to release capital for further expansion, while retaining a management contract in all cases. The final element was to establish worldwide standards of service excellence by training and motivational programmes.

Questions

1 What reasons might Ladbroke Group have had for establishing two brands and relaunching Hilton International after the acquisition?

2 What can be deduced about the travel expectations of Hilton International's clients?

3 What synergies might a successful transport operator gain from acquiring a hotel group, and what problems would you anticipate?

Relevant chapters

3, 4, 5, 6 and 8.

Promoting England Holidays

Introduction

The English Tourist Board (ETB) was established as a result of the 1969 Development of Tourism Act. An aim of the ETB has always been to encourage domestic holiday-taking by British people. In 1971, as part of its strategy to achieve this aim, the ETB produced a brochure to promote the market for holidays of four or more nights. Its twin objectives were to influence undecided holiday-makers, and to provide a cost-effective vehicle enabling advertisers to reach targeted market segments. Underlying these objectives was a belief that awareness of the wide variety of holiday opportunities in England was rather low. The holiday operators advertising in the *England Holidays* brochure sought clients who would book their services, or a means to stimulate potential clients to contact them for detailed information ahead of making direct sales.

It contained a mix of display advertising for specific holiday operators, hotels and resorts. The main method of distribution for the first editions of the *England Holidays* brochure was to travel agents. It was to be placed on their racks alongside commercial tour operator's brochures, but it did not, in most cases, offer the travel agent an opportunity to earn a commission on sales.

Development of the approach

The results of this approach were encouraging, and it was decided to develop the *England Holidays* concept further. The original *England Holidays* brochure concept had weaknesses for each of its three main interest groups, the principals who bought advertising space in it, travel agents who were expected to give it space on their racks without commission opportunities, and the holiday makers who used its contents in making their holiday choice but had to contact principals themselves for further details. A million copies of the 1972 edition of *England Holidays* were produced. At that time there were few Tourist Information

227

Centres (TICS) in Britain, and so a circuit around the country was planned to promote the brochure. This was based on a restored 1927 Dennis open-top bus. The campaign was launched outside the Houses of Parliament, and MPs were invited aboard. The consequent publicity resulted in all brochures being distributed within a week, and the bus circuit had to be curtailed.

Very little advertising was used after the first decade, as both the media space and subsequent fulfilment of enquiries was expensive. Instead *England Holidays* was distributed mainly through the retail travel trade. But the ABTA domestic committee was pressing for a financial return to agents and as a result commissionable products were flagged in later editions of the brochure, although all products remained bookable direct by clients.

Changing market conditions

Since the inception of *England Holidays* the vacation habits of the British population had changed significantly. There had been an overall increase in holiday-taking, but the proportion taking their holiday in Britain had fallen from 50 per cent to 40 per cent by the mid 1980s, while overseas holiday taking had increased from 10 per cent to over 30 per cent. The popular overseas destinations seemed increasingly likely to promote smaller scale, specialist opportunities such as the inland cities of Spain, rather than the mass markets resorts which had less appeal for increasingly discriminating clients.

The structure of the travel distribution system had also changed, the total number of outlets had increased, while the multiples had gained power. Travel retailers were also adopting more sophisticated approaches to their business activities, and in particular were becoming selective amongst the several thousand brochures from which they could stock their display racks. The criterion for displaying a particular brochure on their racks was the revenue they expected it to produce, but *England Holidays* offered rather limited commissionable product for travel agents to sell, and consequently they had always tended to distribute it to enquirers rather than work to sell its products.

Further developments

In the face of their advertisers' needs and the changes occurring in the market for holidays the English Tourist Board decided to establish a direct marketing vehicle, as well as to strengthen its traditional distribution through travel agency racks.

At the annual ABTA convention held in Queensland in 1986, ETB announced that it would produce a travel agency version within two years which would contain only commissionable products. The 1988 edition of *England Holidays* largely met this by listing only commissionable tours, apart from a section on resorts. In addition, the ETB produced a direct sell brochure entitled *England 88* for door-to-door distribution and a smaller version which included response coupons. These were not supported by advertising in view of the high fulfilment costs which would have been incurred.

A travel agents' brochure called *England 89* was produced in 1989, for distribution to enquirers. It had shorter listings and no contact addresses to encourage clients to book its commissionable holidays through retail travel agents. The agents also received an A5 booking manual. However, its small size meant that it was easily lost in the busy conditions of travel agencies, and in the following year it was printed in A4 format, but without a client brochure.

In 1989, a different brochure was published for distribution to the public and an innovative media plan was devised. This version of *England Holidays* contained whatever services its advertisers wanted to feature. It was printed slightly smaller than previous editions, in order to facilitate its back-to-back banding with the magazine *Good Housekeeping*. It included a reader reply service for the first time, freepost facilities and an incentive competition to encourage responses.

Good Housekeeping was selected for the banding exercise because the profile of its readers offered a close match to the demographics and lifestyle of those people known to enjoy English holidays. In addition, the style and approach of the magazine was felt to be compatible and the volume was correct for the distribution plan. Readers gained an added benefit from the *England Holidays* brochure included with their purchased copy of the magazine, the first time this approach had been employed in Britain. The banded copies were complemented by other distribution methods detailed in Table I1.

Table I1   Distribution plan for 1989 England Holidays brochure

400 000	Banded with February issue of *Good Housekeeping*
200 000	Inserted into selected *TV Times* areas (January)
135 000	Distributed to TIC network
100 000	Distributed door-to-door in selected areas as a retest against a previous year's campaign
100 000	Distributed to ETB's data base
65 000	Mailed in response to requests following a small scale national press campaign

Targets

Targets were set for the campaign. £400 000 of advertising revenue was forecast, although a higher figure was actually achieved. The reader reply service was forecast to generate 35 000 requests, each enquirer asking for approximately four brochures from a central distribution service, and a further 20 000 enquiries directed to the advertisers. These resulted in 160 000 requests, costing an average of £2.50 each. At the mid-year stage, it seemed likely that a total of 300 000 brochures would be requested, bringing the average cost down to under £1.30.

An integral part of the 1989 campaign was a tracking mechanism linked to the reader reply service. Analysis showed that the highest response rate was achieved from brochures mailed as a result of the small-scale press campaign. Responses from the database mail out were also high, but these people were already known to be UK holiday-takers, while the other distribution channels reached people who may not have taken a holdiday in England recently. The costs of generating responses varied, and Table I2 provides an analysis according to the distribution channel used.

Table I2   Reader response costs analysis

Distribution method	Cost	Responses
Press advertizing	226 000	11 300
Good Housekeeping	125 000	19 200
Mailing	70 000	13 600
TV Times inserts	55 000	5 300
TICs	54 000	6 300
Door drop	49 000	3 100
TOTAL	£579 800	59 660

Distribution decisions

The varying costs of gaining responses by different distribution methods indicated the need for a decision to be taken about the distribution channels employed for future editions of *England Holidays*. On the one hand significant savings in costs could be made by limiting distribution to banding the brochure with selected magazines, and that would release funds which could be used for increased print runs. On the other hand, a media campaign inviting readers to request a copy offered other advantages. An individual's response to advertising was a good indication that he had an interest in the specific product requested, and it seemed likely that his enquiry would coincide with the time when he was actively making holiday decisions. Against that, costs per enquiry were relatively high, as can be calculated from the data given in Table I2.

There were also a number of drawbacks to obtaining responses through media advertising for the *England Holidays* brochure. A continuing campaign is implied by this method, as the consumer would not respond unless the advertisement was fresh and readily to hand. However, as more people respond as an advertising campaign progresses it becomes relatively more expensive to reach any remaining potential customers. It follows that it is necessary to define the purposes of a campaign in planning how to reach prospective customers, and to determine a cut-off point for advertising investment.

Evaluating results

A key aspect of the *England Holidays* strategy for 1989 was a reader reply service and this was encouraged by a freepost facility and by a competition through which respondents were entered in a draw for a new car. The reader response analysis also provided an insight into the effectiveness of advertisements according to their size, by the type of advertiser and characteristics of the enquirer. Display advertising produced a higher response rate than the cheaper and smaller Factfinder listings. Some of the findings are shown in Table I3.

Table I3   Actual conversion rates

| Decision taken | Distribution methods | | | | |
	Press Advertising	TIC	Good Housekeeping	Mail	Door drop
No holiday	26	27	28	26	33
Holiday in England	48	45	36	39	42
Other UK holiday	11	9	11	17	7
Overseas holiday	15	19	25	18	18

The ETB conducted a study of the marketing expertise brought to bear by its advertisers. One hundred of its *England Holidays* advertisers were polled, the findings were somewhat disconcerting. Fifty-one per cent had not considered the response rate they hoped for from the space they had purchased. Eighty-four per cent had not calculated a cost per enquiry, and 28 per cent did not build a database from their enquirers.

The 1989 campaign was evaluated for its overall effectiveness and against the results which the ETB had hoped it would achieve. The effectiveness of the *England Holidays* campaign varied for different market sectors, as is indicated in Table I4 and by region, shown in Table I5.

It was determined that the 1989 *England Holidays* campaign had been successful in stimulating some £12.5 million of business and that 58 per cent of people the campaign had reached had taken a holiday in England. On the basis of this experience, it was decided that the 1990 campaign would be broadly similar to the methods adopted in 1989, but with a print run of 1.2 million. Two separate reader response cards would be included, one enabling an enquirer to send for up to four resort brochures, the other for two holiday operators' brochures.

Table I4   Tourism sector performance

Sector	Advertisers as % total	Responses %
Regional tourist boards	1	3.7
Package holidays	2	4.4
Activity holidays	3	3.3
Counties	6	13.1
Towns	7	6.2
Boating	9	3.9
Hotels	12.9	11.5
Self-catering	13	30.6
Caravans	13	2.2
Resorts	27	20.9

Table I5   Results by region

Tourist boards	No of advertisers	% of enquirers
London	5	5.2
East Midlands	9	2.2
Northumbria	9	4
Cumbria	10	5.4
North West	13	5.3
Yorkshire and Humberside	13	12.6
Thames and Chiltern	14	7.1
Heart of England	17	7.2
South East England	22	5.2
East England	22	7.2
Southern	36	6.6
West Country	113	32.8

Sources: Data in all tables based on internal ETB report, 'England Holidays 1989, Interim Report', September 1989

However, the previous year's competition to encourage responses was dropped, as was the freepost facility. It was felt that this would confine use of the response cards to those who were genuinely interested in the product.

Questions

1 Analyse the rewards available to the various participants in this tourism system.

2 What additional marketing tools could ETB adopt to support the *England Holidays* approach, other than those reported here?

3 How would you determine the reasons for the varying results shown in the data tables for this case study, and what changes would you recommend in the strategy for the next edition of *England Holidays?*

Relevant chapters

2, 3, 4 and 5.

Public Relations in Texas' Marketing Communications Strategy

Introduction

The climate, scenery, and variety of Texas attract many tourists, and provide many promotional opportunities. Its visitor industry generates more than $18 billion annually, and supports nearly 300000 jobs.

The vigour of the State's economy, despite problems (notably in the oil sector) is such that the State's Gross National Product would rank twelfth in the world, were Texas an independent nation. Partly in response to oil industry fluctuations, it has diversified into high technology and service industries, including finance and tourism. The integrated circuit, foundation of the modern electronics industry, was invented in the State by Texas Instruments in the 1950s. The State also has some of the leading medical research institutes of the world, and is a centre for space technology.

The Texas Department of Commerce's mission is to build and maintain a diverse economy for Texas, and to stimulate job creation by using the State's resources, building public and private partnerships, and instituting programmes and activities. The Texas Tourism Division is part of the Department of Commerce.

Public relations

Within America, the State of Texas employs public relations methods, especially media relations, as a key element in its marketing communications. Three thrusts were identified in the 1990 Media Plan; to present an appealing and accurate

233

image of Texas' attractions, to defeat any stereotypical notions of Texas harboured by potential visitors who had never visited the State, and thirdly to maximize the impact of advertising and gain credibility with consumers through editorial comment on Texas. The strategy was to educate journalists about Texas, and make it easy for them to find out more. This was to be achieved by a series of tactics indicated in Table J1. Various measures were specified for assessing the value of publicity resulting from the media tactics, which were carefully monitored.

Table J1   Media relations tactics

Monthly press packet*
Media site inspection tours
News releases
Information and editorial assistance
Photography
Trade shows
Division support
Clipping/distribution services
Calendar of events listings
Tourism Division Newsletter*
Collateral material for press corps
Public relations campaign
International media relations

*Tactics used in the US, but not the UK

UK public relations campaign for Texas

Texas is very well served by air connections from Britain. British Airways, American Airlines and Continental Airlines between them offer a minimum of four wide body services daily throughout the year to its two international gateways at Houston and Dallas/Fort Worth. Texas was the fourth most popular American State for British visitors in 1988, with 230 000 arrivals indicated by United States Travel and Tourism Authority (USTTA) statistics, and 260 000 expected in 1990.

It was considered that the British market should be developed systematically, and a British company, Raitt Orr Associates, was retained in 1989 to tailor Texas' promotional techniques to local conditions. The approach which Texas adopted in the UK was to stimulate interest in the destination by the public and the travel trade, after the initial product launch, five tour programmes had been developed in conjunction with leading tour operators and British Airways.

Five strategies were developed to heighten awareness of its attractions amongst the travel and business communities in Britain. These were seminars on relevant aspects of Texas' tourism and business, media support facilities, site inspection visits for selected journalists, the preparation of brochures targeted to the trade and to the public, and a major presence at the World Travel Market (WTM) for Texas.

Seminars

A series of informative seminars was arranged for targeted audiences. Specialized topics varied from Texas as a centre of interest and research into wild flowers, to a presentation highlighting the opportunities for business with the State. Each seminar was led by experts on their subject, often flown in specially for the purpose from Texas and was supported with a detailed press information kit. The seminars were followed by a visit to the State for a selected group of journalists who specialized in that particular field.

The purpose of these seminars was two-fold. In the first place, each was seen as a method of developing specific awareness of travel opportunities for a specialized segment of the overall market. Secondly, the cumulative effect of the seminars, together with journalists' coverage, and other public relations and marketing methods, was expected to stimulate general interest in Texas as a destination, amongst both travel trade members and the travelling public.

'Doing Business Texas Style' was the second of the series of special interest, targeted workshops. Its main aim was to acquaint selected British executives with business and travel opportunities in Texas. Eight hundred overseas companies, including 200 based in the UK, were already involved in start-ups, joint ventures and wholly-owned subsidiaries in Texas. The seminar explored the themes of banking, high technology (particularly computer business), import and export, real estate, trade shows and conventions, as well as travel. Speakers were drawn from the Board of the Texas Department of Commerce, Texas-based banks, financial services, and travel groups such as the Texas Association of Convention and Visitor Bureaux. UK-based managers of Texan companies such as Compaq Computer Corporation presented their views and the British Department of Trade and Industry was also represented on the panel of speakers. Nearly 200 professionals attended the one-day workshop held at the London Chamber of Commerce.

Media visits to Texas

In Britain, a series of group and individual media trips was arranged, each patronized by an airline. Although each press trip had specific objectives, selected participants and specialized itineraries, the following is typical in many respects. It was entitled Wild West Texas, and hosted by the Texas Department of Commerce in collaboration with British Airways, which provided the inter-national flights. Eight journalists were selected. They represented national and regional daily papers, local and national radio stations, and relevant special interest magazines such as *Departures*, a full colour magazine distributed to American Express Gold Card holders in the UK and to Platinum Card holders in the USA. Certain freelancers who had a reputation for placing effective articles in relevant media were also invited.

The tour was accompanied by a British Airways press officer, the Media Tour co-ordinator from the Texas Department of Commerce, and the Texas Account Director of Raitt Orr Associates, its UK public relations agency. A major objective of this press tour was to heighten awareness of the Panhandle area of Texas. Table J2 indicates highlights of the itinerary for the Panhandle section of the tour, which was also accompanied by a local photographer and a local journalist.

Table J2   The Panhandle itinerary

Monday	Light breakfast at hotel (in Fort Worth). Depart hotel by 08.30. Morning flight to Lubbock (Southwest Airlines flight 224, departs 10.20, and arrives 11.15). Noon, lunch in Lubbock. 13.30: visit the Ranching Heritage Centre, seeing the evolution of ranching in Texas. (Bus takes bags to hotel during museum tour.) Tour Teysha cellars. Drive by Buddy Holly statue. 16.00: check in at Hotel (Holiday Inn Civic Centre, *address, phone and fax given*). 17.00: depart for sunset dinner at McNeill ranch (cowboy cook-out), near Crosbyton. 23.00: back at hotel. Overnight in Lubbock.
Tuesday	07.30-8.30: breakfast in Lubbock, load luggage. Photo stop at prairie dog town, and meet Prairie Dog Pete. 09.00: morning drive to Hereford. Stop at Cowgirl Hall of Fame. 12.30: lunch in Canyon at the Hudspeth House. Drive on to Amarillo area. Visit the stockyards, then the nearby saddle shop. Check in to Hotel (*details given*). Evening reception at the Don Harrington Discovery Centre to see *Panhandle Promise*. Dinner at the Big Texan Steak House. Back to Hotel for overnight in Amarillo.
Wednesday	07.30: departure from Hotel. Breakfast at the Christian Ranch for 'Cowboy morning' on the rim of Palo Duro Canyon. Then, back downtown to Amarillo to refresh at the hotel. Noon, light lunch, then a brief city tour, including old Route 66 and the Cadillac Ranch. Mid afternoon: drive on to Canyon for a tour of the Panhandle Plains Museum. Then down into Palo Duro Canyon for a ride on the Sad Monkey Railroad. 18.30: end the evening at the opening night of *Texas*, the musical drama in Palo Duro Canyon. Back at the Hotel by 00.30.
Thursday	Breakfast at the hotel. Depart at 09.45 for Southwest Airlines flight 25 to Dallas/Fort Worth.

After the tour, the UK agency monitored the resultant editorial coverage through a clippings service, and by contacting each journalist after an interval to ask for samples of their work. Participants were also invited to comment on the arrangements made for them during the press trip, as an input into planning future visits.

During the year, four group press visits and a number of individual visits were organized for British journalists. The total coverage from all public relations activities amounted to the equivalent of some $6 103 000 of paid advertising at the standard rates of each of the journals, radio and television stations where Texas gained exposure from this exercise. Using Texas' enhanced credibility factor for editorial coverage, this media exposure has been evaluated as worth over $42.7 million.

Tour brochures

Forty-seven UK tour operators offered the State in their brochures for 1989/90, usually as one amongst many American or long haul destinations. The resultant lack of prominence for tours to Texas was identified as a weakness and highlighted for rapid attention early in the campaign. British Airways had gained its Texas route when it acquired British Caledonian, and it needed to promote the service. A joint Texan and British Airways brochure was produced, bringing together tours from several companies which had two features in common; they were all centred on Texas, and they all used British Airways services across the Atlantic. The brochure was produced quickly, as the first of a series. It employed a simple format, using generic copy to describe the attractions of Texas and featured pages selected from the brochures of six major tour operators. It was entitled 'Texas, its like a country within a country', and carried BA's logo on both covers. The contents page indicated the tour operators it featured, giving their contact details. The range of tours it offered included fly drive, escorted coach tours, both around Texas and including other States, dude ranch holidays, and city extensions to holidays. It was launched at the World Travel Market and advertised to the travel trade in the trade press and in selected newspapers such as *The Sunday Times*.

World travel market

Texas brought one of America's largest delegations to the annual international World Travel Market in London in November 1989. The delegation comprised executives of the major cities, resorts, airports, hotels and tourist ranches. A pre-opening media breakfast was held for America's Heartland, a regional marketing group including Texas as its major gateway.

This grouping of six states (also including Kansas, Louisiana, Missouri, New Mexico and Oklahoma) had existed before, but was now seeking to gain mutual advantages from their marketing efforts. A Heartland brochure was produced as a source of information for the travel trade. This gave contacts for each State, together with an introduction to each, and suggested itineraries. A double-page spread provided a calendar outlining three events each month, for each State throughout the coming year. For Texas, these ranged from the Cotton Bowl Parade and Game in Dallas in January, to a Black-Eyed Pea Jamboree, held in Athens in July, and a Dickens festival in Galveston in December.

The *Travel Trade Gazette* had produced an insert in the form of a counter guide for agency staff which was included in a November edition. Offprints of this 16-page full colour guide were distributed at WTM, and provided a speedy introduction to the scope of Texas' tourism. The show business side of public relations emerged strongly at the World Travel Market. Texas' stand was designed to represent the Alamo, its most famous building, and a large styrofoam map of the Heartlands was displayed by the delegates of these States for photographs, which subsequently featured prominently in *Travel News*,

Travel Trade Gazette, and other publications. The Director of the Texas Division of Tourism was interviewed by the LBC radio travel programme. The interview was run back-to-back with coverage of Texas taped during one of the Texas media visits.

Further developments

Incentive and conference traffic to Texas is considered to be a potential market worth developing, but to promote this aspect of Texas' tourism effectively further research was required on behalf of the client, into the needs and expectations of conference managers.

In America, the individual Texas towns are in competition for convention business, and can use a variety of trade shows, specialist magazines and other tools to generate business.

However, they are less well known in the UK, and it is much less convenient for a potential client to research them individually. Consequently, a different approach was recommended for the UK, where a brochure and a promotion of conference facilities would be more effective if it were to feature Texas as a whole rather than individual destinations.

Questions

1 At one time Texas applied a credibility multiplier to calculate the value of the media exposure it gained through public relations. Explain the thinking behind this concept, relating it to theories of source credibility.

2 Examine the public relations practices of an organization with which you are familiar, and assess the strengths and weaknesses of the approach adopted.

3 Why are trade focused promotions important in the marketing communications strategies of destinations?

Relevant chapters

1, 3, 5 and 12.

The Development of a Modern Management Style at British Airways

Introduction

The crises facing British Airways (BA) in the early 1980s have been documented by many analysts and acknowledged by BA. The roots of the problem lay in the ownership (by Government) of BEA and BOAC, the airlines from which BA had been constituted and its failure to cope with the range of challenges facing it after they were merged in 1974. The development of the airline's organization was such that BA's chairman, Lord King of Wartnaby, was able to say in 1986, 'The aim of BA is to be the best and most successful airline in the world'.

Crisis and the need for change

Until 6 February 1987 BA remained a commercial enterprise owned by the UK Government. It had been set up in that form by the 1971 Civil Aviation Act to take over the activities of BOAC and BEA. The merger proved difficult to manage as the two companies from which BA had been formed had been organized in very different ways, and according to the Monopolies and Mergers Commission report the merger was not effectively completed until the 1977 BA Board Act which empowered British Airways to operate air transport services both within the UK and overseas.

However, in 1978 an internal BA study reported that it was less efficient than its main rivals. One problem facing BA after the merger was a substantial overmanning surplus, despite not having increased its staffing since 1972. The strategy which the airline's management proposed in response was to expand the company so that existing staff could be deployed more efficiently. The two-fold implications of this recommendation were: BA needed to grow faster than its rivals, and secondly it needed to encourage more customers to use its services. The tactical solution was to adopt lower prices.

239

These 'gap-filling' approaches failed for reasons which were partly internal, including allegedly slack management, and because of the effects of two major external events. One was the OPEC oil crisis which caused the cost of fuel to double (for all airlines). The second was the resultant worldwide depression. The combined effect was that the planned growth in demand did not materialize, consequently revenue fell short of targets and profits suffered. Operating profits in the year to March 1979 fell short of budget by nearly 25 per cent. In addition, the replacement programme for its ageing fleet caused heavy borrowing.

The restructuring programme had already begun; it involved reducing the routes which BA served, divesting its property interests, closing the college of Air Training and transferring catering operations to outside contractors. The fleet was reduced and the Government decided that the airline was to be prepared for sale to the private sector at a later date.

BA at that time had been described as offering 'a "peasant class" of travel on European routes ... and showing a general subservience to trade union pressure' (Campbell-Smith, 1986). Many of its international routes were losing money. Managers' jobs were highly specialized and interdepartmental communications were very poor. Seniority was the basis of promotion and the split between BOAC (with a tradition of stylish service) and BEA (emphasizing cheap service) continued despite their merger in 1974. In March 1982, debts were declared to be 108 per cent of assets, and accordingly, British Airways was technically bankrupt.

In addition to its privatization programmes, which had identified BA as a target as early as 1979, the UK Government also espoused the deregulation of international transport. Similar policies had been adopted in the USA, with the overall result that airlines gained freedom to bid for routes, schedules and capacity, but lost the protection of their governments on those routes. The consequence was that the pace of change on major revenue routes increased and the nature of competition between airlines altered.

The pressure of increasing competition, resulting in part from deregulation, together with increases in industrial disputes and stoppages at BA further undermined the company's competitive position as its potential passengers opted for alternative carriers' services. Airlines were also affected by changing operational technology and subjected to operating constraints at airports and by Air Traffic Control centres as the volume of traffic neared capacity. The cumulative result of these external conditions was that individual airlines' survival was seen to be at risk in the new market conditions for scheduled air travel where airlines had to compete for their passengers' changing preferences.

This was the background when Lord King of Wartnaby was appointed Chairman in September 1980, and the restructuring of BA began.

Culture and structural change at BA

Lord King appointed Colin Marshall as Chief Executive (now Sir Colin Marshall). Sir Colin came to BA convinced that success in service industries depends on putting people first. His previous success at Avis had been widely recognized amongst service managers. The Avis slogan and operating code was 'Trying Harder'. Clients had been invited to phone named managers in the event that everything was not perfect. *All* Avis managers were expected to work at the counter to remain in contact with their customers.

In February 1983, Sir Colin established a steering group to look at ways of improving the level and consistency of customer service which BA offered. The framework for the steering group was set by BA's expressed aim of becoming the best airline in the world. Customer service was identified as the key corporate value and meeting customer needs was the key area requiring radical change.

In February 1983 two decisions were taken which shaped the subsequent development of BA:

1 A Marketing Policy Group was established. This became known as the Gang of Four and was also charged with the reorganization of BA. An external consultant advised on the reorganization, and other BA managers were co-opted to the Group.
2 A presentation on Putting People First which was accepted by Sir Colin Marshall led to a series of courses implemented throughout the company.

On 11 July 1983 the new organization was announced in two White Books which remain confidential. Volume One set out the Job Specifications for senior positions which those selected were asked to accept on that day, not then knowing who occupied other positions on the new organizational chart. Volume Two set out the company's philosophy for each division. The airline's management was overhauled and the new structure installed in the course of a single day when 60 of the then 100 top managers left the company, and some managers were brought into the airline to fill high impact jobs. The new management team had an average age of 41, in contrast to the average of 20 years in management positions typical under the previous regime. The internal managers who survived were those who displayed entrepreneurial abilities and were prepared to take risks: these were characteristics which the old management had not rewarded. Table K1 shows the revised departmental structure for BA.

In order to achieve an improved responsiveness towards their customers, a cultural revolution had to be carried out in a mature and functioning company. The objective was achieved through programmes of staff and management development programmes.

1 Staff training starting from the bottom up

> In the old days airline managers had concentrated on the backwheel of the corporate bicycle; they had invested in the power end of the business and training had concentrated on product knowledge. Now the interest focused on the front wheel. This did not drive the cyclist forward, but the skill of avoiding obstacles by precise steering was as important as pedalling powerfully ... it was not good business for a transport company to run into its passengers. (Farnham, 1986)

A company-wide rolling programme of training towards customer awareness was introduced. The programme was developed by Time

Table K1   British Airways departmental structure (1983)

Lord King (Chairman)
Colin Marshall (Chief Executive)
Director of Marketing
Director of Operations
Chief Financial officer
Director of Investor Relations and Market Place Performance
Director of Engineering
Director of Safety Services
Company Secretary
Director of Human Resources
Director of Public Affairs
Legal Director
Director of Information Management
Director of Medical Services
Director of Planning
Director of Flight Crew

Management International, an earlier version having proved successful for SAS, the Scandinavian airline. Starting in December 1983, all 37000 BA staff went on the 'Putting People First' course, the first stage of the programme to orient staff towards a customer perspective.

- *Putting People First*
  PPF (1) was a two-day event presented to about 150 people at each session, drawn from a range of customer contact positions. Over a two-year period all employees were covered, not just the contact staff who were its original targets. Its central focus was the basic personal feelings of staff during their encounter with passengers, and ways of coping with stress.

- *Customer First Teams*
  Volunteers formed quality circles to identify ways to improve the customer service experiences in their area of work. The positive outcomes were two-fold:
  a) Staff offered significant suggestions for work improvements based on their experience.
  b) People felt they had gained some measure of control over the service they deliver.

- *Customer First Training Review*
  The implications of developing contact staff sensitivities to customer service was that it became necessary to review all the existing training programmes.

- *Putting People First (2)*
  A one-day training event, similar to PPF(1); but intended for functional staff who did not deal directly with passengers. Its purpose was to demonstrate the importance of effective customer contact.

A Day In The Life of . . .
PPF(3) took the form of 'an internal exhibition', a participative programme in which each department showed the rest of the company what it does. This followed a desire expressed by people taking the earlier courses to find out more about what other departments did.

In a Press Release BA summed up the purpose behind this major investment in training:

> The philosophy is that staff who have a greater awareness and understanding of the business should be able to provide high, professional standards of customer service, and also be in a strong position to act as ambassadors for the airline. Messages delivered at PPF courses are reinforced and the concept of teamwork at BA is encouraged.

2   Management changes and training

A three phase Managing People First programme was devised for BA's management.

- *Research amongst managers*
  A study was commissioned to discover what senior managers considered to be important in their role, and what the shortcomings were. It identified five common aspects, shown in Table K2.

Table K2   Key aspects of
managerial roles

Trust
Teamwork
Taking responsibility
Clarity of vision
Motivation

A five-day residential programme was devised centring on the right things for managers to do, rather than the operational methods involved.

- *Training*
  A series of courses were concerned with the implementation of the appropriate management style.
- *Performance-related pay*
  Management remuneration was based on regular appraisals against pre-agreed criteria. This generated an appraised-appraiser report which, together with company reports, provided the basis of calculation for individual annual financial bonuses.

Marketing research

Underlying the changed philosophy of the company was a programme of market research. This formed the starting point for a fully integrated campaign to improve standards of service. The researchers were concerned with the views of both customers and staff and they focused on where customers' goodwill, and hence their business, could be generated.

The research was conducted amongst airtravellers including BA and other airline passengers to identify BA's image. BA emerged as aloof, detached, not caring, not friendly, but technically competent, showing British cool and ability to cope with crises.

The second phase was an internal research project using repertory grid techniques on customer contact staff to find out their views of customers. The major result of this survey was to identify a strong tendency to jump very quickly to stereotypes and then to deal with the stereotype and not the individual.

A 'Customer Service Department' was established to monitor market research, and analyse staff and customer views. This department has grown in significance and has helped to produce Customer Service Standards and a Service Quality Audit. It has become one of the seven major departments in the marketing section of the company, with line responsibility for all customer contact staff (excluding cabin crew).

Privatization

The philosophy of the Government at that time favoured privatization of commercial operations which had come under public ownership during the decades following the Second World War. The Government provided BA with various forms of support during the run up to privatization including preferential rates of interest on loans from the National Loan Fund, Treasury guarantees to private sector debts and subsidies to Concorde which were estimated at £10m. (Corke, 1986).

The original date set for a public placement of its equity was March 1985, but an anti-trust case brought by the liquidators of Laker Airways delayed it following the events which culminated in the failure of Laker in 1982 – first as a result of the 1984 House of Lords ruling that the defendants (including BA) should appear before United States courts, and then as uncertainties emerged over the Bermuda Two agreements and US anti-trust legislation.

In February 1987, BA attracted 1 200 000 investors when it was launched as a public company, although by the end of the 1986/87 financial year the share register had shrunk to 400 000 investors.

Post-privatization policy

Three related internal one-page documents circulated in 1987 set out BA's mission following its privatization. They are presented in Table K3 in an abbreviated form.

The statement of BA's corporate goals concludes, 'the achievement of all objectives will be managed so as to be consistent with, and contribute to, our earning a profit sufficient to provide an acceptable return on assets employed'.

Table K3   Post-privatization policy

1 The BA Mission – To 1990 and Beyond
- BA will have a corporate charisma such that everyone working for it will take pride in the company and see themselves as representing a highly successful worldwide organization
- BA will be a creative enterprise, caring about its people and its customers
- BA will develop the kind of business capability which will make BA the envy of its competitors, to the enhancement of its stakeholders
- BA will be a formidable contender in all the fields it enters, as well as demonstrating a resourceful and flexible ability to earn high profits wherever it chooses to focus
- Whether in transport or in any of the travel or tourism activity areas, the term 'BA' will be the ultimate symbol of creativity, value, service and quality

2 BA's corporate objectives
The paramount objective is profitability, underpinned by subsidiary objectives:
- To match at least the annual average growth of the total world airline market
- To achieve standards of performance at least as high as the best of our competitors
- To serve existing routes and markets, to identify new opportunities for branded services and products and to ensure BA's freedom to compete in world markets; all being undertaken in such a manner as to meet the paramount and subsidiary objectives
- To attract, develop and retain sufficient well-trained staff with the skills to meet customer expectations
- To be more efficient than relevant competitors in the market places we choose to operate
- To provide a continuity of service from the initial point of customer contact through to the completion of the service

3 BA's corporate goals
- The corporate goal in British Airways is to be the best airline in the world
To achieve this goal, the corporate objectives are:
- To provide the highest levels of service to all customers, passengers, shippers, travel agents and freight agents
- To preserve high professional and technical standards in order to achieve the highest levels of safety
- To provide a uniform image worldwide and to maintain a specific set of standards for each clearly defined market segment
- To respond quickly and sensitively to the changing needs of present and potential customers
- To maintain and, where opportunity occurs, expand the present route structure
- To manage, operate and market the airline in the most efficient manner
- To create a service and people-oriented work environment, assuring all employees of fair pay and working conditions and continuing concern for their careers

Questions

1 Given that the airline was in a serious situation at the time described in this case study, was such a wide sweeping reorganization the only feasible solution?

2 What benefits can you identify for BA's passengers, staff and proprietors from the reorganization?

3 Training was one of the key change mechanisms described in this case study. What is required if such an extensive training programme can be successful in an organization?

Relevant chapters

1, 7, 8 and 9.

Researching Customer Attitudes and Experiences at British Airways

Introduction

> Certainly the airlines as a whole do not always perform as well as they should . . . there are times when our aircraft are neither as punctual as we would wish them, nor as scrupulously clean as we would desire nor as well catered as we feel is essential for every passenger . . . As the average size of aircraft increases, the terminals become more crowded, and arrival and departure slots more congested, so all of this becomes more and more difficult to do well. Our only choice as an industry is to try even harder, for certainly, and properly, our passengers do not wish to hear about our concerns; they only want the assurance that they are going to receive what they were promised in an enticing and caring fashion. (Colin Marshall, Chief Executive, British Airways, 1986)

BA employs a variety of ways to monitor customer perceptions of its services. Some material is generated directly by customers who contact the company with compliments or complaints. Another source is the responses solicited from current customers in a variety of specific studies either internal or commissioned. This information is proprietary to BA, only an indication of recent, rather than current sources is discussed in this case study. A further source is the syndicated studies of consumer attitudes by independent market research companies.

Customer research at BA

An internal BA documented commented, 'Our customers' views are regularly monitored – every year 115 000 passengers are asked how they see us on all aspects of ground service from queue lengths to personal service'. The base studies are the Inflight Survey and the Airport Survey. A variety of analyses are available to BA managers.

Customer service standards monitor

This study provides BA managers with a key measure of performance across all areas of its operations based on selected passengers' attitudes collected in a questionnaire booklet. These views are regarded as 'spotlighting service characteristics, rather than proving their effectiveness'.

Taking one Monitor as an example, some ten thousand interviews with BA customers were analysed. The findings are circulated to BA managers on a quarterly basis, and in this study included:

1 An assessment of overall satisfaction with the (then new) Terminal 4 at Heathrow. It recorded the highest level of satisfaction with any terminal, anywhere. It was felt to be much easier to find the check-in desks and some improvements in staff behaviour were reported.
2 Cabin crew effects on satisfaction were noted and discussed in detail for the main routes operated by BA. For example, inflight announcements were considered from the point of view of clarity and audibility, sufficiency, and the crews' language skills.

Qualitative monitor

A regular survey of Business Travellers is conducted by external consultants. The topics covered vary according to BA's changing needs. Table L1 shows some of the sections included in one study.

Table L1   Sample topics in *Business Traveller* survey

BA's image
Shuttle and other domestic services
Ground handling, check-in and baggage retrieval
In-flight service and entertainment
Catering
Special issues – safety, privatization advertising and Terminal 4
Marketing – a new business class concept for long-haul; automated ticket machines; in-flight telecommunications

The survey methods included self-completion questionnaires and diaries and small group discussions conducted at locations around the UK over a two-month period.

Lessons were drawn from the Business Traveller study for planned future developments:

Some members were very enthusiastic about the idea of having a small screen attached to the seat in front of them to watch films, so that they could decide for themselves whether or not to watch the screen, whether to open or close the window blind, and whether to have their reading light on or off, without impinging on their neighbour's freedom of choice. [Such screens were introduced into service from 1988.]

Competitor comparison

A sample of business travellers identified from the Inflight Survey were invited to rate their experiences of BA and its competitors on some 20 dimensions. Their perceptions were grouped into the categories shown in Table L2.

Table L2   Dimensions of
business travellers'
service perceptions

Human values
Efficiency
Comfort
Food
Aircraft
Safety

Each quarter year, a summary focuses on features then of current concern; for example comparing BA's rating with its major competitors by region of operation.

Advertising and image monitor

Tracking studies to monitor the effectiveness of BA's advertising are conducted in major markets, including overseas. One study had been conducted immediately after the release of the supercare TV campaign. Awareness of BA was compared to that of other airlines operating between Australia and Britain. Image perceptions were examined, contrasting findings emerging for the two major segments in the quota-based sample: business travellers and non-business travellers.

Awareness of the factors indicated in Table L3 were examined as components of BA's image.

Product development

Service changes and enhancements are important elements in an airline's marketing strategy and an awareness of customers' needs and perceptions is central to effective product development. A programme of research relating to Super Club and Club in Europe began in 1984. Despite the fact that they were

249

Table L3   Components
of BA's image

Worldwide offices
Hotels
Car hire
Travel service
Modernity
Expensiveness
Prestige
Safety reputation
Business class
Check-in
Baggage handling
Punctuality
Well-liked
Seat comfort
Friendliness
Meals
Passenger care

constantly improving in terms of the customer service offered, by 1986 BA felt that it was falling behind in terms of physical comfort. A number of major competitors had opted for snoozer seats and research results on these types of seats indicated that they could become the industry norm.

An internal BA seminar examined the needs and preferences of Business Class passengers:

> ... essentially people fly Business Class for reasons of status, comfort and service ... when we looked at what drives people's choice of airline ... we found that whilst businessmen place great emphasis on all aspects of service, including those on the ground, some passengers are driven more by comfort, whilst others are more driven by service or schedule. The key issues for the traveller in the long-haul Business Class cabin are comfort and space; the ability to select a seat, segregation ... priority treatment and the product extras.

The presentation explained the significance which BA placed on customers' opinions in developing the Club World brand:

> Today's British Airways gives you a unique blend of British style and service. In each market we discovered what people like to see in a hypothetical ideal airline; how people perceived BA and what they felt about Britain itself, both favourable and unfavourable. There is always a degree of overlap between each of these, but the overlap is different in each market we studied ... we extracted those areas of common ground and produced a list of descriptors. The research revealed that aspects of comfort were becoming more important, but there is some shortfall in what people want and what BA delivers in terms of key comfort criteria.

Table L4 summarizes the main findings.

The decision was made to relaunch the Business Class product (at the end of 1987).

Table L4   Key comfort criteria

	Ideal %	BA %
Comfort	89	57
Legroom	81	49
Seat width	67	48
Seat recline	57	35
Atmosphere	45	50

Communicating research findings to staff

Although much market research is strategic and long term in its focus, the results often have tactical and immediate significance, as the following example shows. An attractive poster was displayed in BA staff areas at airports, from which Table L5 has been prepared. It showed an 11 item questionnaire with four possible responses for each category boldly ticked to indicate what passengers felt.

Table L5   'How do our customers measure airport service?'

- Staff that are attentive and ready to help
- Polite staff
- Competence in dealing with any eventuality
- Level of tact displayed by staff in difficult situations
- Staff that appear to enjoy dealing with people
- Availability of airline staff
- Response to individual needs
- Being treated as an individual
- Approachable staff
- Staff who are warm and friendly
- Being greeted with a smile

Customer correspondence

BA channels all compliments and complaints through Customer Relations, a management function based at Heathrow. Comments reach the department directly, by mail or phone, or from the video booths installed in some airport terminals; indirectly via travel agents involved in booking flights; or through other BA departments, notably Regional Managers or the Chairman's and Chief Executive's offices. Another route is the comment forms which passengers can obtain either in flight or at the terminal lounges. For purposes of analysis and retrieval, each customer correspondence file is logged by BA's Customer Relations department into a computer database for analysis under more than 100 service headings, grouped broadly into the categories shown in Table L6.

Table L6   Analytical categories for customer correspondence

Reservations and sales
Cabin service
Catering service
Airport service
Operations and equipment
General

The Customer Relations department has two significant roles within BA; it performs a reactive problem solving function for dissatisfied customers, where it has the potential to redeem the situation and encourage the continued loyalty of customers. Secondly, as a proactive marketing unit it identifies opportunities for enhancements or changes to services attractive to customers.

An internal BA consultative document discussed several factors in its work, these are shown in Table L7. The report recommended that all managers should visit the department and read mail relevant to their work (the mail is held secure within this department as a matter of policy). It pointed out that while few did so in 1983, incoming customer correspondence selected at random from the mail is now opened, read, and discussed by groups of managers on a regular basis.

Table L7   Findings of the customer relations department

- Evidence from an analysis of correspondence following known 'service disasters' such as strike bound airports that the complaint rate is variable.
- The varying reasons leading the minority of those who write to do so: suggested motivations range from an attempt to gain compensation, to the high profile of the airline's leaders
- Complaints cannot be regarded as a barometer of customer attitudes, given the varying motivations of correspondents; but the information gathered has potential value to managers.

Executive correspondence summary

The Executive summary issued by Customer Relations for internal circulation presented an analysis of customer correspondence received during two periods, summarized in Table L8.

Table L8   Comparison of customer correspondence

	Month X 198a	Month X 198b
Complaints	2106	2445
Compliments	539	696
Queries	388	482

Confidential company data indicates that premium fare passengers, especially those travelling in first class, are the most active correspondents, both in expressing complaints and praise.

Questions

1 What justification can you offer for the emphasis BA places on understanding its customers?

2 How does the research approach outlined in this case study compare with any other tourism company with which you are familiar?

3 This book has emphasized the central significance in tourism management and marketing of understanding tourists' expectations and subsequent experiences of services. Do you agree with this view?

Relevant chapters

1, 3, 4, 7, 8 and 9.

Bibliography

Ableson, R.P. 'Script Processing in Attitude Formation and Decision Making' in: Corroll, J.S. and Payne, J.W. *Cognition and Social Behaviour*, Erlbaum, Hillside, New Jersey, 1976

Adams, J.S. 'The Structure and Dynamics of Behaviour in Organizational Boundary Roles' in: Dunette, M.D. (ed.) *Handbook of Industrial and Organizational Psychology*, Rand McNally, Chicago, 1976

'The Contribution of World Travel and Tourism To The Global Economy', American Express Travel Related Services Co Inc; New York, 1989

'How Amex Measures Quality'; no author, AMA Forum, 1982

Akehurst, G. 'Service Industries', in: Jones, P. (ed.) *Management in the Service Industries*, Pitman, London, 1989

Allard, I. 'Statistical measurement in tourism' in Witt, S.F. and Moutinho, L. *Tourism Marketing and Management Handbook*, p. 419–24, Prentice Hall, London, 1989

D'Amore, L. 'Guidelines to planning harmony with the local community' in: Murphy, P.E. (ed.) *Tourism in Canada, Selected Issues and Options*, Methuen, London, 1985

'Tourism, The World's Peace Industry', *Business Quarterly*, 1988 (reprint)

International Terrorism, Implications and Challenges for Global Tourism, *Business Quarterly*, 1986 (reprint)

Ansett, R.G. and McManamy, J. *The customer*, John Kerr Pty Ltd, Richmond, Australia, 1989

Ansoff, H.I. *Corporate Strategy*, Penguin, London, 1968

Archer, B. 'The Uses and Abuses of Multipliers' in: Gearing, Swart & Var (eds.) *Planning for Tourism Development*; Praegar, New York, 1976

'Trends in International Tourism' in: Witt, S.F. and Moutinho, L. *Tourism Marketing and Management Handbook*, Prentice Hall, London, 1989

Asseal, H. *Consumer Behaviour and Marketing Action*, Kent Publication Co, Boston, Mass. 1987

Baron, R.R.V. *Seasonality in Tourism: A Guide to the Analysis of Seasonality and Trends for Policy Making*, EIU n2, 1976

Barret, S.D. and Purdy, M. *European Airtransport, Uncabin the Consumer*, Institute of Economic Affairs, Dec/Jan 1987

Baumol, W.J. 'Contestable markets: an uprising in the theory of market structures', *American Economic Review*, March 1982

Baumol, W.J. and Willig, R.D. 'Fixed costs, sunk costs, entry barriers and sustainability of monopoly', *Quarterly Journal of Economics*, August 1981

Bennis, W. *Temporary Society*, Harper and Row, New York, 1968

Blackman, B.A. 'Making a service more tangible can make it more manageable' in: Czepiel, J.A., Soloman, M.R. and Surprenant, C.F. (eds.) *The Service Encounter*; Lexington Books, Mass., 1985

Blazey, M.A. *VALS Typing the Older Adult Traveller,* Travel and Tourism Research Association Proceedings, 1989

Bodlender, J.A. *Tourist Development and the Use of Management Consultants,* City of London Financial Services Seminar, Beijing, July 1985

Bodlender, J.A. and Ward, T.J. 'Profile of investment incentives' in: Witt, S.F. and Moutinho, L. *Tourism Marketing and Management Handbook,* Prentice Hall, London, 1989

Borovits, I. and Neumann, S. 'Airline management information system at Arkia Israeli Airlines', *Management Information Systems Quarterly,* March 1988

Boudon, R. 'Why theories of social change fail: some methodological thoughts', *Public Opinion Quarterly,* No 2, 1983

Brady, J. and Widdows, R. 'The impact of world events on travel to Europe during the summer of 1986', *Journal of Travel Research,* Winter 1988

Brady, R. 'Athens Works Out Miles Cheaper', *Evening Standard,* 6 Feb 1989

British Airways Annual Reports

Burkhart, A.J. and Medlik, S. *Tourism, Past Present and Future;* Heinemann, London, 1981

Buzzell, R.D. and Gale, B.T. *The PIMS Principles,* The Free Press, New York, 1987

Calantone, R.J., Di Benedetto, C.A. and Bojanic, D. 'A Comprehensive Review of the Tourism Forecasting Literature', *Journal of Travel Research,* Fall, 1987

Callies D.L. *Regulating Paradise, Land Use Controls in Hawaii,* University of Hawaii Press, Honolulu, 1984

Campbell-Smith, D. *Struggle for Take-off, the British Airways Story,* Hodder & Stoughton Coronet Books, Sevenoaks, 1986

Carlzon, J. *Moments of Truth,* Harper and Row, New York, 1987

Carter, J. *Chandler's Travels,* Quiller Press, London, 1985

Chase, R.B. and Tansik, D.A. 'The Customer Contact Model for Organizational Design', *Management Science,* v49, 1983

Chatburn, A. 'How BA Intends to Win Over the World', *Campaign,* 13 December, 1985

Chisnall, P.M. *Marketing, a Behavioural Analysis,* McGraw Hill, Maidenhead, 1985

Cohen, E. 'Who is a Tourist?' *Sociological Review,* v22, No4, 1974

Cohen, S. and Taylor, L. *Escape Attempts,* Penguin, Harmondsworth, 1976

Conroy, B.A. 'Approaches to Teaching Brochure Design', *Tourism Management,* September, 1987

Corke, A. *British Airways, the Path to Profitability,* Pinter 1986

Cowell, D. *The Marketing of Services,* Heinemann, London, 1986

Cowell, D.W. 'New Service Development', *Journal of Marketing Management,* v3, No3, 1988

Crimp, M. *The Marketing Research Process,* Prentice Hall, 1985

Croize, J.C. 'Resort Development' in: Witt, S.F. and Moutinho, L. *Tourism Marketing and Management Handbook,* Prentice Hall, London, 1989

Crompton, J. 'Motivations for Pleasure Vacation', *Annals of Tourism Research,* v6, 1979

Crosby, P. *Quality Without Tears,* New American Library New York, 1984

Czepiel, J.A., Soloman, M.R. and Surprenant, C.F. (eds.) *The Service Encounter,* Lexington Books, Mass. 1985

Dann, G. 'Tourist satisfaction, a highly complex variable', *Annals of Tourism Research,* v4, 1978

Davidson, J. 'Strife begins at 40 for the jaded package', *The Sunday Times,* September, 1989

Deshpande, R. and Webster, F.E. 'Organizational Culture and Marketing: Defining the Research Agenda, *Journal of Marketing*, v53, 1989

Deming, W.E. *Quality, Productivity and Competitive Position*, Centre for Advanced Engineering Study, MIT, 1982

Dicken, P. *Global Shift, Industrial Change in a Turbulent World*, Paul Chapman, London, 1988

Doganis, R. *Flying Off Course, the Economics of International Airlines*, Allen & Unwin, London, 1985

Doxey, G.U. *A Causation Theory of Visitor-Resident Irritants, Methodology and Research Inferences*, Travel and Tourism Research Association Proceedings, 1975

Dumazedier, J. *Towards a Society of Leisure*, Free Press, 1967

Embacher, E. and Buttle, F. 'A Repertory Grid Analysis of Austria's Image as a Summer Vacation Destination', *Journal of Travel Research*, Winter 1989

Engel, J.F., Blackwell, R.D. and Miniard, P.W. *Consumer Behaviour*, Dryden Press, New York, 1986

English Tourist Board, *Sightseeing in Britain*, London, 1989
  A Vision for England, London, 1987

European Tourism Year, *Tourism*, October 1989

Evans, F.B. 'Selling as a Dyadic Relationship', *American Behavioural Scientist*, May 1963

Farnham, N. Education for Airlines Proceedings of seminar; 'Transport Studies: What Role in a Tourism Course' Laws, E. (ed.) Tourism Society, October 1986

Farrell, B.H. *Hawaii, The Legend That Sells*, University of Hawaii Press, Honolulu, 1982

Festinger, L.A. *A Theory of Cognitive Dissonance*, Stamford University Press, 1957

Fishbein, M. and Ajzen, I. *Belief, Attitudes, Intentions and Behaviour*, Addison Wesley, Reading, Mass. 1975

Foxall, G. (ed.) *Marketing in the Service Industries*, Frank Cass & Co, London, 1985

Fornell, C. and Wernerfelt, B. 'Defensive Marketing Strategy by Customer Complaint Management: A Theoretical Analysis', *Journal of Marketing Research*, November 1987

Friel, E.J. 'Convention Marketing' in: Witt, S.F. and Moutinho, L. *Tourism Marketing and Management Handbook*, Prentice Hall, London, 1989

Frechtling, D.C. *Proposed Standard Definitions and Classifications for Travel Research*, Travel and Tourism Research Association Proceedings, 1976

Garvin, D.A. *Managing Quality, the Strategic and Competitive Edge*, Free Press, New York, 1988

Gee, C.Y., Choy, D.J.L. and Makens, J.C. *The Travel Industry*, AVI Publishing Co, Westport, 1984

George, W.R. and Gibson, B.E. 'Blueprinting: A Tool for Managing Quality in Organizations' QUIS Symposium at the University of Karlstad, Sweden, August 1988

George, W.R. and Kelly, T. 'Personal Selling of Services: Emerging Perspectives on Service Marketing', AMA, 1983

Georgiades, N.J. and Phillimore, L. 'The myth of the Hero-Innovator and alternative strategies for organizational change', in Kiernan, C. and Woodford, P. (eds.) *Behaviour Modification with the Severely Retarded*, Associated Scientific Publishers, Amsterdam, 1975

Getz, D. and Frisby, W. 'Evaluating Management Effectiveness in Community-Run Festivals', *Journal of Travel Research*, Summer 1988

Good, W.S., Wilson, M.K. and McWhirter, B.J. 'Passenger Preferences for Airline Fare Plans', *Journal of Travel Research*, Winter 1985

Goodrich, S.N. 'Benefit Bundle Analysis, an Empirical Study of International travellers' in: Hawkins, D.E. Shafer, E.L. and Rovelstadt, J.M. (eds.) *Tourism Marketing and Management Issues*,George Washington University Press, Washington DC, 1980

Gray, H.P. *International Travel, International Trade*, Heath Books, Lexington, Mass. 1970

Gronross, C. 'An Applied Service Marketing Theory', Working paper 57, Swedish School of Economics, Helsinki, 1980

Gummesson, E. 'Service Quality and Product Quality Combined', *Review of Business*, v9, No3, 1988

Gunn, C.A. *Tourism Planning*, Crane Rusak, New York, 1979

Hall, J. 'The Capacity to Absorb Tourists', *Built Environment*, v3, 1974

Hamill, B. and Davies, R. 'Quality in British Airways' in: Moores, B. (ed.) *Are They Being Served?* Phillip Allan, Oxford, 1986

Hartmann, R. 'Tourism, Seasonality and Social Change', *Leisure Studies*, v5, No1, 1986

Hawkins, D.E., Shafer, E.L. and Rovelstadt, J.M. (eds.) *Tourism Marketing and Management Issues*,George Washington University Press, Washington DC, 1980

Hawkins, D.E., Shafer, E.L. and Rovelstadt, J.M. (eds.) *Tourism Planning and Development Issues*, George Washington University Press, Washington DC, 1980

Herman, C.F. 'Threat, Time and Surprise, A Simulation of International Crises' in Hermann, C.F. (ed.) *International Crises: Insights from Behavioural Research*, Free Press, New York, 1972

Hirschman, A. *Exit Voice and Loyalty*, Harvard University Press, Mass. 1970

Hodgson, E. (ed.) *The Travel and Tourism Industries – Strategies for the Future*, Pergamon Press, Oxford, 1987

Holloway, J.C. *The Business of Tourism*, Pitman, London, 1986

Hollander, S.C. 'A Historical Perspective on the Service Encounter' in: Gepiel, J.A., Soloman, M.R. and Surprenant, C.F. (eds.) *The Service Encounter*, Lexington Books, Mass. 1985

Howard, J.A. *Marketing Management*, Irwin, Homewood, Illinois, 1963
Consumer Behaviour: Applications of Theory, McGraw Hill, New York, 1977

Howard, J.A. and Sheth, J.N. *The Theory of Buyer Behaviour*, Wiley, NY, 1969

Hunt, H.K. *Conceptualization and Measurement of Consumer Satisfaction and Dissatisfaction*, Marketing Science Institute, Cambridge, Mass. 1977

Hymas, R. 'Marketing Travel Services' in: Hodgson, E. (ed.) *The Travel and Tourism Industries – Strategies for the Future*, Pergamon Press, Oxford, 1987

Iso-Ahola, S.E. *The Social Psychology of Leisure and Recreation*, Brown, W.C., and Co., Dubuque, 1980

Jafari, J. 'The Socio-economic Costs of Tourism to Developing Countries', *Annals of Tourism Research*, v1, 19??

James, G. 'Air Travel in North America – Forecasts for the Market and its Carriers', *Travel and Tourism Analyst*, April 1986, published by The Economist Intelligence Unit, London

Juran, J.M. *Upper Management and Quality*, Juran Institute, New York, 1982

de Kadt, E. (ed.) *Tourism, Passport to Development*, Oxford University Press, London, 1987

Kanahele, G.H.S. *Ku Kanaka, Stand Tall, A Search for Hawaiian Values*, University of Hawaii Press, Honolulu, 1986

Kanter, R. *The Change Masters,* Simon and Schuster, New York, 1983

Kaspar, C. 'Recent Developments in Tourism Research and Education at University Level' in: Witt, S.F. and Moutinho, L., *Tourism Marketing and Management Handbook,* Prentice Hall, London, 1989

Kassarjian, H.H. and Robertson, T.S. *Perspectives in Consumer Behaviour,* Scott Foresman & Co. 1973

Keown, C.F. 'A Model of Tourists' Propensity to Buy; the Case of Japanese Visitors to Hawaii', *Journal of Travel Research,* Winter 1989

Koutsoyiannis, A. *Non Price Decisions, the Firm in a Modern Context,* Macmillan, Basingstoke, 1987

Kotler, P.H. 'The Major Tasks of Marketing Management', *Journal of Marketing,* October 1973
Marketing Management, Analysis, Planning and Control, Prentice Hall, 1982

Krippendorf, J., *The Holiday Makers – Understanding the Impact of Leisure and Travel,* Heinemann, London, 1987

Ladbroke Group Annual Reports, 1986, 1987, 1988

'Ladbroke's Move Piles On The Pressure', *Caterer and Hotelkeeper,* 10 September 1987

Lalonde, B.J. and Zinszer, P.H. *Customer Service, Meaning and Measurement,* NCPDM, Chicago, 1976

Lavery, P. 'European destination Marketing', in: Witt, S.F. and Moutinho, L., *Tourism Marketing and Management Handbook,* Prentice Hall, London, 1989

Laws, E. 'Identifying and Managing the Consumerist Gap', *Service Industries Journal,* 1986

Lawson, F. and Baud-Bovey, M. *Tourism and Recreational Development,* Architectural Press, 1977

Leppard, J. and McDonald, M. 'A Reappraisal of the Role of Marketing Planning', *Journal of Marketing Research,* Winter 1987

Levinson, H. *The Exceptional Executive,* Harvard University Press, 1971

Levitt, T. *The Marketing Mode,*McGraw Hill, New York, 1969

'Production Line Approach to Service', *Harvard Business Review,* v50, 1972

Lewis, R. *The New Service Society,* Longman, Harlow, 1973

Lewis, R. & Morris S.V. 'The positive side of guest complaints', *Cornell Hotel and Restaurant Administration Quarterly,* v27, 1987

Lockwood, A. 'Quality Management in Hotels' in: Witt, S.F. and Moutinho, L. *Tourism Marketing and Management Handbook,* Prentice Hall, London, 1989

Lovelock, C.H. *Services Marketing,* Prentice Hall, Englewood Cliffs, 1984

'Strategies for Managing Demand in Capacity Constrained Service Organizations' in: *Marketing in the service industries;* Foxall, G. (ed.) Frank Cass, London, 1985

'Services Marketing: What Does it Involve?' Paper presented at the Economist Conference, Marketing Financial Services, London, February 1988

McLuhan, M. *Understanding Media,* McGraw Hill Books, New York, 1964

Maister, D.H. 'The Psychology of Waiting Lines' in: Czepiel, J.A., Soloman, M.R. & Surprenant, C.F. (eds.) *The Service Encounter,* Lexington Books, Mass. 1985

Makens, J.C. and Marquard, R.A. 'Consumer Perceptions Regarding First Class and Coach Airline Seating', *Journal of Travel Research,* 1977

Mathieson, A. and Wall, G. *Tourism Economic, Physical and Social Impacts,* Longman, Harlow, 1982

Mathisen, H. 'Adjusting the Aircraft Product to Emerging Customer Needs', Travel and Tourism Research Association Proceedings, 1988

McCallum, J.R. and Harrison, W. 'Interdependence in the Service Encounter' in: Czepiel, J.A., Soloman, M.R. and Surprenant, C.F. (eds.) *The Service Encounter;* Lexington Books, Mass. 1985

McEwen, D. *The Economic Impact of Tourism in London,* LTB/Schlackmans, 1987

MaCannell, D. *The Tourist, a New Theory of the Leisure Class,* Macmillan, London, 1976

Marshall, C. (Sir) 'The Airlines and Their Role in Tourism Developments in the United Kingdom'. Proceedings of 'The Prospects for Tourism in Britain', Financial Times Conferences, 1986

Mayo, E. *The Social Problems of an Industrial Civilization,* Harvard University Press, 1945

Mitchell, B. *Geography and Resource Analysis,* Longman, Harlow, 1979

Mill, R.C. and Morrison, A.M. *The Tourism System, an Introductory Text,* Prentice Hall, Englewood Cliffs, 1985

Middleton, V.T.C. *Marketing in Travel and Tourism,* Heinemann, Oxford, 1988

Milburn, T.W. Schuler, R.S. and Watman, K.H. 'Organizational Crisis, Strategies and Responses', *Human Relations,* v36, No12, 1983

Miller, J.C. & Sawers, P. *The Technical Development of Modern Aviation,* Routledge and Kegan Paul, London, 1988

Mills, P.K., Hall, J.L., Leidecker, J.K. and Marguiles, N. 'Flexiform, a Model for Professional Service Organizations,' *Academy of Management Review,* v8, 1983

Mills, P.K. 'The Control Mechanisms of Employees at the Encounter of Service Organizations' in: Czepiel, J.A., Soloman, M.R. and Surprenant, C.F. (eds.) *The Service Encounter;* Lexington Books, Mass. 1985

Mitchell, A. *The Nine American Life-styles,* Macmillan, New York, 1983

Minter, C. 'Travellers as a Target Market', *Admap,* June 1988

Moutinho, L. 'Consumer Behaviour in Tourism', *European Journal of Marketing,* v21, No 10, 1987

Murphy, P.E. *Tourism, a Community Approach,* Methuen, New York, 1985

Narayana, C.L. and Markin, R.J. 'Consumer Behaviour and Product Performance, an Alternative Conceptualization', *Journal of Marketing,* v23, 1975

Nightingale, 'The Hospitality Industry, Defining Quality for a Quality Assurance Programme, A Study of Perceptions', *Services Industry Journal,* v5, No 1, 1985

Nyquist, J.D., Bitner, M.J. and Booms, B.H. 'Identifying Communication Difficulties in the Service Encounter: a Critical Incident Approach' in: Czepiel, J.A., Soloman, M.R. and Surprenant, C.F. (eds.) *The Service Encounter,* Lexington Books, Mass. 1985

Olshavsky, R.W. 'Customer-Salesman Interaction in Appliance Retailing', *Journal of Marketing Research,* May 1973

Okoroaka, S. 'Branding in Tourism' in: Witt, S.F. and Moutinho, L., *Tourism Marketing and Management Handbook,* Prentice Hall, London, 1989

Ogilvy, D. *Confessions of an Advertizing Man,* Pan Books, London, 1987

Pearce, D. *Tourism Today, a Geographical Analysis,* Longman, Harlow, 1987

Pearce, P. *The Social Psychology of Tourist Behaviour,* Pergamon Press, 1982

Parasuraman, A., Zeithmal, V.A. and Berry, L.L. 'A Conceptual Model of Service Quality and its Implications for Future Research', *Journal of Marketing,* v49, Fall 1985

Raitt, I. 'Tourism Prospects for 1990', *Tourism,* February 1990

Rathmell, J. *Marketing in the Service Sector,* Winthrop, Mass. 1974

Reynolds and Daden, 'Mutually Adaptive Effects of Interpersonal Communications', *Journal of Marketing Research,* November 1971

Ries, A. and Trout, J. *Positioning, the Battle for your Mind,* Warner Books, New York, 1986

Riordan, J. 'Leisure, the State and the Individual in the USSR', *Leisure Studies,* v1, 1982

Ronkainen, I.A. and Farano, R.J. 'United States Travel and Tourism Policy', *Journal of Travel Research,* Spring 1987

Rudney, R. 'The Development of Tourism on the Cote D'Azur, an Historical Perspective' in: Hawkins, D.E., Shafer, E.L. and Rovelstadt, J.M. (eds.) *Tourism Planning and Development Issues,* George Washington University Press, Washington DC, 1980

Sawers, D. *Competition in the Air,* Institute of Economic Affairs, London, 1987

Schlissel, M.R. 'The Consumer of the Household Services in the Marketplace: an Empirical Study', in: Czepiel, J.A., Soloman, M.R. & Surprenant, C.F. (eds.) *The Service Encounter,* Lexington Books, Mass. 1985

Seward, B. *International Airlines,*Philipis and Drew, London, 1986

Shaw, G. and Williams, A. 'Firm Formation and Operating Characteristics in the Cornish Tourist Industry – the Case of Looe', *Tourism Management,* December 1987

Shaw, S. *Airline Marketing and Management,* Pitman, London, 1987

Sheldon, P. and Var, T. 'Residents' Attitudes to Tourism in Wales', *Tourism Management,* 1984

Shostack, G.L. 'How to Design a Service' in: Donnelley, J.H. and George, W.R. *Marketing of Services,* American Marketing Association, 1981
'Planning the Service Encounter' in: Czepiel, J.A., Soloman, M.R. & Surprenant, C.F. (eds.) *The Service Encounter,* Lexington Books, Mass. 1985
'Service Positioning Through Structural Change', *Journal of Marketing,* v51, January 1987
'Breaking Free from Product Marketing', *Journal of Marketing,* v41, No 2, 1977
'How to Design a Service', *European Journal of Marketing,* v16, No 1, 1982
'Designing Services That Deliver', *Harvard Business Review,* Jan/Feb 1984

Smart, V. 'Why bargain hunters are no longer sitting pretty', *The Observer,* June 1988

Smaoui, A. 'Tourism and employment in Tunisia' in: de Kadt, E. (ed.) *Tourism, Passport to Development,* Oxford University Press, London 1987

Smith, S.L.J. *Recreation Geography,* Longman, Harlow, 1983

Smith, V.L. *Hosts and Guests,* Blackwell, Oxford, 1978

Stein, C. (interviewed) 'You Can Buy Companies, But You Have To Earn Growth', *Leaders Magazine,* April, May, June 1988

Swinglehurst, E. *Cooks Tours, the Story of Popular Travel,* Blandford Press, Poole, 1982

Thomas, M. 'Coming to terms with the customer', *Personnel Management,* February 1987

Tiebout, C.M. *The Community Economic Base Study,* Committee for Economic Development, New York, 1962

Tirvengadum, H. 'Tourism and the Airline Industry', paper presented at the Seminar on Tourism and Development, University of Mauritius, November 1986

'Tourism Pacts Protect Parks', *Countryside Commission News,* No 40, Nov/Dec 1989

Twedt, D.W. 'How Important to Marketing Strategy is the Heavy User?' *Journal of Marketing,* v28, Jan 1964

Tymson, C. and Sherman, B. *The Australian Public Relations Manual,* Millenium Books Pty, Sydney, 1987

Uhl, K.P. and Upah, G.D. 'Services Marketing, Why and How it is Different', v1, *Marketing of Services,* AMA Chicago, 1983

Um, S. and Crompton, J.L. 'Measuring residents; attachment levels in host communities', *Journal of Travel Research,* Summer 1987

Wagner, J. and Hause, S. 'The Efficiency of Family Life Cycle Research', *Journal of Consumer Research*, 1983

Wanhill, S.R.C. 'UK Politics and Tourism', *Tourism Management*, March 1987

Waters, S. R. *The Big Picture, the Travel Industry Year Book*, Child and Waters, New York, 1988

Weitz, B.A. 'Effective Sales Interactions: a Contingency Framework', *Journal of Marketing*, v45, 1981

Wells, A.T. *Air Transportation, a Management Perspective*, Wadsworth, Belmont, 1984

Wells, W.D. 'Psychographics, a critical review', *Journal of Marketing Research*, Month? 1975

Wells, W.D. and Gubar, G. 'Lifecycle Concept in Marketing Research', *Journal of Marketing Research*, November 1966

Wilkie, W.L. *Consumer Behaviour*, John Wiley and Sons, New York, 1986

Williamson, O.E. 'Selling Expenses as a Barrier to Entry', *Quarterly Journal of Economics*, v77, 1963

Witt, S.F. and Martin, C.A. 'International Tourism-Demand Models, Inclusion of Marketing Models', *Tourism Management*, March 1987

Witt, S.F. and Moutinho, L. (eds.) *Tourism Marketing and Management Handbook*, Prentice Hall, London, 1989

Woodside, A.G., Cook, V.J. and Mindak, W. 'Profiling the Heavy Traveller Segment', *Journal of Travel Research*, Spring 1987

Woodside, A.G. and Ronkainen, I.A. 'Tourism Management Strategy for Competitive Vacation Destinations', in: Hawkins, D.E., Shafer, E.L. and Rovelstadt, J.M. (eds.) *Tourism Marketing and Management Issues*, George Washington University Press, Washington DC, 1980

Woodside, A.G. and Sherrill, D. 'Traveller Evoked and Inept Sets of Vacation Destinations', *Journal of Travel Research*, v20, 1977

Young, G. *Tourism, Blessing or Blight*, Pelican, Harmondsworth, 1973

Zaleznik, A. 'Managers and Leaders, are they Different?' *Harvard Business Review*, v55, No 3, 1977

Zallocco, R.L. 'Marketing plan' in: Witt, S.F. and Moutinho, L. *Tourism Marketing and Management Handbook*, Prentice Hall, London, 1989

Zhang, G. *Ten Years of Chinese Tourism, Profile and Assessment Tourism Management*, March 1989

Zeithmal, V.A., Berry, L.A. & Parasuraman, L.A. 'Communication and Control Processes in the Delivery of Service Quality', *Journal of Marketing*, v52, April 1988

Zeithmal, V.A., Parasuraman, A. & Berry, L.A. 'Problems and Strategies in Services Marketing', *Journal of Marketing*, v49, Spring 1985

Zemke, R. and Schaaf, P. *The Service Edge, 101 Companies that Profit from Customer Care*, NAL Penguin Inc, New York, 1989

Zipf, G.K. 'The P1P2/D Hypothesis, an Inner City Movement of Persons', *American Sociological Review*, 1946

Author Index

Index